A Soldier Muses
Ponderings of WWII

Richard E. Young

Judith Ann (Young) McNamee

ISBN: 1548455695
ISBN-13: 978-1548455699

INTRODUCTION

Dad not only wrote of his WWII memories, but for a number of years he composed a poem and wrote letters at Christmastime to send to family and friends. His faith was always evident in the poems. He loved to write poems for other occasions, too. He honored his parents at their 50th Wedding Anniversary celebration by writing many verses that told of their fifty years together. It is a treasured historical account for future generations to learn about Herbert and Alta Young.

Dad was still a young man when he returned from WWII, and his full life is obvious in the way he wrote about his business and family through the years. After Dad passed away, we found files that contained many of his other writings tucked inside. It was evident that we had discovered a treasure trove of Dad's experiences throughout his life. Dad looked forward to the day when his WWII memories would be in book form. Daughter Judy typed all of the WWII memories from Dick's handwritten notebooks and other odd pieces of paper. We want to honor that dream in this book.

However, we couldn't publish a book with only the WWII memories when there were so many other stories from Dad's life that would be worthy of telling for future generations in the family and for those who also knew Dad in his spiritual and business life.

These are my father's words which I have in some instances rearranged somewhat for clarity. It was not my goal to have perfectly-structured sentences throughout the book as these are my father's memories as he recorded them over many years. I realize that some of Dad's writings were sometimes repeated in different accounts. I decided to leave all the stories/poems as he wrote them and not try to meld them into one. Dad wrote about these incidents for different occasions and it would be very difficult to make one memory out of two or more writings.

It is my hope that you, the reader, will also enjoy reading the WWII memories and all the other writings of and about Richard Emory Young.

DEDICATION

Dick's wife, DeLoris Dorothy Emily (Butenhoff) Young

Judith Ann (Young) McNamee, husband, Michael James McNamee, son; Scott Michael McNamee, wife, Katrina Louise (Cooper) McNamee, grandchildren, Arielle Lyn McNamee, Amber Katrina McNamee, Savannah Rose McNamee, Caleb Scott McNamee, son; Daniel James McNamee, wife, Patricia Ann (Bonnet) McNamee, grandchildren, Rachael Joy McNamee, Megan Nicole McNamee, son; Paul Andrew McNamee, wife Amy Jo Ann (Stoltz) McNamee, grandchildren, Tanner Michael McNamee, Trinity Jene McNamee, Macy Jo McNamee, daughter; Kirsten Joy (McNamee) Dionne, husband, Paul Daniel Richard Pierre Dionne, grandchildren, Alexis Quinn Dionne, Monique Mackenzie Dionne, Kira Cameryn Dionne, Vienna Joy Natalie Dionne

Richard Charles Young, wife, Lorna Evelyn (Zenner) Young, son; Jeffrey Paul Young, wife, Cynthia Ann (Koehn) Young, grandchildren, Declan Andrew Young, Isaac Bodi Young, son; Brian Kenneth Young, wife, Noemie Young-Studer, grandchildren, Calder Giacun Young, Kieran Antieni Young

David Carl Young, wife, Beth Marie (Sundby), daughter; Michelle April (Young) Cullen, husband, Timothy Graham Cullen, grandchildren, Tyler Graham Cullen, Emma May Cullen, Abigail Morgan Cullen, Elizabeth Grace Cullen, daughter; Jennifer Hope (Young) Grandouiller, husband, Thomas Christopher Grandouiller, grandchildren, Matias Richard Grandouiller, Theo Armand Grandouiller

CONTENTS

ACKNOWLEDGMENTS

Roseanne Bliss - First met with Dick in June, 2006 at Perkins in Grand Forks, ND, about publishing his WWII memories, through her sister, Joy Bliss.

Joy Bliss - Began collecting content for the book - photos, other official documents and the manuscript in the fall of 2006.

Michael L. Harvey - Michael spent many hours standing near Dick as he worked on various machines at Young Mfg. Dick shared his work and WWII experiences with Michael. In early 2015, he began weekly meetings with Judy as he gave her much needed technical assistance and, most of all, patience in the dozens of hours it took to organize the book to its final printing.

Karen Fahey - Invaluable help in the many hours of proofreading and conferring with Judy through phone calls to make spelling and punctuation corrections.

Photos supplied by: Charles Crummy - Jennifer Grandouiller - Cynthia Young - Joy Bliss - Bonnie Kossow - David Young - Dick Young, Jr.

Judith (Young) McNamee - Dick's daughter - In 2007 started typing the manuscript from his handwritten notes. She researched other writings of Dick, his family and friends, as well as newspaper articles about his time spent in Europe during WWII and his business and spiritual interests.

Bonnie Huff - Daughter of Bob Padgett, a war-time buddy to Dick, supplied the information about her dad and photos from her brother.

Family - David (son) and Roland (brother) - facts and history. Granddaughters Jennifer (Young) Grandouiller, and Kirsten (McNamee) Dionne.

Friends - for encouraging Dick to put his "stories" into printed form.

Printed articles - permission granted from Grand Forks Herald, Fargo Forum, and Encyclopedia Britannica.

This poem was written at the war front in 1945

by Sgt Richard E. Young

A SOLDIER MUSES

It's not very long that I've been here
Nor much of this war that I've seen.
But I've seen enough to convince me
That conditions at home were serene.

I've quarreled with family and friends
And sought out my selfish desires.
But believe me- it will be different
When the ruthless old "War King" retires.

I was proud of the day that they took me
And gave me my set of " ODs".
Of course I'm still proud to be able
To help with my countries needs.

But my pride NOW is very much different.
I strive for a peace that will last.
Then I'll take my pride in achievements
We've attained from dreams in the past.

I've stopped looking for personal glory
And admiration from friends.
All that I hope now and pray for
Is the time when this night-mare ends.

I haven't been very religious
Nor followed ALL lessons I've learned,
But when bombs are bursting around me -
My thoughts then in prayer are turned.

Soon we will all be returning,
To the GOOD old USA
And may God protect us and keep us
Til the dawn of that glorious day.

WWII MEMORIES

The basics have been part of every recruit following the day he or she receives the famous greetings from the president of the United States, but the fact is that every recruit had unique experiences that he feels are just that much different to make them worth telling. I was a tanker. Here's my story.

My wife and I were married just 42 days before the attack on Pearl Harbor, December 7, 1941. Within days, the United States was thrown into bedlam, adjusting to the rigors of war.

Every eligible young man and some not so young, were required to take the physical exam. My father secretly wished I could escape the service and preferred that I not qualify physically – (4F?). I wanted to be strong and able, and I was pleased after my exam when Doc Duncan slapped me over the shoulder and said, "I wish there were more guys like you going through here."

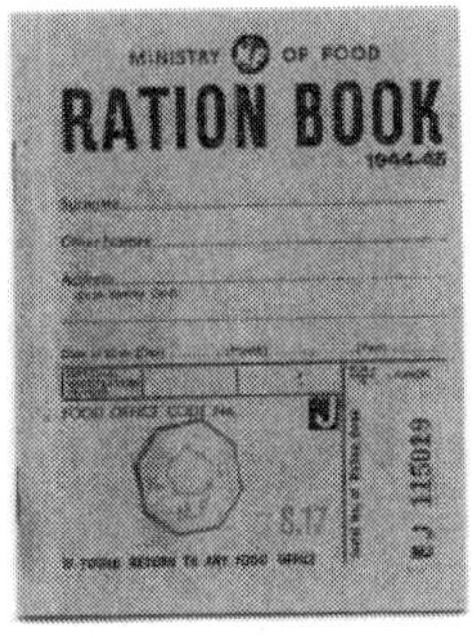

Rationing became the order of the day. Cigarettes and coffee disappeared off the shelves. I worked with one man who bought 100 pounds of coffee – strictly out of selfishness.

Factories came alive with contracts to produce materials of war: tanks, guns, ammunition, planes, trucks, and clothing to name a few. The shortage of experienced machine operators created another major problem – training men for war industry.

To aid in the war effort, the machine shop where I worked in Moorhead, Minnesota was converted from a repair shop to a training school for men to receive experience for entering into war industries. The Minnesota Board of Education took the lead in establishing a curriculum. Many men in varying ages did not qualify for military service. In a very short time, the shop-school received about a dozen men who eagerly took to the coveted trade of machinist.

Using experienced machinists for instructors, I was called on to fill the position as I was foreman of the shop. This was a unique experience. Working with men from the school system, we used tools and machines on hand to create a sort of crash course for men who did not qualify for military duty. These fellows eagerly took hold of a coveted trade and many were placed in defense plants.

Through the school system, employment agencies knew my skills. I received notice that I would be deferred for a period to enter a defense plant. My young bride and I, married only weeks, found it adventurous to move to Minneapolis, Minnesota where I became employed at the Minneapolis Moline Tractor Company as a tool and die maker. The contracts for the company included steam cylinders for the Navy and anti-aircraft guns for the Army. This was in 1942.

The impetus of the early war months brought into our lives, as with hundreds of other couples, our first child, Judith Ann. I could enjoy my new daughter for only a short while because it was not long before my number came up. I had to leave the defense plant and report to Ft. Snelling, Minnesota to begin my military duty on 5/12/1944.

FORT SNELLING, MINNESOTA INDUCTION CENTER

The first day at Ft. Snelling was a revelation. One soon discovered that all men known as recruits were reduced to a common denominator. Long lines of totally nude men filled the induction center as we reported for a quick physical. For the record, that exam covered two subjects – venereal disease and hemorrhoids.

You could not tell the well-to-do from those with less, as the only thing we carried through the examination was a sheet of paper with our name and preliminary scheduling. Some used that single sheet as a cover up – no explanation necessary.

Military jargon suggests that 'sergeants' are a tough lot, and to support that, I believe those in the induction center made good use of it. Sergeants, in particular, gave the orders for any related activity and we heard the sharp command when ordering anything, including shoes, to sound off our name, serial number and shoe size. We were threatened with having to take shots again for a failed report. Reportedly, the needles were large and square and injections given in private parts of the body.

This was a sobering experience and a backward glance reminds me of how silent the men were, lining up for each activity, especially shots. It took only two or three sergeants to handle the entire groups of men because of the reported nature of these 'tough guys'.

Having received socks, shorts and shoes and wearing only these clothing articles, we lined up at the dispensary for shots. Suddenly, we heard a loud lament "No, Sarge – no!" In addition, to our consternation, two large sergeants were dragging a smallish soldier, who struggled to be free, and continually saying "No, Sarge" as he was shoved through a door that all of us would enter for shots. He heard once more that he should have remembered his numbers. We heard a yell and a thud and all was quiet. I doubt if there was one man in that line-up who could not recall his number. We suspected and later learned the episode was staged.

In time, we were outfitted with heavy woolen clothing commonly referred to as ODs (olive drab). Having to wear such clothing in May was not too comfortable, but a quick glance back at the sergeant in charge dispelled any notion to complain.

After shots and wearing the heavy clothing, we were ordered to enter a barracks and scrub floors. From my observation, the floors were already spotless, but scrub – we did.

The shots caused me to have a severe headache. I asked our sergeant about some relief and he said, "Go on sick call." When I questioned where, his terse answer was, "7:00 AM at the dispensary." I lived out the day with the headache.

Much of the activity of a recruit was routine and not too exciting. Living in barracks was a matter-of-fact experience with the needs adequate but not plush. We had canvas Army cots with typical military bedding, a cotton mattress, sheets, a pillow and the only blankets issued were the scratchy wool blankets we all love to hate! Every man made his own bed and the order of the day was to have the top cover so tight that a coin would bounce when dropped on it.

After three days at the induction center, different branches of service – infantry, artillery, signal corps, armored, paratroopers and supply - were made known to us. There were variations to all and I may have missed listing some. There were also the Air Force and Navy that had many facets. My civilian records may have influenced the decision-makers, but I was sent with a few men to Fort Knox, Kentucky, which was an armored command training post.

FORT KNOX, KENTUCKY

Old time steam locomotives were used to transport, and it is worth telling that smoke and cinders were a normal part of riding the rails in the 1940s. The train ride was in old-fashioned coaches with limited facilities. All coaches were crowded and had no air conditioning. Realizing that we were headed for basic training, I am reminded that there was a sense of uncertainty, and the trainload of men were well aware that combat loomed in our sights. Truly, I do not recall a lot of joking and glib talk.

Everything seemed to revolve around expedient moves and the scheduling moved rapidly. From the train, we were loaded into waiting buses and the NCOs (non-commissioned officers) were carrying the roster of names that created the unending calling out of names for direction to destination.

As we approached the main gate at the Army post, we were greeted with a grisly sight. An Army jeep, in the ditch near the entry gate was all shot up with bleeding bodies hanging out and some slumped in the seats. A curved sign over the entrance read THIS IS WAR – ACT LIKE IT.

There seemed to be a constant sorting of names as to who went where and the alphabet was ever a factor. Andersons, Browns, Carlsons and Dailys were called out first and the Wilsons, Youngs, Zeeks, and Zimbas were always last. Once inside Fort Knox we trucked past stately brick buildings, which we believe, were headquarters – plus a circular outlay of buildings, which we learned were officers' quarters.

We moved quickly into the barracks area, which consisted of four barracks, a supply building and the "orderly room", which for the uninitiated could be considered the office. I was assigned to barracks #4 and our title was simply "4th platoon."

Every soldier may have a different slant on how he sees things in the military. Nevertheless, there is a sameness to training and I found that a willing spirit is very beneficial.

Fort Knox was like a city. There were thousands of men and women in many assignments. There were many females on the post also as nurses and WACs (Women's Army Corps). As with any city, vehicular traffic and constant moving of troops created the climate for accidents. Several were killed while I was at Ft. Knox.

Men who desired an easy Army life often became the victims of heavy labor. It was common to have some goof-off ordered to dig a hole – three feet wide, three feet long and three feet deep. That means moving approximately one and one half tons of earth.

Equally tedious was scrubbing building sidewalls with a toothbrush. If a soldier had some ingenuity, he may have some assignment that calls for some head work and I can explain that.

I was asked to help change mattress covers on several hundred beds. Sound like a big job? You bet it was. To understand the project, one must realize the beds were single and to work alone is truly exhausting. Fortunately, the fellow who worked with me was a willing worker and we learned some worthy techniques.

Stripping the covers off was relatively easy, but pushing a mattress into a cover was another story. I was tall, about six feet and I learned that if the mattress was folded lengthwise, the cover went on easily. By experimentation, placing the mattress on top of my head and grabbing the sides, it could be bent into a V shape. My buddy could slip the cover over the end about three feet and with both of us grabbing the cover, we could bounce the mattress into place. We enjoyed the job but nobody said thanks.

STARTING OUT AT BASIC TRAINING

Training started immediately. A sergeant called for assembly in the street and commanded, "fall in." We lined up by ranks four deep and with sixty men in the building that was four ranks with fifteen men per rank.

Absentees were unheard of. To be absent called for some very unusual needs – illness, death in the family, or some special assignment. The command 'At Ease' meant we could stand – relaxed, but no talking. We waited for further instructions.

The sergeant called out, "Do we have any typists?" Several hands went up. He then asked for truck drivers and again there were several volunteers. The typists were given lawn mowers and the truck drivers received wheelbarrows. It seemed they invented work for obvious reasons, namely training. One could not be sure if volunteering was a wise idea, but it became more acceptable when we were accustomed to the whole system.

I marvel at the ability of a few men to handle so many. I alluded to the fact that most 'non-coms' were the no nonsense types and the general response to orders was – do it now with a military bearing.

I had no idea that I was to be chosen early to become a Lance Corporal. I never had the rank of PFC (private first class). Which is a beginning rank for prospective non-coms. There was no change in pay, but a sort of testing for possible leadership.

RANK

Since some who read this account might not be familiar with military terms, it seems to be of some value to give a rundown on rank and other jargon (language) - like the use of acronyms and abbreviations common to soldiers.

A soldier (not officer) is commonly referred to as a GI (Government Issue) – a rather dubious title. The first title to anyone entering service is recruit. Once in uniform, the next and unglamorous title is private (pvt), then private first class (pfc). Each rating implies an advance in a more involved workload – plus a pay increase.

After pfc is corporal (cpl), then sergeant (sgt) or (sarge). There are five ratings for sergeant. The first is buck sgt – the most coveted rating because entering into the sergeant status implies a sense of authority. Buck sergeants are commonly thought of as being tough with a bold nature. Some could be mean-spirited, but generally, soldiers recognize that the sergeants are also under authority. Following buck sergeants in this order are staff sergeants, technical (tech) sergeants, first sergeants, and finally master sergeant. Each of the ratings is identified with chevrons worn on both upper sleeves between the elbow and shoulders.

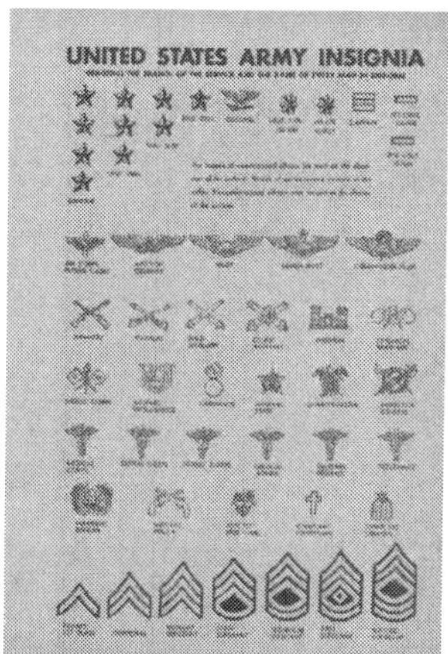

The first rating with a chevron is pfc; this requires one inverted V shape on all clothing and jackets. Next is corporal with two stripes. Corporals may be used in numerous tasks that will give those in authority the opportunity to discover who may be entitled to be advanced to another job rating. Third is buck sergeant – the most coveted rating of all. The three stripes is notoriously a tough character and have the main job of directing work assignments.

Following is staff sergeant – with three stripes up and one bottom rocker. His work may be more in the administrative line or platoon sergeant. Next is technical sergeant – with three stripes up and two bottom rockers. He may be used in various jobs as needed. One would be working with trucks and other equipment such as weapons and engineering tools.

Topping enlisted men ratings are two sergeants with similar chevrons. The first sergeant uses three stripes and three bottom rockers with a diamond centered in the chevron. Master sergeant uses three stripes and three bottom rockers, but lacking the diamond. His authority is recognized as topping all ratings, slightly above a first sergeant. A first sergeant normally centers his activity at company level, while a master sergeant may be at battalion headquarters – or as needed. Sergeants generally are referred to as non-commissioned officers – 'non-coms'.

All military personnel quickly learn the lingo that is common to all branches of service. When a corporal or sergeant calls any body of men to some assignment, the fully understood word, sounded off loud and clear is

"ATTENTION". Seasoned non-coms learned the slang, shortened version, easier to say – "TEN-HUT". From my own experience, it seemed easier to say if one was a bit short of breath in parades.

Standing at attention meant feet together, with arms down, eyes forward and no talking. Parade rest was nearly the same except feet spread about fifteen to eighteen inches and hands behind your back. "At ease" meant to retain position but a bit more relaxed in stature and visiting was permitted. However, each commander was free to establish some of his own requirements. Oddly enough, referring to a commanding officer, as "The Old Man" is acceptable.

Officers are rated in this order; 2nd lieutenant, 1st lieutenant, captain, major, lieutenant colonel, colonel, and general. There are five ratings with generals starting with one star up to the top at five stars.

TRAINING SCHEDULE

A typical day started with a sharp signal over an intercom at 5:00 AM – everybody up. There is no need to describe the center rush to a washroom with only two toilet stools and a six-foot common urinal, two sinks for sixty men and everybody shaved – completely (no facial hair allowed)– using safety razors.

The shower was a metal lined room, probably zinc, about five feet by eight feet with perhaps four showerheads and all of us learned to be good-natured in the many bodies soaping down and trying to get finished in a very short space of time. Need it be said? No mess allowed in the washroom.

Getting dressed plus bed making and a completely organized clothing rail in minutes was the standing order. I learned early to be up and get ahead of the rush.

The next order was "FALL IN" - all men in the street were to form ranks alphabetically. The 1st sergeant would meet for roll call. When your name was called you would sound off "Here", or "Here, Sir" if it was an officer. All eyes were straight forward with no one talking. Total attention was given when general orders were announced or even a lecture. I cannot emphasize enough the need to be alert and cooperative. Survival depended upon it.

CHOW AND CIGARETTES

After roll call, we all welcomed the snappy order of *"dismissed for chow"*. When chow was over, we were not free to loiter, but grab a smoke if you were a smoker. I should mention that smokers were given strict orders. Every post in the barracks had a butt can hanging on a nail with water in it. Throwing cigarettes on any property was a no-no. I believe enough officers smoked so they felt obliged to figure out an acceptable system. We had to field strip the cigarette. The glowing end of the cigarette was flicked off and a fast foot maneuver extinguished the fire. The paper wrapping was torn and all unburned tobacco could be dumped out. It was hard to see in grassy places and was of little concern otherwise. The paper was to be rolled between the thumb and finger until it was an inconspicuous little ball about half the size of a pea and could be tossed anywhere.

However, enough men ignored the flicking order, so a unique little duty was created that ALL men took part in. I will say it with a bit more dignity than was customary. When the sergeant yelled “Okay guys, rear ends and elbows”, everybody was down on his hands and knees looking for cigarette butts or any other cast-off item. With all men available, the job was only about five minutes and the lesson learned was obvious.

LANCE CORPORAL YOUNG

As Lance Corporal, I did not dare "pull rank" as seasoned sergeants did. I believed all sergeants were fearless. They cultivated commanding voices and when they sounded off – men moved. I believe they were chosen because they understood military jargon.

The fellows in my squad knew I was just another soldier and they knew I was called on to lead certain assignments from higher authority. Out of nine of us in one squad, I would be called on to send four men or so, and I would always pick one short and fill that slot myself. I escaped having anyone say, “Hey, Young – you ain’t any better than the rest of us."

LECTURES

Much of our activity was carried on in orientation buildings. These were similar to theaters where training cadre could show film plus lectures. Using training film, we learned much about Army life. Weapons could be demonstrated, but films were also used to show something like temporary bridge building and some activity that was not convenient to have on the Army post.

BAILEY BRIDGE

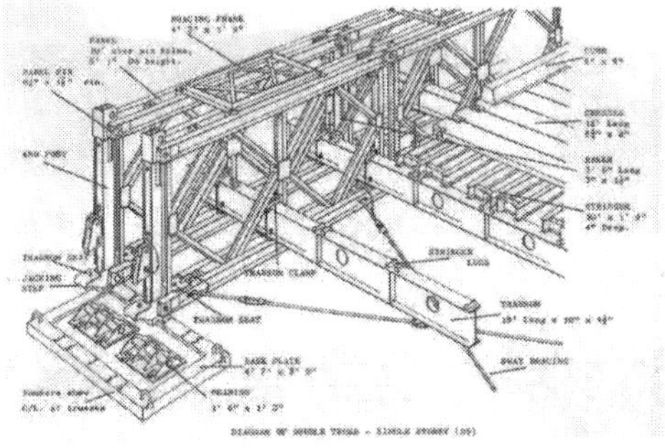

One such film taught us about the Bailey bridge. It was a prefabricated unit using steel angles, beams and rods. In the unassembled form, the bridge could be hauled to the job site on flatbed trucks. Using a company of men, the bridge could be assembled on dry ground in sections. The unique design allowed all side panels to be inter-changeable, and this was true of the tread members.

A system of skids was used to set the bridge members in place and after several sections were assembled with pins and bolts, the engineers used heavy tractors to push the bridge across the stream. It took many extra sections to make the bridge long enough to reach the other side.

Once it reached the far side, engineers would secure the bridge and in an incredibly short time period, troops, trucks and tanks could cross over. This operation was accomplished within hours. We could sit in the comfort of an assembly hall and see how it was done.

A NIGHT ON THE TOWN

One item of importance came early in our Army life; many men experienced certain freedoms after leaving home. Many of the troops were married, however a great number of men were single. After a few weeks at camp, it was the desire of almost everyone to get a pass and go to town.

This prompted the high command to warn of hazards lurking in the cities. Army chaplains spoke to full companies of men and explicit films were shown portraying the effects of venereal disease and loose living. It has been said that we can't legislate morality, but hopefully the warnings were meant to be a strong deterrent.

HIKES

Hikes were a part of training. The day came for a 25-mile hike. As I recall, it was mostly on gravel roads mixed with the red soil of Fort Knox. The day was bright and sunny, following a heavy rain during the early morning hours. Roads were sloppy wet. The mixture of soils made a gooey mess.

We carried a field pack and a canteen of water. Everyone was required to have a raincoat. If it was not raining, the coat was folded and strapped to our back.

Some fellows could not handle a 25-miler. The guys coined some of their own phrases and these were called the "sick – lame – lazy". These were unkind thoughts but authorities knew that help was needed for many. Trucks were available to pick up the tough cases. During the day, many chose the easy way back to camp.

Towards evening, that last truck was dispatched and only eight of 240 men completed the hike. I was one of them. Boots were muddy and full of water. There were blisters, too. Our clothing was sweat soaked and especially under the folded raincoat.

My seven buddies were in good spirits and, in retrospect, we maybe gloated a bit that "we made it". The fact is that we should have said, "Praise the Lord for the strength and ability." The hikes were intended to build up our bodies. Many of the fellows entered service with run-down physiques. There continued to be constant reminders that weaklings were going to be in trouble.

When we reached camp, the eight of us were told to clean up and go to chow. Following that we were free. All the rest of the company was sent to the arms warehouse for cleanup duty. Nobody ducks out of duty.

DUTY STRAIN

The details of basic training may be boring to report, but some things turned into real drama. We had a fine sergeant platoon leader that we all respected. We were shocked to learn that the strain of duty caught up with him. He slipped over a ridge in the near woods and shot himself.

TRAINING CONTINUES

Nevertheless, training went on. Some of the more elementary training needs included map reading, field sanitation and bivouac (temporary camp). From this, we learned scouting and patrolling – studying the habits of the enemy.

INFANTRY TRAINING

All infantrymen know the machine gun obstacle course. A piece of ground in an open field was prepared with many strands of barbed wire stretched across from side to side. The wire was quite close to the ground with only enough space for a man to crawl under on his belly. Machine guns placed at the head of the course were mounted to send a stream of bullets just over the top of the barbed wire. To rise above the wire could be fatal. The gunning continued until we reached the far side. It seemed like a city block or more. I asked a friend what he would do if he encountered a snake. He said he would choose the lesser of the two evils – namely the snake!

Almost every explosive device was included in our training. The weapons were the type that could be carried by individuals: hand grenades, rifles, rocket launchers, machine guns and side arms. The big stuff came later – anti-aircraft guns, tank guns and artillery.

It is somewhat difficult to point out all the "ins" and "outs" of basic training after the years have passed. However, I feel it does have a place in reporting because what we learned was to our benefit. I have already named activity, which preceded the use of firearms. The sound of machine guns became our lot in the machine gun obstacle course even before seeing one of them.

RIFLES

For infantry soldiers, perhaps the most important part of training was the care and use of rifles. Disassembly was the first actual contact any of us had with any rifles. They were kept very secure in the arms warehouse. Only ranking non-coms had access to rifles, which were locked in place. Each of us was issued a rifle, and a very important order was given to learn the serial number.

Smaller groups of us were used in the start of training rifle functions. First was the disassembly and learning each part and function. Following that was oiling and reassembly. The name of the rifle by manufacture was Garand. The military personnel called it the "M1". It weighed ten pounds and used a clip for the ammunition. Another popular rifle was called the Carbine. It was smaller, weighing about half that of the M1. Both rifles were 30 caliber.

Even before we were allowed to have ammunition, it was necessary to go through some practices which were very demanding. In an open field with all natural terrain, we were to hold the rifle at port arms – one hand on the trigger grip and the other on the wood, which housed the barrel. Then, on command, we were to run forward until the signal from an officer "hit the dirt" at which time we were to use the rifle to break our fall by jamming the butt of the rifle in the ground. This, no doubt, was a maneuver for ground troops when enemy soldiers were encountered.

All this was done without ammunition in the rifle to avoid any possible mishap. Several times after doing the hit-the-dirt routine, I discovered I broke two watches. Following this, it was back to the cleaning and oiling. All of us could see that using the rifles as we did could easily make some of them inoperable.

FIRING RANGE

After the "feel" of these fine rifles, next was the rifle range where we first received ammunition. We were trucked to the range with the rifles in our possession. Each firing range was equipped with perhaps 24 positions. The distance appeared to be about 100 yards from the firing line to the targets. Every target was white paper about four or five feet square. Each was mounted on a wooden frame, which could be raised and lowered from the pit in front of the target. The pit was deep enough to protect the men tending the targets.

Targets were designed with a bull's eye in the center – eight inches in diameter. Outside the bull's eye were circular rings, which aided in scoring hits. A loudspeaker system was used to direct activity on the range. We had to learn to shoot from several positions. The first one was prone. The next was sitting and the last was squatting. We did not have rifle training from a standing position on the range, but this came later with targets at a close range in the form of a man.

Every shot fired on the range was by the command of the range officer. The procedure may have varied with different officers in charge. My memory tells me that every shot fired was a single round. There would be a "ready" signal and the officer would command "fire at will". Everyone fired at the same time, which helped to maintain control. No one was free to do his own thing but to wait for orders. As the bullet hit the target, it made a cracking sound and it was possible to see exactly where it hit.

After each shot, the target was lowered and marked with a three inch diameter spot on a stick which entered the hole in the target. Each rifleman could see the results of his work. Since every rifle was subject to the sights being out of adjustment, each soldier, to obtain a "shot group", fired at least three shots. Consistency was hoped for, as this was the system used to determine the accuracy of each man. A close grouping of shots was desirable for checking sights.

At times shots fired would hit the wooden frame causing splinters to fly into the pit. I was with a buddy who had one of the large splinters stick in his neck. It was not serious, but the fellow at the firing line needed to know that he missed the target. Each pit had a red flag on a wooden pole, which could be waved in front of the target with the message.

Humor seems to be second nature to soldiers. The names given different operations became so much a part of every outfit. The red flag was named “Maggie’s Drawers” and in my experience, I never heard it otherwise.

Additional target practice was done on the range where targets were placed out as far as 800 yards, which is somewhat less than one-half mile. Men operating the pits used telephones to report results. Should a phone fail, the operator was doomed to stay in the pit until he was certain of the "all clear".

Infantry training always precedes other types of military assignments. It is rigorous and often separates "men from the boys". I believe ground troops are of the best in uniform. I have seen courage in infantrymen, which seems to be natural to those who are exposed to the worst conditions expected of fighting men. What is learned in infantry training is beneficial to anyone in other branches of service. There are times when even tankers in a combat zone may be called on for close fighting. I know.

It happened to me when we had to leave our tanks and go on a house-to-house search. I will explain more of this later.

Almost every known explosive device was included in our training. For infantry, the weapons were the type that could be carried by individuals. Examples would be rifles, submachine guns, hand grenades, rocket launchers and side arms – pistols. The training included the use of all sorts of explosive devices. In the field were storage sheds for ammunition.

It seemed that most soldiers smoked. When near the ammo dumps, smoking was forbidden. Can you imagine a sequence of human behavior that led to a disaster? The ammo dumps had sheds built with a slanting roof – almost flat. During operations, fellows would get up on the roof, to have a smoke. Cracks in the roof seemed a natural part of these shelters and the improbable happened. Someone let a cigarette fall through the crack and a fire started followed by an explosion, which killed several men. The fellows on the roof escaped harm even though the explosion tipped the shed roof over.

In spite of the somber nature of combat training, humor was always welcome. Near the training area, someone had set up a small mock cemetery with white crosses on the graves. Some of the names were HERE LIES DIR T GUNN, M. T. HEAD, SLEE P. JOE and others, which have slipped my memory.

TANKS

Perhaps detail of activity can become wearisome, but there came an end to infantry training and we were introduced to tanks. Tank training followed as the last major item on our schedule. There were three types of tanks – light, medium and heavy. We were not given any training in light tanks. The need, it seemed, was Sherman medium tanks (named after General Sherman) which had two types of engines. The first was a 9-cylinder radial engine and the next used a 500 horsepower Ford V-8 engine.

The older tanks with the radial engine used a 75 mm tank gun, with muzzle velocity at 1900 feet per second. The newer Sherman tanks with the Ford V-8 engine mounted a 76 mm gun with 2700 feet per second muzzle velocity. With the increased firepower, the 76 mm gun could shoot a projectile 18 miles. I had experience with both sized guns and later, towards the end of the war, we were given the latest tanks, much larger by weight and 90-millimeter gun with a muzzle velocity of 5,000 feet per second. Truly, they were devastating weapons. Some tanks were outfitted with a 50-caliber machine gun on the top of the turret. This was to be handled by the tank commander as needed – even against planes.

Sherman tanks were designed for desert fighting. They were very hot in summer. Air was sucked through the hatches to cool the engine oil. It helped to cool the occupants also, but when these tanks were moved to the European campaign and cold weather set in, the tankers had to wear clothing to match the situation.

Sherman tanks weigh 95,000 pounds, almost 50 tons. Every tank required a five-man crew – a driver, an assistant driver, a gunner, a loader and the tank commander. The assistant driver had the responsibility of operating a 30-caliber machine gun in his side of the tank. The loader, seated to the left of the main tank gun was to place ammunition in the big gun as ordered by either the tank commander or the gunner. The two main types of ammunition were armor piercing (AP) and high explosive (HE). The main tank gun was center mounted in the turret and could be raised or lowered as needed. The entire turret could be turned either to the right or to left to position the gun. This was under the control of the gunner.

Medium tanks used a five-man crew commonly called tankers. Each tank has three hatches. Hatches on the top were the means of entry. Small and slender men could mount up with ease compared to some of their buddies. The hatch in the turret is for the three men assigned to gunnery – the gunner, ammo loader and tank commander. In the lower part of the tank were two hatches. One was for the driver on the left side of the tank. The hatch on the right was for the bow-gunner who was also the assistant driver. One other hatch was the escape hatch on the bottom of the tank. This was rarely ever used unless the tank had rolled over on its top or side.

Finally, to wrap up information regarding tank training, the open field used for all purposes was mostly for driving. The reddish topsoil was ground to powder and not a blade of grass in sight. As we drove our tanks in this powdery condition, the dust was so bad that we could hardly breathe. We had to be careful not to run into another tank, and at times, we came close enough that we could feel the exhaust in our face of the tank ahead. I asked our officer why they used such soil for tank training. The answer could be expected. I was told that <u>any</u> soil turned out the same. After a rain, walking in the muck was almost impossible.

Crew drill, mounting and dismounting was first. Next was driver training followed by weapons school. This was a carefully planned training since the high explosives – an integral part of gunnery - required the utmost in caution. Firing tank weapons needed much supervision. It was necessary to have proper impact area that stray shells would not cause damage beyond the range.

Each phase was taken in stride. The element most often brought up was the safety for each one to practice. When one realized a loaded tank has 200 gallons of gasoline, nearly 100 rounds of tank ammunition, several dozen hand grenades, a number of smoke grenades and finally, upwards of 10,000 rounds of belted machine gun ammunition, a mistake could spell disaster.

BARRACKS HI-JINKS

Much activity has not been recorded in this report. I have not said much about barracks activity. My temporary rank as Lance Corporal remained with me throughout my stay at Fort Knox. I am sure the title had an effect on my behavior. In addition, the men in my squad must have sensed a need to show some respect. At age 24, it was common for younger men to call me "Pop".

As a married man with a baby daughter, I tried to live as would be expected. Most of my men carried on with trips to town to visit pubs and some spent long evenings at the Post Exchange (PX) drinking beer. I am not trying to prove me the nice guy who doesn't do these things, but some activity may be worth reporting. Often, I spent evenings alone in the bunkroom. That left it open for me to engage in some behavior that I am sure would have received disapproval from my commanding officer.

Men in my squad were so bent on the booze trail that they would come in late every night. The second floor housed thirty men and it seems incredible that there would be nights when I would be the only man on deck for several hours. Two fellows in my squad named Wooten and Wooley were the worst for coming in drunk.

My attempt at a reprimand may have been out of order, but I went to their bunks and rolled up their bedding – mattress and all. I put the rolls up against the wall where they hung their clothes. Beds were metal frames and could be folded up.

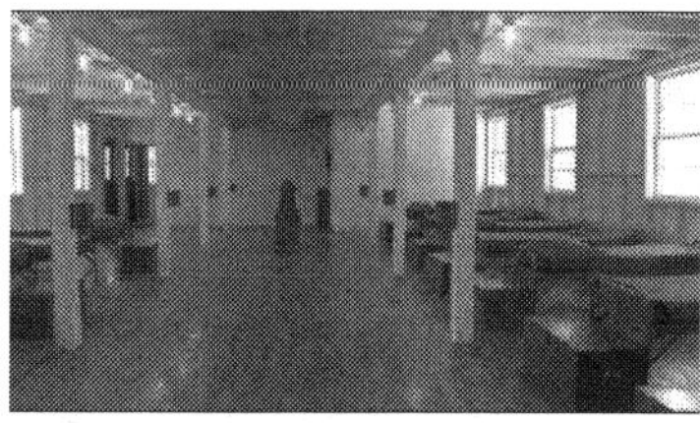

Down through the center of every barracks was a metal heat duct hanging from the ceiling with metal straps. There was a space of about four or five inches above the duct. After folding the metal beds, I could easily slip them over the top of the duct. No one would see them after dark. That was the extent of my mischief.

As other men returned to their bunks they saw what had happened. None dared to accuse me, but they added to the prank. They went to the clothing rail of Wooten and Wooley and tied knots in all of their shirts and jackets. It all seemed relatively harmless.

However, it was lights out and men kept straggling in. When the booze twins finally showed up – I could hear the "cussin'" in low tones - "Where the hell is my bunk?" They wound up sleeping in their bedding on the floor.

At the far end of the second floor was a tall man named Wilson. He seemed to invite problems. Also being practical jokers, Wooten and Wooley decided it was Wilson that engineered the bed trick. Footlockers are part of everyone's gear. This includes personal items – pictures, clothing and whatever. The booze pals waited one night and now it was their turn. They tipped over Wilson's footlocker – scattering everything. That triggered more footlockers being tipped over. (Mine was not).

I was a bit ashamed that I had started all this, but I escaped reprisals. The final episode was by Wilson. The same night of the footlocker tipping, at 3:00 AM, Wilson took a slug from the firing range that weighed several pounds and starting at his end of the barracks, he dropped the slug several times. The booming sound woke the entire barracks – both floors. The metal heat duct contributed an extra sound chamber, which made the episode more effective. Wilson's sense of humor included him yelling, "Everybody up and urinate, the worlds on fire!" I do not recall any further action, but we can rest assured that the sergeants in charge brought things back to normal.

Another thing that seems to be a natural part of a soldier's life is being kept in the dark. Rumors were ever present. After a hectic number of weeks at Fort Knox, Kentucky, it became obvious that our stay was coming to a close. The men in "B" company became buddies as it was the first experience for all of us, but we faced separation. None of us knew what to expect. We all learned that rumors are a natural part of Army life.

An excited soldier entered the barracks one day and sounded off, "We are going to Alaska. We just got in a shipment of long underwear." Newcomers were the target for such pranks and few of us believed the rumors. We truly were not always informed about many things. We had to be ready at a moment's notice to pack up to ship out.

The fact is that we were scheduled to ship to another camp here in the USA, but we were not told until we arrived. Certainly, the non-coms knew, but maybe some of us were not listening.

My wife visited me during my stay at Ft. Knox and I recall the worst part of the visit – for my wife – were the bedbugs! They did not bother me at all!

MOVING ON – CAMP CHAFFEE, ARKANSAS & FORT MEADE, MARYLAND

Camp Chaffee, Arkansas was next after Fort Knox, but I do not recall any special training that was to enhance our experiences. The fact is that we were there for only a short space of time. It was very hot in later summer 1944. The one benefit we all experienced was the rapid drying of our laundry. Nevertheless, it seemed like a sort of "excuse me" move before orders to move on to Fort Meade, Maryland.

As fall approached, the temperature drop from the Arkansas camp was quite abrupt. We experienced a lot of rain at Fort Meade. Training took on certain "extras" we did not receive at Knox and Chaffee. Fort Meade was a beautiful post with a great variety of trees and hilly terrain features. This made our camping out very enjoyable.

Of course, barracks were always the main point of assembly from where all orders originated. We were trucked to the point of field activities. The evening came for us to take to the field where we set up pup tents as they were called. Each tent consisted of two men sharing a portion of his equipment. Material used was a type of canvas made into a shelter half. When joined with another shelter half, it became a complete tent. It was only sufficient for sleeping or resting, but soldiers are innovative and candles or flashlights made the difference.

Meals were served in daylight. The men assigned to food service set up field kitchens. I was always glad when the food served was substantial. I am sure that this activity was also part of training. Certain activity stands out in my memory. Much of military training was routine and not too exciting, although there were times when activity became extremely exciting and dangerous.

Tankers normally are not required to dig foxholes. However, the time may come when it may be necessary. A maneuver used at Fort Meade called for a company of men to dig foxholes in an open field. Fortunately, it was sandy soil. At a given signal, sirens screamed as tanks hidden in the woods roared out, and every man was to take refuge in his foxhole.

FIGURE 30.—Prone shelter.

Tanks were to pass over the foxholes – straddling the opening as the men in the hole ducked down low covering his head with his steel helmet.

Truly, it was scary. One tank driver either missed his mark or tried a bit of mischief. Instead of straddling the foxhole, he passed one track directly over the hole. The soldier in it was helpless. The sides caved in burying the hapless victim. Immediately a number of buddies rushed to the scene and frantically dug him out with bare hands. He was spared any injury by Providence, but as could be expected there was a lot of laughter and poking fun. Personally, I dug my hole so close to a tree that no tanker took up the challenge.

Our stay in the wooded area included one more night. Pup tents were still set. As evening chow was served, we all welcomed the early evening to relax and prepare for nightfall. We either crawled in under blankets or used sleeping bags. One feature that may have been welcomed by most of the fellows is that we could sleep fully dressed – boots and all. Of course, that simulated combat readiness.

None of us expected the torrential rain after midnight. It is nearly impossible to accurately assess the results of a heavy rainfall. Trenches had been dug around each tent but were inadequate. At first, it seemed we were okay, but as the rain continued, our tent was soaked. Water entered our bedding, then our clothing and, by morning, there was not a dry stitch of clothing on any of us. My wallet was so soaked that my few dollar bills turned brown.

The daylight was very welcome, but we shivered hoping to find enough tinder to start bonfires. The thought of trucking us back to the barracks for comfort was not even a consideration. We were learning to be hardened soldiers.

The rain had stopped, but heavy clouds prevailed. Bonfires helped us dry out while the enterprising cooks put together a great field breakfast. Field exercises geared to simulate combat conditions continued to conclusion. The stay at Fort Meade included many of the routines we went through at Fort Knox, so it will not be necessary to elaborate.

We were in the countdown for the next move. I believe most fellows would welcome a trip to California. Word came down that Fort Ord in California was our next station. As I have mentioned before, rumors seemed to be a way of GIs entertaining each other. Surely, we were headed for the Orient.

FORT ORD, CALIFORNIA

We shipped to California by train. We were becoming accustomed to smoky trips, and learned to leave the details to the men in charge. Upon arrival, we were bussed to the barracks that all had a similar styling. We adjusted easily to the different Army camps. Here, too, it was the rainy season and it was difficult to do our laundry and expect it to dry in an average period. We washed our clothing by hand in large tubs using soap provided by the quartermaster. That soap was not the kind any of us would have spent our money on. It was very strong and gained the title of "GI soap". Clothing was dried on lines outside the building.

At Fort Ord, we had more rifle training. The day we went to the range was a very interesting day. Perhaps being near the ocean made the difference. The day was mostly sunny with the usual fluffy white clouds that looked like cotton. With very little wind, we settled into the routines of the firing line. With previous experience, everything moved along very well.

About mid morning, we could see it coming. One of those cotton clouds settled right down on the ground in front of us obscuring the targets. It was as dense as thick fog. The cloud covered about half of the targets, mainly on the side where my buddies and I were engaged. Needless to say, we enjoyed the rare experience.

The move to Fort Ord gave us every reason to assume that we were headed for the Pacific operations. We were at Fort Ord only a few days, but once more we were trucked to a position for a tent setup. It was a nice clear night. We trenched around our tents by lantern light. Sounds of steel tent pegs being pounded into sandy soil leaves strong memories of that night. We did not have a chance to occupy the tents.

Out of the blue, we hear the order "Wrap 'em up – we are heading east." The emotions that followed were varied, but the Pacific war did not please any of us. How would they use tanks in the jungles?

CAMP SHANKS, NEW YORK

Again, we boarded a train for New York and the port of embarkation – Camp Shanks. Most of the fellows did not object to the train ride as it did take up time. We were treated to great scenery in Colorado. We learned of a train wreck somewhere in the West, which caused the rerouting of our train that took us as far south as Texas. One remarkable experience greeted us when we passed through a canyon on a moonlit night. High above us we could see a suspension bridge that looked like polished silver.

In time, we reached our destination Camp Shanks. Once there, it was a complete blackout. No phone calls. We could receive mail but could not send any. Mail received came from other Army camp addresses as our position was not to be revealed to family members. It seemed every Army camp left memories that characterize it. I do not recall men allowed access to liquor. Card games were one of the main pastimes.

I played a lot of chess but could not always find a chess partner. Card games were not my kind of pastime, but in a tight arrangement, it seemed we do things not in our normal routine. I entered a poker game and with only $2.00 and some change, I was quickly wiped out. Even during that dreary evening, we heard the welcome report "Mail call!"

Eagerly hoping for something, I received a small envelope from my parents. It was near Christmas and as could be expected, it was a card wishing me a Merry Christmas. Enclosed was a five-dollar bill. To my parents even a $5.00 bill was a lot of money in those days. My sense of reason seemed to evaporate and I thought that ***maybe*** I could win back my loss from earlier in the evening.

I was welcomed back into the game. The short space of time it took for me to lose those five dollars haunts me to this day. My parents, very religious people, never knew what happened to that gift. I actually grieved over the loss. Here was a camp of soldiers waiting to be shipped overseas to a combat zone, and me – gambling away my precious gift. Such behavior was without excuse.

I learned later that my wife was having complications with pregnancy during my stay at Camp Shanks. She tried desperately to get me to return home, but to no avail. Phone calls and even telegrams were ignored. Perhaps a doctor's recommendation would have helped, but it seemed that anyone could trump up a reason to get out of the trip overseas.

After being at Camp Shanks for about a week, there was a sense of relief when orders finally came down to board ship. Preparing our belongings into a duffel bag became routine practice no matter what was our destination. Every soldier had a prescribed listing of needs that seemed adequate in the eyes of the high command.

The alphabetical listing of our names had some benefits. We learned to know certain fellows well enough to think of them as buddies. Perhaps that element may be expected no matter whom we are with. The time came for the boarding announcement. If ever there was tight security, it was then. Military police were used to keep lines moving and nobody could take a shortcut out of line. Going aboard varied with different ships – but we entered on a gangplank that was lowered to the deck. The next chapter will explain activities on the ship.

ABOARD SHIP

Our "home" for the next seventeen days would be aboard a Liberty ship – styled for Pacific waters. According to reports, Liberty ships were round bottomed. The difference in styling would be up to ship builders who understood the type of weather to contend with. In any case, a ship is subject to rolling and pitching in heavy seas. It seems that the shortage of ships required the use of whatever was available. That was of little concern to a bunch of military men – fresh out of basic training.

Much planning by the high command was necessary in preparing a convoy of ships. There were forty-five ships in New York Harbor – anchored in readiness for the voyage. Our ship was the largest, and the only troop ship in the convoy. I do not know the dimensions or the tonnage, but the ship could hold 4500 men, and the Navy personnel assigned for duty. It was a known fact that ships were vulnerable to attack, and some were lost before us. With thousands aboard, a crippled ship is a major disaster. Extreme security was the order of the day when troops were guided up the gangplank.

After boarding, Navy personnel instructed us in smaller groups in the procedure for "abandon ship". With a limited number of lifeboats available, we had to learn how to jump into the sea. It was very scary. Personal belongings would be left behind. The distance to the water would depend on which deck we were positioned. The special orders for our personal safety called for us to cup one hand over our nose and the other hand to protect our crotch. Should the order be announced to "abandon ship", we were ordered to jump feet first. Diving was NOT an option.

The convoy was football shaped. Our troop ship was the largest and centered in the convoy. Surrounding us were cargo ships, destroyers, and destroyer escorts. The escorts were the smallest and more maneuverable. They carried depth charges for protection against sub attacks.

Even before spending the first night in our quarters, four of us were assigned to operate the naval guns in the upper level gun turrets. Since only a few of us had tank training, our experience with tank guns qualified us for this dubious task. Here we were taking our place on board ship with Navy men who we believed were highly qualified for the duty. The largest guns we had experience with were 76 mm – about three inches. Since we were still in port, the training on the five-inch naval guns would wait until we were in deeper water.

As we took our place in the gun turret, it was a very unusual night. The sea was calm and to the south toward Florida, a full moon was to our benefit. Even in December, the air was very mild and we could spend time getting better acquainted. Personally, I was very excited for having some reason to be there, but realized that others were depressed at the thought of what they were facing at the end our journey.

The men picked for the gun crew were taken from the bottom of the roster. That included Wilson, Zeek, Zimba and Young. I will never forget Zeek. He was a very handsome, sturdy young man. Clearly, in the moonlight as we shared, he said, “Young, when I get home, I am going to eat a steak this thick!” He held his thumb and middle finger apart at least two full inches. Remember Zeek. His name will come up later.

One of the elements in being on a ship is the problem of seasickness. Perhaps much of it is caused by rumors that motion causes the problem. Those of us on gun watch learned an important lesson. When we were high above the water, we could see when the ship would pitch and roll. The men below deck in cramped quarters could hear the waves beating against the ship. In addition, it gave the impression that the compartment was tilting when they could not see the action. Those of us on the gun crew seemed to fare quite well and we all escaped going on sick call. Of course, we had to take our turn below deck, but remembered what we learned above deck.

All of us were constantly learning the ways of military life whether it be the Army - state side - or now the Navy. Perhaps our view of the Navy was limited to what we saw without knowing what sailors experienced in comparison to soldiers. Life aboard ship was not luxurious. Quarters were very cramped. My memory tells me that we were at least four levels high in the sleeping quarters. We heard that upper bunks were best, simply because if you were in a lower level and somebody above you was seasick, he may not have time to find a latrine. A great help for an emergency was to have our steel helmet close by.

It seemed we were always facing wind. For the most part, the forward motion of the ship was causing air currents. Sea gulls were ever present. They hovered near the ship alert to food cast overboard. The gulls did not flap their wings but allowed air currents to keep them aloft. Gulls did not come aboard the ship, but it puzzled me where they were at night. They always returned in daylight.

Cooking for more than 4500 men was a major undertaking. All we knew of it was to listen for the welcome sound of the glockenspiel to let us know it was chow time. Boiled potatoes and wieners could be expected as a main course for the enlisted men. We learned that the officers had an entirely different menu. However, that was of little concern to the soldier boys. We did not receive any special training on board ship. Due to the different branches of service, that would have been rather involved. As tankers, we were in the minority. The time came to fire the five-inch guns at imaginary targets. The noise was deafening and caused thunder throughout the entire vessel.

After two weeks aboard ship, we experienced some very rough water. Those inclined to seasickness got worse. One fellow, named Red, lay on the deck – so sick – he prayed to die and was afraid he would.

One early evening as we approached the European mainland, we were alerted to the deafening sound of depth charges from our destroyer escorts. The charges were used in defense of submarines. As I have mentioned before, very little of the workings of military affairs is made known to the average soldier. This was undoubtedly a defensive operation by the Navy. At night, the explosion causes a bright light even under the water. If a submarine was near, the explosion could crush the hull even if it did not actually come in contact. The noise inside the ship was very unnerving. The fellows had no idea what was happening. The sound of the explosion travels through the water as we learned that the density of water causes the sound to travel for miles.

This was not a pleasure cruise. Generally speaking, we were well taken care of. There was a hospital ready for emergencies. Food was adequate. Sleeping quarters were warm. Taking a shower with salt water was not a pleasant experience. The special soap did not do the job. We felt 'sticky' for several hours.

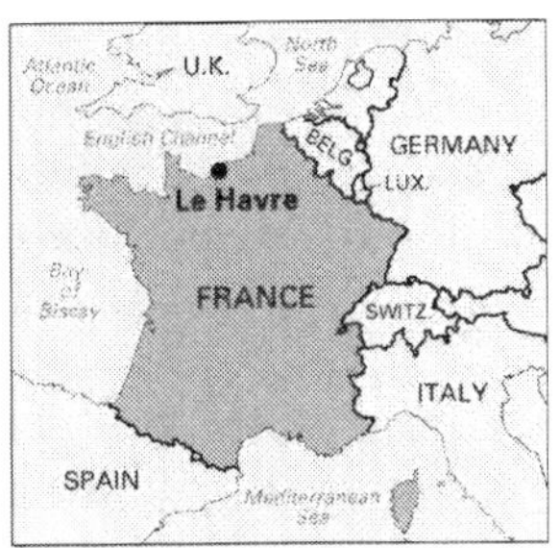

I am sure we all looked forward to docking. As we approached the harbor at Le Havre, France the various ships with cargo and other functions gradually left the convoy. Our troop ship was the only vessel to enter the harbor.

It is not possible for everyone to be on deck, but for those of us who had opportunity, we were shocked at what we saw in the harbor. Several ships lay on their side and it appeared they had been for the most part, sunk. We were greatly relieved to learn that they were 'fakes', built by the Germans as fortresses when they were in control of that area, with heavy artillery for armor. Fortunately, they were all disarmed.

The order to disembark came next. Normally, those at the head of the alphabetical order were first in line. In this case, the Yorks, Youngs, Zeek and Zimba were first to leave the ship. This was an advantage in that we did not have to sweat out long lines of men listening to the unending calling out of names. Following this, we were trucked inland to prepare for meeting combat forces.

FOREIGN SOIL – COMBAT ZONE

Setting foot on foreign soil was truly an experience – hard to describe. This was not a culture exchange or a sightseeing tour, but the hard cold facts of facing combat. A look about us in France showed the scars of war. Action before we arrived was evident. We were replacement forces and we could see bombed out buildings and piles of rubble. How the troops ahead of us fared we may never know, but they were engaged even at the point where we entered the scene.

Sounds of artillery appeared to be ever present. Both forces used the long-range guns. France was a part of Allied forces, so we felt somewhat secure – at least for the present. As we were waiting for further directions, we could reflect on the comforts left behind. Our homes were our castles and even the Army barracks as well as quarters aboard ship provided adequate needs.

The period of time from our first day in the stateside camp until our entering foreign territory was relatively short. Most of the men in the group just off the ship were quite young. Many were in their late teens and early twenties. It appeared that food was available to a satisfactory degree, but the one missing element that caught us all was the lack of toilet facilities. More than anything was the shortage of roll paper.

The war was still hot in late 1944. As replacement troops, we had no idea where we would be sent. We had to trust the sergeants or officers in charge for direction. A quick truck ride to an assembly point began our involvement.

The first item of business was a rifle issued for personal use. In freezing weather, our first job was to clean the heavy grease from our weapon. Large garbage cans filled with heated water provided the means to rinse the grease from all parts of the rifle. Our training at camps in the USA was helpful in getting the job done. While rifle parts were still hot, getting rid of moisture was necessary before we could oil and reassemble the rifle.

A lieutenant named Jones was our first contact when preparing for the trip into France. He said he was a Jew and he made sure that we understood the use of the word liaison, a word commonly used in military assembly direction. Lieutenant Jones said emphatically "the word is LEE-A-ZON and don't let me hear you say it any other way". He seemed sincere, but there may have been a bit of humor in the comment. I don't recall much else from Lt. Jones, but it was late afternoon and after a quick meal, we loaded up in a truck and headed for Southern France.

Here was the culmination of eight months of training. Need it be said that the total purpose of our training was to subdue the enemy? I am not sure how the general response struck the average soldier, but we were trained to kill. When we review the many weapons, **all** were geared to accomplish some form of destruction.

WOOL CAP

We had unloaded from trucks and marched through the strife-torn city of La Havre, France. Snow covered the ground. Streets were slushy and the chilly wind whined through our helmets. Small faces peered through the crowd of civilian onlookers in sheer wonder at the sight of American soldiers who, in their thinking, were filthy rich. Their inexhaustible source of chewing gum, chocolate, and cigarettes never ceased to amaze, especially the younger set. Hollow-eyed youngsters, many of them orphans, were among those who watched hundreds of well-fed soldiers march in full combat garb to the bivouac area in the outlying parts of the city. Trying hard to give a moment of feeling towards those in need, the reality of the situation climaxed as a small boy dived after an apple core tossed by a soldier. I knew I would never see that little fellow again, yet he left an indelible imprint on my mind – that hunger gripped Europe. Another element entered into the picture, the lack of warm clothing.

Some situations may seem unimportant, but they are all part of our experiences. Personal items of clothing are important to any of us. During my first night in camp my wool knit cap – worn inside the helmet - was stolen. Perhaps I should say it was merely transferred to a head that needed it worse than I did. It was not the work of a GI, but some youngster. Small boys hung around all military establishments looking for candy or cigarettes. Nearly all of them smoked regardless of age. A smoldering cigarette had only to lie for a few seconds when it was promptly snatched up for a few more puffs.

I needed a wool knit cap. There were none in the supply truck and neither could I find anyone who had an extra cap. A slight French boy, about nine or ten years old was standing near the PX truck. He wore no coat; his shoulders were hunched from the cold. He was puffing a cigarette he had just picked up. The cigarette was really too short to be held, but the boy managed. He asked me for "chocolate" and a cigarette for "Papa." I was more interested in the wool-knit Army cap he wore. "How much for the cap?" I asked. His only answer was "Cigarette um Papa."

I bargained for the cap. It was not the one I had lost. My own was plainly marked. The boy must have worn it day and night for weeks. The rim inside the headband was thickly coated with grease from his hair and inside the earflaps, he had stored wads of chewing gum – for future use. After I made the deal, I nearly changed my mind, except, I did need a cap before going to the front. I carefully carved the gum out of the earlaps and washed the cap in cold water using face soap. The perfumed aroma remained in the cap almost all winter serving one purpose – to remind me of a little lad in want. He no doubt could have used the cap, but he had an unusually thick head of hair. His real need was a coat.

A SORE THROAT? NOT ME

No doubt, the driver knew where he was going, but we had to travel under the cover of darkness. Our driver stopped in front of a small French home. I am sure he had been there before.

It was headquarters for the 756th tank battalion company B. Nine of us entered the home and were greeted by a tall slender lieutenant. I believe we were somewhere near Alsace-Lorraine in eastern France.

The point of contact was the Colmar Pocket where Germans held out in trenches and foxholes, stubbornly resisting the American forces. We learned later it was a swampy area where movement of troops was difficult and perhaps very nearly impossible for tanks.

I have trouble to this day to understand fully the procedure at times, but the first thing was a quick exam amounting to taking our temperature and a look at our throat. Why this was important before entering combat was a puzzle, but we learned that orders are orders. The lieutenant looked at my throat and said, "Soldier, you have a sore throat. You will stay here tonight." Frankly, I do not recall having a sore throat, but I learned to respect orders.

It must have been about 8:00 or 9:00 PM. Four of the men from the nine were immediately sent out for duty at the front. Remember Zeek? He was among those sent to the front. I never saw him again. He became a casualty his first time out and none of the other four returned. The word I got was that they were killed while crossing a canal.

What about my red throat? I did not fake it. That was a medic's decision. Frankly, I do not recall that it hurt or felt sore. However, it has come to my thoughts – hundreds of times - I may well have been a victim along with Zeek. That mental picture of Zeek in the moonlight on board ship haunts me to this day.

In the early morning hours after we lost Zeek, still dark, I was assigned to a medium tank alongside of another tank. We were to point our tank guns toward enemy positions and fire many rounds of ammunition in that direction. This was covering fire for infantrymen – creeping along the ground to reach enemy emplacements.

The anxiety of it all – we could not see what we were doing as it was still dark, but we followed orders. In time, we heard from forward observers the mission was accomplished. As a tank gunner, I could only see what was in my telescopic sight. It was like looking at the front through a pipe, but nearly impossible when dark. The first action, where I was involved, was a success.

A lieutenant standing behind me in the tank placed his hands on my shoulders. By pulling back a bit meant to raise my gun. Pushing forward meant to lower it and the direction either to the left or right was given by him twisting a bit – left or right on my shoulders. We learned very quickly.

Most of our tank warfare was at night. As I said earlier, we could not even see our target at times, but somehow, by telephone – the command picked up the messages. Every time we anticipated action, we lined up for orders in a point behind the lines and when the hour arrived we pushed off with infantry men and other tanks to accomplish our mission.

Here we were, truly green troops, hopefully learning fast. Our lieutenant had told us there were many casualties, but he said, "We are learning to be more cautious." That sounded good to us. However, who could predict the enemy?

To be more cautious was a vague comment to those of us only a few hours at the front. Some things we learned by default rather than by a scheduled lecture or training period. Only about 20% of troops were at the front at any given time, a comment made by an officer. The rest were deployed in some other activity such as supply, reserve troops, hospitals and/or headquarters.

48 HOURS ON; 96 HOURS OFF

The same lieutenant that told us things would improve, also told us that with enough men we would be at the front 48 hours and could be away from action 96 hours. That is the ratio of guard duty – serve two hours and off four. This was normally a one-day stand.

Nevertheless, we believed our lieutenant and after being at the front for 48 hours, we all checked the time. It grew to 96 hours – and several days - and even weeks and we were <u>still</u> out there. I can tell you that it never happened. We were not relieved all winter. We stayed in our tank, as it became our mobile home. At that point, we were becoming accustomed.

Supplies were brought to us so we had ammunition replaced and food in the form of canned rations. Most cans could be opened with a key that came with the same can. With a little self-help, we were able to heat the beans or stew over a small gas stove using white gas. Starting fires had problems as it had to be done outside the tank.

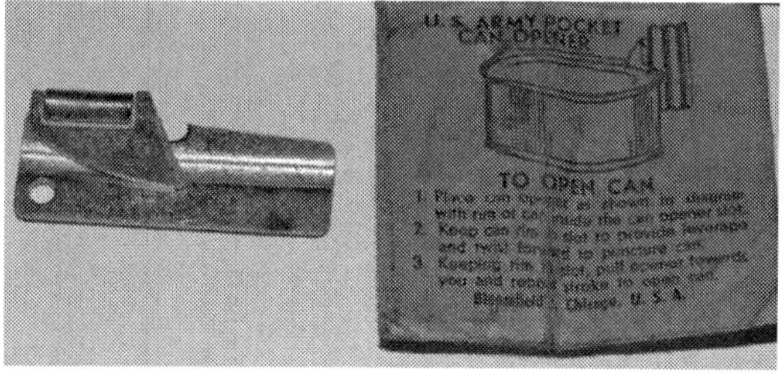

Not wishing to have a chore with eating utensils and clean up in cold weather, I took a soup spoon from my packet and used it for every need. I could eat soup, cut meat, or spread butter, if we ever received bread. Soldiers learn to put up with less. I kept the spoon in my pocket so I did not have to look for it.

I will try to give account of certain action without being excessive. Actual sequence of events is not easy to recall after over 60 years away from action. However, I can be truthful that the different actions I wish to comment on are indelible in my mind.

Our job was to support infantry. We had the undesirable situation of being under the control of infantry officers. Many of them were fine, upstanding men, but they assumed tanks were invincible – that we could do anything. That may have varied in different pockets of activity, but those of us in tanks were not close enough to other tanks for companionship. We were, however, in touch with infantry soldiers as much as our own tankers. We worked together in teamwork. We were stuck to be in our tanks while foot soldiers could be in bunkers, foxholes, or buildings as conditions allowed.

I did not envy the infantrymen – they were exposed a great deal of the time. We learned that they had mixed feelings about tanks. The noise drew attention from enemy sources. Foot soldiers saw tanks as death traps. If a tank was hit, shrapnel was the deadly element – feared by tankers. I saw tanks that had been hit that burned for two or three days.

HEY, LET'S LIGHT A MATCH!

Military units do not stay in one location very long lest the enemy learn their habits. Our tanks were constantly being moved – sometimes a few city blocks; sometimes several miles.

Toward evening one day just before dusk, we were alone on a gravel road along a bank of small trees. This was our first major combat assignment. I believe the trees blocked the view from the enemy and we were thankful for that. To our consternation an infantry major came to our tank and ordered us to head across an open field to "knock out" four tank destroyers on the opposite side of the field.

These behemoths were far and above us in firepower. They were outfitted with the feared 88 mm tank guns that were able to shoot a projectile one-mile per second. Our tank gun was hopelessly incapable of hurting hidden tank destroyers say nothing of facing four with their positions dug in. Our little 75 mm gun could only do 1900 feet per second – hopelessly incapable of doing the job against tank destroyers.

What do we do? We obey orders as able. Our nineteen-year-old tank driver, Corporal Hardy, started his engine and was cool and collected as we mounted up and slowly headed for certain defeat toward an opening in the trees. If we were moving towards them, we would be like sitting ducks. They could have their guns trained on us from their dug-in position. Further, if we were moving, it would be extremely difficult to see our target much less fire our weapon from a moving tank. We were all shaken by the order.

It was a very cold day in January with snow and ice covering the road. When Hardy reached the point in the road to turn left towards our target, the tank slipped off the road. The shoulder in the narrow road did not support our tank and the tank slid sideways off the road to the left in a precarious position in the ditch – leaning at about a 45-degree angle. Every attempt to dislodge the tank failed. We took sticks and branches to try to make a footing for the tank tracks to give traction but to no avail. The tracks on our tank were rubber covered, totally unlike the tracks on farm tractors. All the while, we were unarmed and exposed to the enemy, but the tank only wallowed deeper in the futile attempt. Darkness set in.

The infantry major ordered us to at least turn our gun towards the enemy, but here again the angle of the tank was a hopeless case. The infantry major was furious but we did the best we could.

With the tank leaning one way, we were unable to bring the gun into a favorable position. The weight of the gun tended to swing the turret in the direction of the tilt of the tank. I was the gunner. I tried to power the gun into position but it caught on something inside the tank and was somehow incapacitated. I worked to turn the turret by hand as I truly tried to please the major.

Someone said we should try to see why we could not traverse the gun into position. We did not have flashlights. However, we did have matches. It was always "lights out" at the front, so at best if we lit a cigarette, we had to use care not to reveal our position.

One of the guys said, "Light a match so we can see what's wrong." Here to our horror, a 75 mm tank shell had broken loose when the tank slid in the ditch and got caught in the turret basket. The brass shell had become crushed and released all of the gunpowder, scattering it all over the floor of the turret. The fact that we were not blown to kingdom come is a miracle – especially after we lit a match! The major left in disgust!

SCATTERED CREW

It was very dark and the only light was the light of fires created by artillery shells. We were not able to determine if the artillery was friendly or from enemy sources. It was inky dark and the hope of salvaging our tank was useless. All our gear, weapons, personal belongings were left to fate. What next? The crew scattered as we left a hopelessly crippled tank and we took off for what we hoped was towards safe territory. We did not stay together as we were separated in the night. I could not understand why we as crewmembers did not stick together.

I wandered around in the heavy woods trying to make some decision. I came across a large pile of ammunition – large artillery shells – left by the Germans. I got so weary, I crawled on top to get a bit of rest, but artillery was bursting nearby and in the darkness, it made me nervous.

I kept moving on, not knowing where I was. The snow made it somewhat easier to make out images, but the chances of falling into a trap was very real. Finally, I came to a tent not knowing if it was enemy or friendly. American soldiers had a familiar odor about them – namely cigarettes. I took the chance when I was not challenged as I felt I was among other U.S. troops. I slipped on under the flap just to get out of the weather and cold. As men lit their cigarettes, I got a glimpse of things. Oddly, there was no conversation. Inside the tent were men lying on the ground huddling under

Army blankets. I left all my personal belongings in the abandoned tank, so here I was, with only the clothing I wore and in the company of strangers. Someone allowed me to pull part of a blanket over me and I just simply crawled in with them – not knowing who, what or where. I fell asleep, as I was exhausted from the ordeal, for a few hours until daybreak.

In the early morning, a lieutenant entered the tent and woke me. He said to me, "Soldier, take a hold and help carry out this fellow." I did not know that near me was a dead GI, killed with a horrible chest wound. He was covered with a blanket, so I did not see him. I grabbed under his armpits to lift him while another man took his legs. His body buckled since there was no strength in his midsection as we lifted him – his whole midsection blown apart. I have no idea of how many lying on the floor were alive or dead. This was my first encounter with a combat casualty. It was an infantry outpost and I had no reason to remain there. After a short session near that gruesome tent, I found my way back to my own outfit. I must say I was relieved to be back in spite of the hazards each day presented.

RECONNECTING

The uncanny part of all this – our crew did reassemble but I learned early, if you lose a tank – there is another just waiting. However, to our good fortune, we got a new tank – larger – with a more powerful gun. It was a Sherman tank with a 500 horsepower V8 Ford Engine. The tracks were wider and the cleats were steel giving a better grip in various terrain features.

The area of our operations was in southern France. We were assigned to the proud Third Infantry Division that had great experience in the African Campaign and up through Salerno in Italy. We felt that the officers who survived the early months of the war were qualified to make major decisions. Our tank unit was only a battalion, just four companies, so we were not capable of a massive armored attack, but as I mentioned earlier, we were to support infantry soldiers in close encounters.

SNO-PACKS

Soldiers had a constant concern for the chill of winter and all I had to wear were leather boots. My feet were getting colder by the day and I sorely needed sno-packs, but they were in short supply. I still had not received sno-packs and the original leather boots I wore became covered with the blood of that unfortunate soldier. I carried blood on my boots for several days until I received my sno-packs. The supply trucks would come around and if they didn't have what we needed, we would put in a request for that. Getting my sno-packs was very welcome. I do not recall if I had a choice for size, but the ones I got were size 13. I could put on about six pairs of heavy socks, which made it feel like I was walking on a mattress all the time.

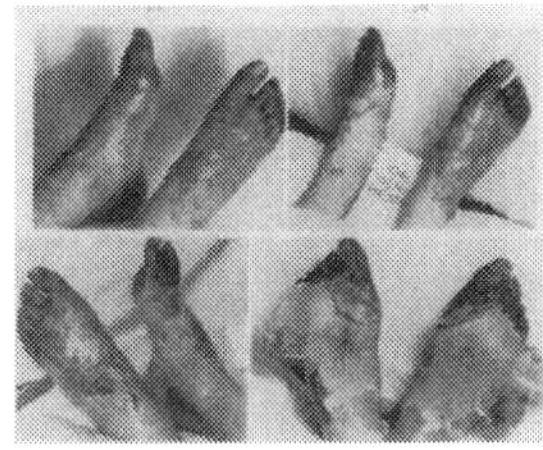

An extended period with feet being extra cold can result in trench foot. Trench foot is not a disease but the lack of circulation. It cost some foot soldiers their feet when gangrene set in. Tankers were not able to do much foot travel so the inactivity was a problem. I was within a few days of the dreaded trench foot. The bottom of my feet had turned a deathly white like cotton with no feeling, no blood. Only by a miracle did they begin to regain normalcy and have feeling again. My feet tingled like being asleep for months. But, thankfully, it left no lasting problem.

COLMAR POCKET

The Colmar pocket was a holdout with Germans at the same time as the Battle of the Bulge raged. I believe I would have preferred the Colmar pocket, but here again we were just a platoon of tanks under orders from higher authority. The area in France was a mix of hills and valleys and the trouble area was referred to as the Colmar pocket.

After the first morning, we were engaged using tanks plus infantry to rout Germans. I am reminded that the tank to our right was also one of our platoons and the tank commander was hit in the eye. Only a few hours at the front, and he was removed for medical attention.

On one assignment, we were ordered to take a black top road up a mountain trail. Ours was the only tank taking part. Snow and ice were on the roadway. Our tank weighed nearly fifty tons. As our driver edged up the curving trail, we felt the tank starting to slip backwards. A steep bank to our right was a true concern. Hardy stopped the tank and fortunately the slipping only took place when the tank was in motion. The tank commander told all of us to leave the tank except the driver. He felt that if the tank slipped over the edge, it would be best if only the driver stayed with it.

Putting the tank in low gear, Hardy worked the levers to move the tank toward the edge of the road to gain the advantage of traction with one track outside the blacktop. That was scary because it was much closer to the drop-off. However, it worked, and the rest of us walked up the grade until the driver reached a point where we could rejoin him. We stood a chance in the open terrain of being a target for snipers or anti-tank guns. I am not sure of the distance, but we rolled on into a French community. Buildings on the outskirts of many of the towns were actually small farms with a few cows.

"APPLE JACK"

After the mountain climb, we moved into several small French villages. Bear in mind that even though the war was going on, civilians in any of these towns were trying to carry on with their daily routines.

Because of previous raids, we often were able to occupy a town without direct confrontations. We were quite welcome in many of the French homes – so it seemed. Food may be shared to some degree, but one thing very common in French homes was the very large wine vat in the basement. Homes reeked of wine, which caused some of our fellows to find a suitable container and stock up.

Some fellows called it "apple jack" not too strong from an intoxicating point of view, but I thought it more like cider. It was not my kind of thing and at best, I only tasted of it.

Not known to most people, the use of alcohol was a factor in certain situations. I am not in a position to state that officers in charge advised liquor, but if anyone was in a position to obtain liquor, it was officers.

THEY MADE IT OUT – TANK MINE HIT

Our job as a battalion was to probe some uncharted areas. That is what reconnaissance is all about. We loaded foot soldiers on our tank as many as could hang on and poked into areas to test enemy strength.

We spent one day on a daytime raid. One thing everyone understands is a white flag. While we were in a slightly wooded area seeing the results of our action, a bunker of German soldiers came out waving a white flag. One of our tanks proceeded down a fairly steep hill ahead of us to join up with the infantry.

Feeling a bit relaxed after taking some prisoners, we were watching our buddies in the tank ahead when WHAM – a violent explosion rocked his tank. The blast was the result of dreaded tank mines, carefully dug into the gravel road. No one spoke, but gazed at the scene where the cloud of dust created was enough to cover a football field and we shuddered to know our buddies were in there.

Suddenly, to our great relief someone yelled, "There goes one!" Then another fellow came running out of the dust blast and when number five made it, if we didn't shout "Praise the Lord" – we should have. Amazingly prompt was the delivery of the replacement tank for our buddies. They seem to drop out of nowhere.

PERSHING TANKS

We were subject to the advent of new equipment and that included new tanks. It may be assumed that the larger tanks had more firepower, but the medium tanks were more to our liking. It may be due to our training, or experience. The light tanks were used at times to take care of some stubborn pockets, and we never were near when they were in use.

The same may be said of the heavy or Pershing tanks. They were available, but we only were given orientation and the "feel" actually was not part of my experience.

RED HOT GUN

The men in every tank crew became buddies. They were like brothers. Much of the terrain in the war zone was heavy woods. One night we were cut off by some twist of fate, and we were ordered by phone to keep shooting in the direction of the enemy to ward off an attack by foot soldiers. They can hurt a tank with bazookas. I was the gunner and kept traversing the turret. We fired over 10,000 rounds of 30 caliber machine gun rounds and our gun became red hot. Since all machine guns were fed by belted ammunition, we were shocked to see that the gun would continue to fire by the red-hot chamber setting off the ammo. We had a runaway machine gun. The bullets no longer left the gun in a straight line, but took a crazy pattern, like in a nondescript flight pattern. We could see the tracer bullets in their erratic flight.

The gun was directly over the driver's hatch. Fortunately, our tank driver was short – only 5'2". Had he been any taller, he may have been killed. When firing our machine gun ceased, he opened his hatch and stood up.

WHAM! The red-hot gun fired again and little Torchia (Joe (Joseph) Torchia – T/4) dropped into his seat – yelling like everything at those blankety-blank gunners, but the slug missed him.

I had to twist the belt and hang on to prevent it feeding another shell into the chamber. Oddly, after some heart-pounding operation that had all of us on our toes, a rehashing of the episode was the natural reaction. Only a few days into the war and we began to feel like old GI Joes. Night fell and we rejoined our other tanks in the morning.

CARMELLO, FRANK PFC (KIA)

For a space of time, Carmello was my ammo loader. This unusual soldier was about 5'10" tall, sandy blond with a trim mustache, and even at the front, he looked like a garrison soldier. His shoes were clean and polished and his clothing always neat. He never attained rank above private first class and was one of those Casanovas – like Willette, Reed and Torchia – just a few of the men who regularly entertained girls – even during combat. The crew discreetly left the tank once, while Carmello would spend a half hour or so with a French or German girl. Nobody could control these fellows.

We stopped our tank on a hill near a provincial home. It was a bright spring day and Carmello brought a chair out of the house to use as a barber chair. He was a barber among other things and did a good job with just scissors and a comb. I could look to the south and see a strange sight. We were in full view of a few German soldiers who were taking a break – having coffee or some other liquid – who knows.

I feel it much a part of combat experiences to mention that war is not really as depicted in the movies. I do not believe German soldiers were any more anxious to be at the front than we were. This was especially true toward the winding down days of conflict.

Suddenly, Carmello turned to me and yelled, "Cut that out!" He thought I had hit him with something. The fact is that he was shot in the rear end and it became real when blood ran down his leg. I do not recall how that ended, but it was time to move on and Carmy survived with probably minor medical attention.

On very rare occasions, we got our hands on real American style foods. In a few days, we had acquired some eggs, bacon and white bread. The front line soldier is very enterprising and when you need a gas stove, plus cast iron griddle, spatula et al, you get it - perhaps from an abandoned home.

This versatile Carmello also became a fry chef. During a short break, when we were all in our tank, Carmy started the gas stove in the middle of the turret floor. Soon the sputtering sound of bacon frying brought with it the wonderful aroma that turns anyone on. We all anticipated a touch of home and a late breakfast as eggs were cracked and though everyone was anxious to eat, we were willing to wait our turn.

Before the coveted breakfast was ready, the very unwelcome order came - crank 'em up. Our driver, Torchia, started the engine and we moved up a few hundred feet. Carmello had set the griddle off to one side and snuffed the flame. We moved quickly to a new spot. I believe the cast iron griddle was still warm when Carmy pumped up the gas stove again. Enthusiasm ran high as breakfast time seemed certain.

Almost as if by demonic force, a repeat order came again to move on, for reasons known only to the commanding officer. Carmello's composure was weakening, yet he performed as before. Changing location was for strategy, but the distance moved may have been less than a mile.

For the third time, Carmy went through the motions but with a subdued spirit. The eggs looked like yellow tire patches and the bacon - perhaps it was still edible.

Unexpectedly, the third report came to move out. When an angry fry cook goes into action, watch out! I am sure he depleted completely the expletives so well known to most military men when not under attack. Out through the open hatch went frying pan, bacon, eggs and even the stove as well as the coffee. It all lay in the ditch as we pulled away. Carmello had lost his cool and no one had the courage to challenge Carmello's behavior.

Later, when we were in Bamburg, Germany waiting for orders, in broad daylight, all seemed very calm. We heard a tank engine start up. To our surprise, Carmello had access to an extra tank, and he rolled on by. Seated in the drivers' seat with the hatch open, grinning, with a cigar in his mouth and headed for downtown, he was alone. Whereas such behavior raises an eyebrow, how does one correct it?

Everything seems quite normal, but it started turning dark and the usual procedure was for each man to satisfy his own food needs. There was in fact an eerie calm. No lights were on in town.

Soon, we would hear a small airplane, which seemed quite natural. Without warning, a huge light from a flair lit up the town. Suddenly, all hell broke loose as personnel bombs, designed to kill people and not destroy an object, rained down on our position.

Tank hatches were slammed shut and all we could do was hang tough. The bombs were designed to kill foot soldiers. Several hit our tanks, but in time all this unwelcome action ceased and we tried to regroup as best we could.

About an hour later, our driver Torchia, also adventurous, stuck his head in the main hatch on our tank and said, "Well, they got Carmello." Thus ended the tour of duty of a truly renegade soldier. This ne'er-do-well soldier often complained that he was denied the job of being in charge of a tank.

MAGINOT LINE

Perhaps most people have heard of the pill boxes or bunkers in France called the Maginot Line. The Maginot Line was built by the French before WW II as a defense from the east in southern France, but easily outflanked by the Germans. The defense system runs along a line that was intended to halt invading forces. The Germans made use of the defense line against the French.

As I said elsewhere, much of our activity was at night. When a town or village was secured or in American control, it is the common practice for tanks to line up on a given street – spaced apart about 200 feet or perhaps a city block.

Infantry soldiers accompanying the tanks would be in wait in ditches if possible with rifles and gear. A ditch made a good place to provide extra protection, as we never knew when a renegade enemy soldier or sniper would see someone and take a shot at him. Often, the infantry would creep on the ground under the tank shells, and we learned that they loved us and hated us – depending on the net results. We had the utmost respect for those who had the frightening job of taking enemy positions and taking prisoners. Casualties were high on both sides.

We were in southern France and prepared for a night attack. An assignment came for our unit to enter a French town after dark. Here again we worked with infantry soldiers in a mop-up operation. There was a constant sound of machine guns and artillery. Tank officers were shifted from one company to the other constantly. In this instance, it was Lieutenant Melfi's turn to command our tank on this one occasion. I believe he and Bob Padgett knew each other before Bob came to our tank.

SECOND LIEUTENANT MELFI, ANTHONY F. (KIA)

The town we entered on this eventful night was quite generally on fire from air strikes. Our job was to move in and secure it. It was very dark outside the town, but the burning buildings in town lit up the lieutenant's face, under the steel helmet he wore, as he stood in the hatch from where he gave orders.

Conversation was difficult in the roar of the tank, but we learned to communicate in other ways and when specific orders were required, we learned to pay close attention. As the gunner, I was given direction by the hands on shoulders routine. The lieutenant in charge of operations used our tank for leading the attack. He kept pointing out targets for me to fire at. Truly, we had no way to assess the damage.

Tank commanders were almost required to be exposed from the shoulders up to do any kind of a job. They were about eleven feet above ground and many were lost because of the exposure. Several times, I looked back at our lieutenant and observed facial expressions and I could see him blink now and then, as if to wonder how it would feel to be hit. He blinked quite a bit, but we made it through the night without a problem.

Our close work with the infantry presented many challenges. Armor gave us maximum protection against small arms. Infantry officers in contact with us explained that a pillbox in the Maginot Line was full of enemy soldiers. The pillbox or bunker was covered with earth and sod to hide its identity from the air. Our job – knock out the bunker.

The condition prompted an infantry officer to call on us to blast a pillbox full of Germans. We placed our tank about a city block from the front of the heavy steel door of the fort. Lieutenant Melfi ordered me to fire at the door! Shells burst against the door but no damage was done. It looked like a standoff.

Using binoculars, the lieutenant observed a dark spot near the top of the bunker. He believed it might have been an observation slot where a lookout kept track of enemy moves. Lieutenant Melfi asked that I try to put a few rounds of 30 caliber tracer bullets from our machine gun into that spot. We could see the bullets enter what proved to be a lookout. Next, he asked that I place a 76 mm high explosive shell in the targeted opening. Since the machine gun and tank gun were coaxially mounted, I was already lined up so I let it fly. The shell found its mark causing dust and smoke to squeeze out around the steel door.

Within moments, the door burst open and a German soldier came out waving a white flag signaling that the crew surrendered. I have no idea if anyone was killed in the bunker, but the American infantry soldiers did the mop-up and took prisoners. We were all glad for daylight.

Later in the day when things settled down some of us had opportunity to see inside the bunker. It had two levels, but I chose not to inspect farther into the crude structure. There were liquor bottles, a supply of sausage in a special white cover and some of the best chocolate I had ever eaten. The food items seemed to be properly covered and therefore none of us feared being poisoned. After breaking the cover off the sausage, I can report that it also was of the best quality. The sleeping area was just a flat plank bunk with only a pile of straw for a bed; no blankets or mattresses. It was probably as comfortable as our tanks or better, but we had no interest to use the facility. I believe there was a cache of liquor bottles also in the bunker – all empties.

Lieutenant Melfi moved on to another tank company that day. My buddy, Bob Padgett, told me later that the handsome platoon leader did get killed down line in a different tank. He was an extremely handsome fellow – small in stature. I considered him a very brave man. It may be of little value to report, but all of us had favorite officers, and surely, Lieutenant Melfi was one of them. We were saddened indeed to learn of his death.

FIREWOOD RAILINGS

In France, a very questionable bit of behavior was to gain firewood by pulling railings off porches of private homes. No one seemed to question it. Removing railings did not wreck the house. As I recall, building a fire in a home was done to prepare food and even share some things. What a paradox. How could we retain relations?

HOUSE GUESTS

We stood a chance in open terrain of being a target for anti-tank guns, but we rolled on into a French community. Decision-making was always a concern. The very presence of a tank may have caused enemy soldiers to lay low. We came to a two-story home, similar to American homes of the 1930s and 1940s, on the outer edge of a small French village and decided to use the home to get some rest. It was common for us to use a house to fry eggs if we had any and catch a wink of sleep if time permitted.

As tankers, we were not free to go into homes by our own decision, but the preliminary work by recon elements determined our assignments. With only a few weeks of experience, we were glad to abide by directives, trusting that such orders were to our benefit.

Houses in Europe were often heavy stone and mortar work or brick. It seems the homes were built to stand the ravages of war. The house had been hit by artillery, leaving a gaping hole to the south. Just inside was the stairway, and all the treads were all blown away. Some plastic sheeting had been used to help close the opening in the south wall. Residents were still in the home. They realized we were friends. Military advance forces had informed them of our use of the property and they cooperated. Other soldiers joined us with their tanks. Before nightfall there were perhaps thirty men assembled.

Fortunately, the average GI tends to look at the humorous side of things. Joking or seeing someone in a predicament evoked laughter. None of us expected the next item of activity. To our welcome surprise, a PX supply truck caught up with us carrying goodies – like candy bars, cigarettes, gum, razor blades, watches, lighters and even beer. Each man received only one bottle – a "stubby" as it was called. There were no refusals. I probably could have sold mine for good money but we all had a "here today – gone tomorrow'" philosophy. This happened only once all winter.

By the time the refreshments were gone it was dark. Imagine a house full of soldiers, perhaps thirty or more, sleeping where they can. Rooms were full of GIs sleeping on beds or wherever there was a space to roll out a sleeping bag. There were no bathrooms. We needed the space upstairs. Only the most minimum of lighting was available, but we were able to take our sleeping bags and made it up the main stair stringers, hazardous to say the least. We were happy to get a few hours of coveted sleep. I don't recall how many men were lying in their bags on the floor, but we were packed in like a bunch of weenies.

Keep in mind that even one bottle of beer in January caused considerable concern. About 2:00 AM, the beer started to catch up with the sleeping troops and the men were seeking relief. One enterprising tanker named

Ervin Zentz (Cpl – KIA) did a little research and thought he had salvaged an awkward situation when in one room he found a tall vase with a narrow neck and limited capacity. It may have been capable of holding upwards of a gallon or more of liquid.

Realizing the stair situation in the dark was not practical, I could hear as a few men used the impromptu vessel. Erv used his own invention, as he was standing in the opening of his sleeping bag when all of us could hear the unmistakable sound of the vase filling. Much laughter and fun poking erupted when Erv was the victim of the container overflowing right on his sleeping bag. In favor of the nature of soldiers, humor prevailed, and I do not recall any cursing in the situation.

Our experiences in the early days in the combat zone matured us rapidly. Some lighthearted behavior is always welcome. Poking innocent barbs at each other took the edge off tension. This was a countryside home with a path – not a bath. Other needs befell the large number of soldiers in the morning as they flocked to the small one-seat outhouse near the barn. Of course, during cold weather, freezing prevented normal action in the outhouse. In no time, it was full to overflowing and a large number of men sought relief up against a board fence leading to the barn.

Seasoned combat men had learned to take situations in stride, but as normal activity took place, the woman of the house appeared with a milk pail, heading for the barn. She passed very near the men who were busy with what should require privacy. She greeted each with a cheery, “Good morning!”

If the subject has not become too offensive, permit me to wrap it up with another comment or two. We all learned that in the old country, "honey carts" as they were called were used to collect waste for future fertilization of the gardens in summer and the same milk maid who greeted the indisposed soldiers, willingly gathered up after them for use at a later date.

HOUSE-TO-HOUSE SEARCH

Fighting men feel the most secure in whatever they were trained to do. Infantrymen had their foxholes and tankers had armor for protection. Strangely, in combat, if a tank crew lost a man, we learned early that asking a foot soldier to fill in a position in the tank made him very uneasy. Some could not wait to be released. To them the tank was a death trap. They had seen tanks burning in battle and the crew lost.

Conversely, when tankers entered a village, if the need arose, we could be asked to leave our tank and go on a house-to-house search for the enemy. It was easy for me to understand the unrest of an infantry soldier in a tank after experiencing the exposure we were subjected to when we took on the house-to-house search on foot.

Infantry soldiers were trained to go on foot to flush out the German soldiers from homes and buildings. At one point, after we had stopped our tanks in the center of a small town, the order came down for all tankers to dismount from the tanks, take a submachine gun, and go on a house-to-house search for holdouts.

We were to go alone – not in pairs. To this day, I cannot understand why we took on the assignment without using the buddy system. I was very nervous at such a practice since we had no training in the States to prepare for this. How does one take the first step? Many homes had been evacuated in this small French town in the Colmar Campaign.

Once you set foot in a street to hunt down the enemy, there is no protection against a well-hidden sniper. It reminded me to pray. There I was, armed with a submachine gun used by tankers. The styling was totally unlike submachine guns used by infantry soldiers.

I went to the front door of a modest home and kicked the door open. It was no time to knock. Better to keep both hands on the gun. There was no one there. As I went on, I gained a little courage. It became easier to repeat the system. I do not recall how many buildings I checked, but I received a real shock when I entered a home and found a dead man sprawled on the living room floor. He may have been a French soldier. I left when I determined there were no live German soldiers there.

This sort of activity was the lot of infantrymen of the Third Infantry Division. I returned to my tank and was truly thankful that I had completed the job without confronting a German. All of the fellows from our tanks returned without any known problem except some prisoners were rounded up. I believe the activity in that part of France had softened the German soldiers to where many of them were happy to surrender. It was interesting to note that captured men were very docile.

WINE VATS IN FRENCH HOMES

While in France, for some reason, we did not sit at a dinner table with the family. It appears to me that customs change from one country to another. However, our experience with the French was acceptable as the country was considered an ally – or friendly.

It seems many folks in that corner of the world, not necessarily only the French, appeared skilled at making what I felt was a mild or even a beverage wine. It appeared upon entering a French home there was one thing in common with other homes and that was the large wine vat in most basements. Fermenting wine left a distinct odor in homes that practiced wine making. I do not recall having much experience with their beverage wine, but overindulgence did not appear to be a problem with the French people. Many of the GIs seemed to get enjoyment from the wine which was colorless, but did not appear to be highly intoxicating.

FRENCH TRAIN RIDES

There is nothing very special about trains from my Army days, but there was a difference in trains in Europe and England. In London, I rode some of the better-built trains of the times. The tracks were very smooth and the starting and stopping were very comfortable.

Air conditioning was not part of trains in those days. However, riding in some of the bumpy cars in France included the four-wheeled cars called the 40 and 8's – which meant 40 men or 8 horses. By chance, if any of them were passenger cars, a little incentive was to receive a little of their beverage wine. You could taste it or not and nobody was offended at a refusal.

MOVING INTO GERMANY

I was impressed by the fact that with all the New Testaments given to us at the induction center, I have no record of seeing any man use one. Oh yes, I prayed a lot. However, my Bible was in a duffel bag – somewhere. Our equipment was just jammed into limited space in the tank.

We finished up in the southern France operations and began our move up into Germany. The names of towns were not made known to tank soldiers. There were many signs made up for military use and thankfully, the infantry officers understood where different units were located or where action was designated.

Moving into Germany was a routine operation with tankers and infantrymen sharing certain activities. The behavior of men seemed to follow certain types. As noted previously, there was no evident use of Bibles or religious activity and men entered into card games as the ready means to be entertained. There was always a card game or two when time permitted. We were not fighting all the time. We entered vacated homes to fix meals or just take a break and rest awhile.

Other situations came about with infantry soldiers. I had great respect for the men who were exposed to the elements as well as the enemy. Rain or snow, heat and cold were all a part of the ground troops. Casualties were far greater with infantry than with tankers.

As a tanker, I could expect anything that goes with war. How German planes would drop personal explosive bombs on our position and engage in firing at our tank when we parked close to a German home and disregard the safety of their own people is questionable. The tank may be able to withstand the machine gun activity, but what about the German people? It occurred to us mostly to protect our own hides.

MUZZLE BLAST FROM A MAIN GUN

There were times when we, as a crew, were called on to do something that most of us would have done differently, had we known. The earlier tanks had main guns that fired high explosive shells as well as armor piercing projectiles. Sitting in the tank, it was of no concern when the newest tanks had a muzzle break.

One thing that always impressed us was the relative cooperative spirit of the German civilians who showed a genuine interest in working with us and even extended a helping hand. As our tank parked very close to a small, very nice, clean home, the main gun was up close to a window. We received the order to fire at some target and the unexpected happened. The muzzle blast smashed the window and caused much damage to the items in the cupboard.

I do not recall what took place after the kitchen-wrecking blast. Nevertheless, my memory causes me to feel relieved that nothing extra took place that we felt was of major concern. The man and his wife were pleasant people. Our sorrow for their problem did not repair anything. I could not feel any desire on their part to see us get what we deserved after the mishap. All we could do was to be ready for the next command from headquarters and move out to join other forces.

GERMAN WOMEN COOKING

When the German women prepared a meal, we always had the impression that they used their skills in providing the best, as we did not feel that the entire German populace considered us as enemy or unfriendly. I believe the greater bulk of German civilians seemed desirous to avoid conflict. Truthfully, had it not been that most of us felt that our presence was acceptable, it could have created much discontent.

PAPA, WHERE IS THE GOLD?

Some accounts from war experiences appear to have somewhat of a flavor of men getting out of order. It is difficult to describe what enters a soldier's mind to engage in activity that he would ordinarily consider out of order. Wartime generates feelings that seem to be born of the notion that being called to take part in a foreign country suggests conflict. As a result, it is easy to see that little, if any, consideration is given to avoiding misdeeds.

My memory notes suggest that I experienced another soldier engaging in such behavior. To ask an elderly man "Papa, where is the gold?" suggests gaining something, not earned, by demanding he give it up, not wishing to engage in conflict. I have no idea just how much of such activity went on.

SILK STOCKINGS FOUND IN RAILCAR

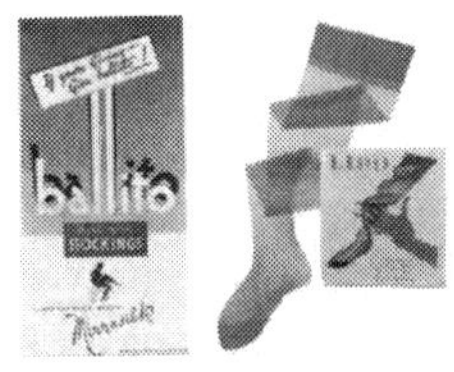

One thing that seems to be natural for soldiers is rumors. Near the area we were stationed in Germany was a railroad yard with cars ready to be unloaded. The word was that one car had a substantial load of silk stockings. Promptly a number of GIs got wind of the "trading stock" and dared the elements to open the car and check the contents. Our tank was near enough we could see the performance, and the soldiers involved were anxious enough to overlook the hazards to take a chance.

Whether we, in our tank, were cowards or not does not alter the fact that it was a bright day and the period when planes checked the activity and fired in the railroad yard. I have no record of any action, but men get hurt in such conditions. As tankers, we were a minority group. Often foot soldiers took the challenge in questionable activity. Within a short space of time, new orders changed our activity.

HITCHHIKER

We all tried to be friendly to the civilians. Some may have made some decision that they were not prepared for the results. With one hand, a hitchhiker steered his bike and with the other hand, grabbed some bracket to get a free ride. When a tank turns, it does not go around corners like a car or truck. It pivots and the back of the tank swings in a wide arc. If anyone were hanging on, he would not know what to expect.

This young hitchhiker, hanging on the right side was promptly thrown in the ditch and ran into a tree. It was not the duty of a soldier to find out if there were any injuries.

BEAUTIFUL GIRL TO GUARD

Sometimes an experience can be puzzling. We were using German homes for taking a break. I recall a young woman who came to our unit and asked for protection against being molested. Perhaps the fact that she chose our platoon had nothing to do with personalities; nevertheless, we all accepted her challenge. I believe the men in my unit were pleased to be considered as having the respect she requested. The reason she was in the area for a while is not clear. Often, we may have been using someone's home and they may have wished for the freedom to return for specific interests. Situations as such were occasional and not of serious nature. Any of us who may be in charge and bore the title of being a leader were subject to handling such matters as best we could.

HEIL HITLER

Occasionally we experienced being in a German home and who would know what to expect. In our country, being in some ones home at mealtime, it would be common to offer a prayer. Most of the times the guests are asked to join in the prayer. Some of us experienced being in a home at mealtime and not being at the table would exclude us from any formalities. It did happen that a family would be around a table and not to be nosy, we could not help but notice some joint conduct that everyone took part. The people were friendly; perhaps courteous would be more to the point. I do not recall – ever – that any attempt to ignore us was evident.

We happened to be in one home at their mealtime and they joined voices in repeating "Heil Hitler". It was intended to be a formal greeting as a prayer. I recall only one experience like that.

PAPER SHORTAGES

We had one front line dilemma – a shortage of paper. Our rations did provide a very small folded piece of paper that was sort of a dull color – rather coarse – to be used as needed.

Sergeant Tom Young (not a relative) received a letter from his wife – neatly folded. Tom was very happy to receive it. After finishing the letter, Tom took care of a personal need. His response to her was amusing as he wrote and thanked her for the letter and apologized for its end use.

All seemed okay until the day Tom received another long letter from his wife. She provided him with a letter written on narrow paper about 30 feet long! In addition, reminded him of what he could do with it when he finished reading it. We all enjoyed a good laugh!

GERMAN CRAFTED BOOTS

Germany is well known for their different crafts. At one point, a middle-aged German man offered to make me a pair of boots for two packs of cigarettes. They fit and I could wear them, but our supply sergeant did not approve them. I have no record of where they went.

I have perhaps commented before regarding how the German civilians seemed easy to be around. In fact, there were times when they packed around our tank so tight, just to be social, it was truly a puzzle.

BOB PADGETT

My story would not be complete without including the personality of a five foot, seven inch soldier I will never forget. He was Bob Padgett from Champaign, Illinois. He became my closest companion. It was late February and he had been in the hospital after suffering from frozen feet. Bob had replaced Carmello, when he rejoined company B. He was younger than I was by about four years. I was 24 years old and oddly, even at that age, younger men called me 'Pop'.

Bob was assigned to my tank as the assistant gunner. Particularly, his duties were loading ammunition into the 76mm tank gun as well as tending the co-axial mounted 30-caliber machine gun. He may have had experience before, but he proved to be the best ammunition handler I had the privilege of working with. He was perhaps the fastest loader in Europe. He could 'slam 'um home' as fast as Lt. Willette called for them.

Bob had a system for everything. He could find any type of ammo in the dark. He could take a breechblock apart with his eyes shut. He was able to relate to the letter any operation in which he had participated. He stood straight with feet slightly spread; helmet cocked jauntily and used inimitable hand gestures to embellish his accounts. He was small in stature, but because of his ability, I could fire faster than any other fellow who held the job.

As we sat, waiting to push off with our engines running, I would look across to Bob and ask the inevitable question; "What do you say, Bob?" In addition, whether or not it was fact, I always felt better when Bob gave that familiar OK sign with his fingers. The roar of the tank prevented conversation and much of our communicating was done with body language.

Bob claimed he was *'psychic'* and could always tell when things would go well and not so well. Bob was the closest of all soldiers I dealt with to giving any hint how he stood spiritually.

He said, "Hey, Young – let's you and me behave ourselves and *WE* are going home." Whether or not his reporting was divinely instilled, it felt good to believe him. I was not sure if it was from his spiritual training, but I accepted the comment as having merit.

We shared a little plan which, when employed, meant we would follow orders; do as we were told; stay in our tanks as much as prudence dictated and believe Providence would see us safely returned home. Though we had not gone into any deeply religious discussions, I felt in my heart Bob was trying to tell me the Lord directed his thoughts, also giving him intuition in matters at the front.

Prior to any encounter with the opposition, the status of Bob's outlook gave me either confidence or a feeling of disquiet. A slight grin, a wink of the eye or the familiar "everything's OK" hand signal usually calmed me to such a degree as to provide for steadier gunning. As skirmishes ended, our regrouping included a critique from Bob, never forgetting to allude to his clairvoyant tendencies. Bob and I were together for several months.

After returning from the war, it was several years before we made contact again. He called me one day when he was about 200 miles from Grand Forks. He was traveling with his family, which now included three small daughters. He said he was bringing the girl "I" chose to be his wife.

Bob & Jean Padgett

I recall him showing me three pictures of three pretty girls and the letters they wrote. My selecting one dark haired girl had nothing to do with common sense, but a haphazard selection. Her name was Jean and she freely admitted that my selecting her was a fact.

Bob had told Jean that she had better be careful when she met me, as I would probably grab her and plant a big kiss on her! When they drove up to the house, Jean stayed on the other side of the car until she realized that I was really not the threat that Bob claimed I was; he was really just teasing her. They proved to be a loving, devoted Christian couple.

Some years later my wife, DeLoris, and I drove to see Bob and Jean at their home in Illinois. Our only contact after that through the years was exchanging Christmas letters.

ERV (ERVIN) ZENTZ – CPL – (KIA)

Learning the names of the different towns and cities in Germany was a tough assignment. I do not recall seeing homes in the outskirts as is common in America. It seemed every roof was red tile. Many homes had plain board fences surrounding the property. Our tanks were nine or ten feet tall, so if anyone was up in the hatch, he could see over the fences.

Traveling through the country was quite an experience. When leaving one town, we could look ahead and see another and sometimes to the right and left. Our job was to scout these villages and secure them, and normally use the town as a staging area for our next adventure.

An example of the crew's reaction to Bob brings to mind a situation in Bamberg, Germany where a sizeable attack force lay in wait on one street leading west, out of town. It was a rather nice spring day. About 5:00 PM, our tanks were lined up on the street – ready for the evening mission. We were to attack a position south and west of us.

Large numbers of infantrymen rested on the ground along the edges of the street. Some leaned against the board fences that were quite common throughout Europe. Several of our tanks were lined up in the center of the road, ready to accompany the infantry on the mission.

Ours was the lead tank. We were spaced about 150 feet apart. Infantrymen were spread out several feet ahead of us near large orchards we were to pass through. Modest homes were on either side of the road, most of which were surrounded by fences. We stopped alongside a home with the plain board fence as I mentioned.

After towns were taken, we could expect to see a certain amount of civilian activity around homes and business places that were intact as was true here. The town was very quiet. I am sure with a number of tanks, and dozens of infantrymen, most folks kept out of sight. These dwellings in Bamberg had been searched for snipers and other troops.

Sitting on top of our tanks, we could easily see a clear view of these "innocent" looking houses, generally feeling quite secure with the "safety in numbers" of our own forces near at hand. Lt. Willette was at the Command Post receiving instructions, leaving our tank without a commander. I stood in the hatch watching and waiting. The house behind the fence was in clear view, but I did not see anyone.

Bob Padgett was in my tank and he was nervous. Joe Torchia ("Torchy") of New York reacted. The "jitters" hit the entire crew as Bob kept repeating, "I don't like it here men. Let's get out of here". I finally agreed to ask the driver, Torchy, to start the engine and move up – just a little – perhaps 200 feet. Crews were chatting just waiting for the order to move.

The other tanks followed suit, but did so on their own volition. Tank number two, drawing up behind us in exactly the same location we had occupied, held the position for only moments when a thunderous explosion rocked the tank, mortally wounding the gunner, mild mannered Ervin Zentz who had been standing in the hatch as I did in our tank. Nearly dark, it was not easy to see. In such action, there was not some rush on the part of the others to go to see what happened.

Bob's pallor and wide-eyed astonishment convinced me he **did** have some knowledge of impending doom. Could he have known that out of one of these houses on orchard row, a lethal weapon in the hand of an expert would hurl a dreaded 'Panzer Faust' at some victim? Bob's reporting had me intrigued and nervous. How did he know? I had to just think – why Erv, and not me?

As we pushed on that night, Bob calmed down and assured me everything would be okay. As usual, he was correct, thereby causing me to include his deductions in every future action as well as orders from the commanding officer.

We pressed on, traveling mostly at night. The clank and squeal of the steel of tanks penetrated many nights as weary forms of infantry men clung to the hulls of the 'Iron Monsters', probing into unknown territory. As directed from headquarters, we either set up road blocks or gave covering fire to advancing infantry.

AMBUSH

March still presented us with a mix of cold and snow, plus some very nice days. Convoys – intended mainly to move to new locations - appeared to be routine. When possible, we moved under the cover of darkness using blackout lights. These lights showed only a few feet in front of vehicles.

The order to move came from higher sources and again a convoy of tanks, jeeps and trucks loaded with men took a gravel road to new operations. It was a mix of equipment – several miles long. None of us knew when some strange situation would arise.

Never fully aware of the assignment ahead, all we could do was make sure our tank was ready for whatever we may encounter. We had not traveled very far when it was reported that some German soldiers were holding up in an area ahead of us and to the right.

A tank seemed adequate to rout a few foot soldiers. An infantry colonel singled out our tank and asked our platoon leader to use our tank to flush out the pocket of Germans. We left the convoy and took a side road leading into the countryside - quite heavily wooded and vehicles traveling through grass and underbrush only marked the trail.

We did not have any ground troops to accompany us so it was up to a lone tank to do the job. The colonel mounted the tank and stood on the engine compartment behind the turret. Our platoon leader joined him. As we edged forward, suddenly, about 100 or so feet in front of us, a face appeared way down near the ground, at the base of a large tree.

The colonel saw him and saw that he had fired a German bazooka at our tank. The colonel literally screamed "BACK UP!"

Our driver quickly slipped into reverse. No doubt, the rapid reverse of the tank perhaps saved the colonel and serious damage to the tank. My job was to immediately return fire with either machine gun or tank ammo. Our tank was hit on the right front corner, but the sandbags did the trick and we were spared any major damage and we were not hurt. Our tank was one of the first to be outfitted with sand bags.

An enemy tank weapon called Panzer Faust – or literally, "tank fist" - was fired at us. It did not travel fast, but backing up our tank perhaps saved a direct hit on the main tank turret. The Americans referred to the tank weapon as a bazooka. I have seen some of our tanks hit that burned for several days.

Without taking time to inspect what damage we did, we returned to the convoy. A later report came out that a German vehicle – similar to our jeeps was found slightly to the right with dead soldiers in it. After an action such as this, it took quite a while for us to settle down and clear our minds. People, especially young ones, have asked me if I ever killed anyone in the war. My best answer has been – "I wish I could say otherwise." Next in line was a holding position in a heavy wooded area deeper into German territory.

SAND BAGGING IT

Every new assignment called for tanks and trucks with soldiers to convoy to a point of action. Sand bagging the tank behind a steel rod network saved many tanks from the feared Panzer Faust. It is important to report that all of our tanks required a special protective system involving sand bags. All tanks were outfitted with a steel framework using round rods to form a network to retain the sandbags to protect the tank from enemy tank ammunition.

After the rods were welded to the tank turret and other vulnerable areas, we were able to fill sandbags with road gravel, and slip the bags in place. All of this was done after months in action without the bags. It may be difficult to explain some things, but the Germans had a devastating weapon that could blow a hole in a tank – killing the crew with red hot metal.

The sandbags created a protective cover that would stop the action of this weapon that used a shaped charge. In order for the charge to be effective, it had to come in contact with the metal of the tank. If a charge hit the sandbag, there would be a terrific explosion, but would not damage the tank. This lengthy explanation has been included since the sandbag protection spared us in the ambush.

TRANQUILITY IN A GERMAN HORSE BARN

Animals become a very large part of war stories, but it is obvious they are unaware of their role as far as war is concerned. Something to consider about horses is they seem to be so easy to engage in duties that they accept as their way of life. They are quite tame from birth and are easily trained as the owner or caretaker deems proper. No doubt, they become accustomed to owners or trainers - something horses possess that makes them desirable to be around.

Those of us engaged in WW II had very little to do with animals, but I recall a day when the area we were in had a barn with several horses. Just entering the barn was a welcome feeling as the horses seemed to be contented in their stalls, and were not aware of a stranger. I was alone that day, and stayed in the barn only long enough to absorb a few minutes of a calm atmosphere.

A SNOWFALL TO REMEMBER

After every action, it was time to regroup and prepare for more assignments. Earlier, I mentioned the convoy and the near ambush. Convoys became more common toward the end of the war as assembling large numbers of troops and rigs during heavy combat would not be practical. It is really strange how some conditions became welcome that normally wouldn't.

Convoys at night seemed most practical to be somewhat veiled from aerial attack. This particular night – again – we were lined up to head for another staging area and all of us were truly delighted that a very heavy snowfall was to our advantage. There was no wind, and snowflakes were coming down like feathers. We could use our blackout lights, which helped some. Our convoy was a mix of tanks and equipment, plus personnel trucks loaded with troops.

A German light plane, nicknamed "bed-check Charley", would take a reading on our position with the net results we could expect artillery or a bombing raid. The cloud cover may have been a factor in protection for us as bed-check Charley was nowhere in sight. We lumbered along at the speed of the slowest vehicles. In spite of the questionable pleasure I got from the snow cover, the narrow road was slippery.

When the convoy started to move, nobody stops. You just hang in there. Our tank was loaded with infantrymen, hanging on as best they could - each one clutching his belongings. Infantrymen would hang on our tanks, as many as could stay there. We would move into woods and towns attempting to identify enemy pockets and positions. Militarily it is called recon or reconnaissance.

Now this very welcome snow did both good and bad. Directly behind us was a truck loaded with infantry soldiers. Convoys as such did not move fast at night, but my heart nearly stopped as I saw over my right shoulder a sickening sight. Totally unexpected, the troop truck lost its footing on the snow covered narrow dirt road, slipped and rolled over on top of two dozen or more men riding in the open truck. All those men – hopelessly incapable of protecting themselves were caught in the tragedy. We could not stop to help.

Remember, I said the convoy keeps moving. The roar of engines prevented us from hearing any call for help, and as we moved on, I winced at the thoughts crossing my mind at what I saw. Our driver did not know and we could not take it upon ourselves to do anything. The strange pleasure of the snowfall backfired.

Incidents like that were not reported to us and all we could do was mentally burden ourselves hoping it was not all that bad. However, such things would occupy our thoughts for hours, trying to assess all facets of the tragedy.

It was still March weather and the tradition of a tank commander standing in the hatch was my lot and that beautiful snowfall had me soaked to the skin. How pneumonia escaped me is still a mystery – or is it? How many of us remembered to thank the Lord for deliverance? I have trouble to remember what happened after the unfortunate accident, but we reached a new location to set up for the next assignment.

WE NEED SOME GASOLINE

Another day we moved to another wooded area. The spring was welcome, however the conditions of the ground made it difficult to get through with tanks. It was necessary to keep our tank combat ready and well supplied with ammunition and keep the fuel tank full. Our tanks used regular gasoline, which was supplied, in five-gallon cans. Delivery trucks would be informed of our needs and we never had to wait long for supplies. Trucks brought our supplies and I must say that the men who drove the trucks were very brave; daring to meet us at refueling sights. They were not fighting men, but were subject to the enemy blowing up wheeled equipment, preventing delivery.

Leaving our tank, we walked through heavy mud to pick up gasoline. These were five-gallon cans and it took forty to fill our 200-gallon gasoline tanks. The large tank capacity was heavy but with the number of troops on hand, the job went fairly well. Sloshing through the mud was very exhausting.

It was a morning about 9:00 AM; we were loading our tank. Nearly finished, an Army jeep entered the scene with a stretcher carrying a wounded man. He was laughing hysterically and yelling at us as the vehicle passed on – "Hey, you bastards, I got my ticket to go home!", as he held up a bloody arm – half-missing.

This type of tragedy was a constant threat to any of us. None of us envied his position, but combat creates situations that are as noted here. We had men in our unit that could not stand the pressure of combat and had to be sent away for help. Seeing buddies killed is traumatic.

I HAVE A SON!

As we moved on to new assignments things were really moving fast. We journeyed to a suburban area and parked our tank near an old red building about the size of a two-car garage. It was March, 1945 with freezing weather still to be reckoned with. We used the building for a place to heat a can of stew and make a cup of hot chocolate, if you could call it that. The evening sky was red from the sun going down, but was also red from fires and shells bursting. We would see a flash and seconds later, a heavy thud would shake the ground. The explosion could be quite a distance, maybe miles. In addition, we could never be sure if it was German or Allied shellfire. The constant sounds of war became our daily diet. It got so that distant sounds did not bother us much. When machine gun bursts could be easily heard, we took note.

While we were still using the red building, we used precious time to reload our tank with gasoline, ammo, water and rations. Darkness was falling fast when all of a sudden, a jeep appeared. The blackout headlamps were almost useless, but gave limited light only a few feet in front. Taillights were not used.

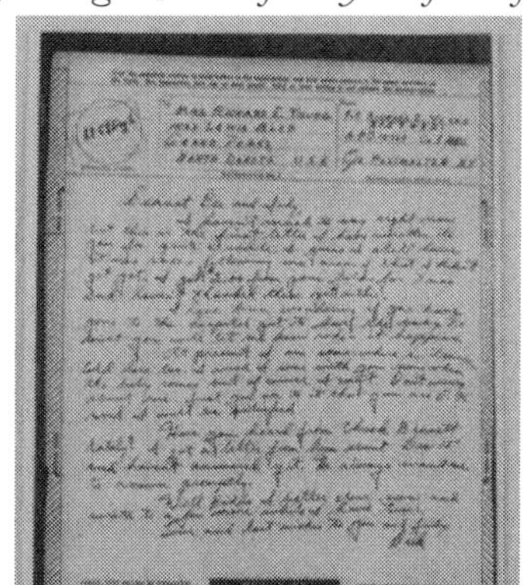

Dearest Dee and Judy, I haven't much to say right now but this is the first letter I have written to you for quite awhile. I guess I still have Xmas boxes following me around that I didn't get yet. I got $2.00 from your folks for Xmas and haven't thanked them yet either.
I have been wondering if you have gone to the hospital yet to have the baby. No doubt you will let me know when it happens.
At present I am somewhere in France. Cold here too. I wish I was with you now when the baby comes but of course I can't. Don't worry about me. Just you see to it that you are O.K. and I will be satisfied.
Have you heard from Chuck Bennett lately? I got a letter from him about Dec. 15 and haven't answered yet. He always wants me to answer promptly. Well Kiddo I better close now and write to a few more while I have time.

Love and best wishes to you and Judy. Dick

(Interesting note: Dick wrote and posted this letter on January 23, 1945 to DeLoris the day BEFORE his son was ***actually*** *born).*

Our company first sergeant found our position. He came with a dual purpose. First off, I received a telegram informing me of the birth of my second child, a son, Richard Charles, born January 24, 1945.

My wife selected his name to be Richard, Jr., in case I did not return from the war. I knew about the addition to our family from mail, but it took until March for the telegram to reach me. I did **not** see my son until he was thirteen months old. It was a hard thing to adjust to a child never seen before. When I saw him the first time, I felt like I was looking at someone else's kid.

Second, he had a passenger – a young, blonde soldier – fresh from the States. After seeing him, all of us became aware of our own condition. By comparison, we looked like bums; unshaven, needing a bath, clothes dirty and greasy and giving the impressions that we were battle oriented.

The sergeant posed a loaded question. He asked, "Are you guys okay? Is anyone sick or looking for a chance to go back for a rest?"

No one answered him, that is, not right away. We looked at each other and no doubt mentally entertained the idea that here was a chance for a break. When I looked at Salty, Bob, Joey and Torchy – the same guys with whom I spent many days, how could I think of looking for a better deal?

No one aired the thought but it must have hit all of us in the same vein. "No thanks, Sarge", I said. I was in charge of our tank and my faithful crew joined in with me.

That young blonde kid looked like 500 pounds had been taken off his shoulders. The sergeant wished us well and both men left. We did not see our first sergeant again until the war wound down.

ACCORDION GIFT

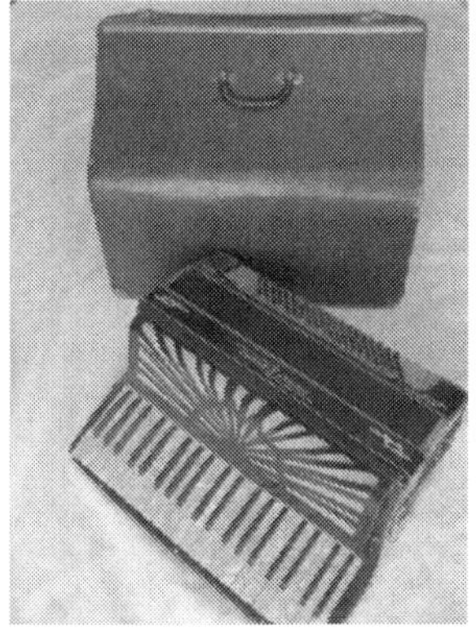

Another infantry soldier had picked up an accordion he found. The nature of soldiers was to find as many ways to be entertained as possible even in dire circumstances. Lugging that instrument along with his normal field equipment was a chore. He asked if we would lug it along on the back of our tank. Of course, he trusted that we would meet at different times. It was a full-sized 120 bass instrument made in Italy.

I asked him if he would sell it some day. He said, "If I find that I don't need it, you can have it." Yes, he too, paid the ultimate price. I was stunned to learn that he too, got killed in action. It was not my pleasure to obtain an accordion that way, but it became part of my gear and I brought it back home with me. I kept it on the back of my tank for the duration.

Different fellows found interest in playing it and I was able to take lessons from one of my tank buddies. Shrapnel from artillery punctured the case with a jagged hole about the size of a half-dollar.

Dick Young, age 89, with accordion

SINGING SOLDIER

One infantry soldier found a piano in a house where we fixed a meal. He sat at the keyboard and started playing familiar hymns. I found it to be a refreshing change in activity, but must confess I did not take part with him.

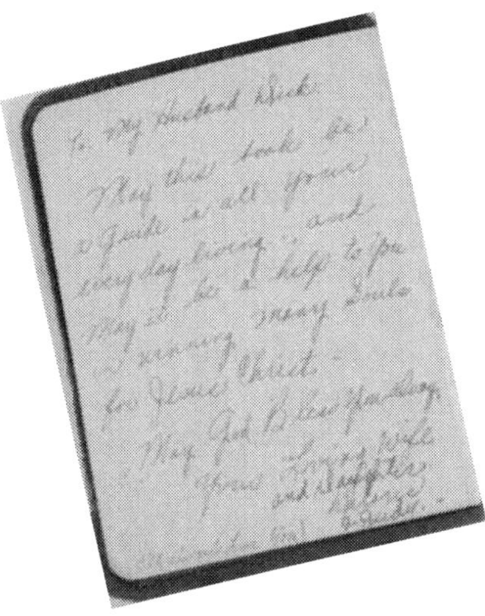

One of our men involved in a card game – a rough, tough fellow – nudged me and said, "That fellow won't last long." He perhaps assumed by the soldier being *religious,* he was prepared for the inevitable and his time was short. Unfortunately, he was later killed in action. That episode remains indelible in my mind.

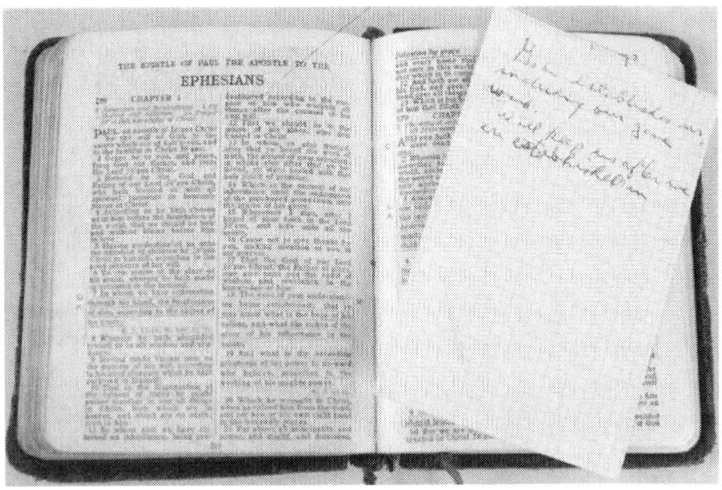

KNOCK IT OFF, JOE

Someone asked me once if I ever killed anybody. I did not take pleasure in taking lives of even the enemy. My best answer was "I wish I could say otherwise." I heard several reports that are bone chilling, but I take no glory in destruction of enemy soldiers. I know that normally we feel it is necessary to silence the other fellow's gun and not his life.

One night we were to cross an open field with our tanks spread out. A distinct order was given – do NOT fire any weapons. We could not see the targets anyway.

Joe, a young newcomer, misunderstood the order and he cut loose with a volley from our front 30-caliber machine gun. The tank officer, a lieutenant, was livid. Our tank could easily be picked off by the anti-tank artillery. Joe could not hear, but a few raps from a stick on Joe's helmet got his attention and he stopped firing.

Ours was always the lead or command tank. An officer rode with us at times and as we moved forward across the field an unknown distance, we could see in the fading twilight several German soldiers, and we were shocked to discover we were in direct line of a powerful German anti-tank gun.

Thoughts hit us that when Joe was firing the machine gun, the tracer ammunition may have been the factor in us being the victim of that feared gun. However, to our amazement, the German gun crew seemed to be in shock. As our tanks closed in, they appeared very willing to surrender. Tankers did not take prisoners. That was the job of our infantry buddies. Soon it was dark and we found the time to grab a few winks of sleep.

Even though there was still a war going on, Allied and U.S. men had taken much territory plus prisoners. There were times when our men had gathered perhaps 200 or more men. At some distant point, a compound was established to keep the soldiers as prisoners. We could not help but note that many of the POWs were really very young. Somehow, we had escaped encounters with the feared SS troops. They were the pride of the German army.

GARBAGE CAN KIDS

Every Army mess was frequented by the hungry. When our field kitchens were able to prepare a meal, kids quickly learned to be ready to find a way

to get something to eat. The incidents of little children wearing tattered clothing and waiting near the chow lines wherever field kitchens were set up was a common sight all over Europe. The scene continued to shift to Nuremberg, Munich, Wolfgang, Salzburg, Linz and others. In Karlsruhe, Germany, a little girl with stringy brown hair stood expectantly, watching men emptying their mess kits of leftovers. She held a battered gallon can and kept a large spoon poised, ready to reach out with a quick swipe at some edible morsel remaining on a mess kit.

When chow was over, GIs of all ranks lined up for cleaning mess gear. All utensils were washed in boiling soapy water after passing the garbage cans. I saw it myself - into the garbage went unused coffee, hunks of bread, small pieces of meat, or a spoonful of cold mashed potatoes topped with a mashed cigarette. Several inches of coffee in the bottom of the can hid the heavier material that went to the bottom. Cigarettes and pieces of bread floated in the coffee. As each man banged his kit on the edge of the garbage can, immediately three youngsters quickly bent over the can scooping out anything they could grab, using both hands like a clam bucket. A gallon can of this mush – to them – was a real treat and home they would go.

The habits of men never seemed to change unless a direct order was given. Most men had something left in their mess kits. It was promptly thrown in the garbage and excess coffee was thrown into the same garbage can. Occasionally, an obliging GI bent down and helped sort out a few remnants from his mess-tray. I believe some soldiers went back for 'seconds' in order to present a more appetizing offering to those little waifs in want. The extra coffee was poured directly into their containers.

Our commanding officer issued an edict, that no cigarettes would be extinguished in mess-trays; and that some consideration is given to hungry youngsters who may have otherwise gone unfed. Our units rarely stayed anywhere long enough to get to know any of these little personalities, yet the behavior of the children of the continent was the same everywhere. I witnessed youngsters and grownups alike, scrounging around the Army mess dumps; and some went home with nothing more than a few potato peelings. Kids had better luck than grownups in the salvage maneuver.

Some of the more enterprising youths had learned to perform some service, thereby qualifying for a more consistent dividend. It was amazing what one could do with a package of chewing gum. As first sergeant of my unit, I was required to see that the area was policed around headquarters.

Unidentified tots, constantly waiting for a handout, stayed in close range of our operation. I recruited five boys and girls, about age six. I demonstrated how pieces of paper or some other refuse, should be gathered and placed in waste containers. The eager youngsters quickly caught on, and did a most satisfying job for the payment of one stick of gum each. It was heartwarming to see the delight registered in their faces. Five dirty-faced little kids hurried down the street when the work was done to tell someone they had some "choon-gum".

PEAT BOGS

Moving on was an ongoing routine. Tanks are tricky. A short explanation regarding tanks is that changing direction with a tank was done with steering levers; you do not turn a tank. Tracks would slide around and hard surface made it easier.

In German territory, we prepared to cross a large field. There did not seem to be any urgency with protecting our tanks or ourselves, so we entered the field and I could see the ground moving several feet in front of the tank – it was very soft and spongy. Actually, it was a real peat bog.

Our tank moved along, but the order came to make a left turn and the action of the tracks cut through the grassy topsoil and our tank bogged down so rapidly, that movement was impossible. It was hopeless to go forth or back.

Water started entering through the bottom and, within a short space of time, water filled the sinking tank until it covered the instrument panel. All we could do was abandon our favorite tank. I did not keep track of the tanks we lost, but it was always a real pain to salvage personal items from a tank in jeopardy.

I had great respect for men who were assigned to salvage. They came with a rig called a T-2 – actually a tank wrecker. It was self-propelled with a large cable drum. The unit weighed much less than our tank so they went up on a hill behind us about 150 yards and anchored the wrecker to a large tree.

The cable was one inch in diameter – capable of some heavy work. They hooked it to our tank and the creaking and groaning of machinery began as this most unusual wrecker actually started dragging the tank out of the mire.

I cannot believe to this day how 100,000 pounds of steel could be dragged out of a peat bog – and the stunning part of it was the enormous pile of earth that formed ahead of the tank. It appeared to be as much as two times the size of the tank. The cable was so long, it never did pull straight, but sagged considerably. Suddenly the cable snapped, and the result was obvious; we had to abandon another tank. Time did not permit us to continue salvage. We could take very little comfort in the fact that other tanks were also lost in this setting.

There was no guarantee that we would always receive a new tank. The affairs were such that we had to adapt to many variables. In this case, we picked up an older tank. That was of little concern as the one we received was in good working order. We had some items salvaged from the stricken tank, but we were always outfitted by a very efficient supply system.

CUT THEIR THROATS

Since our tank was always the lead tank, it was common for an officer to accompany us and take control of other tanks. As the gunner, I was second in command. When the officer was on some other mission, it was my job to be in charge. Truly, I was relieved when major decisions were not part of my responsibility but to carry on as directed. Certain things were in my jurisdiction, like behavior of our men as seemed fit in certain situations. Not every soldier carried out orders regarding treatment of civilians. I was the oldest and the one in charge in our tank. My rank of sergeant gave me some authority. My crew respected my leadership.

I was amazed at how many homes in Germany welcomed us. As we entered homes, it is worth telling that we were welcomed in a remarkable way. It was common for us to see pictures of German soldiers around the house. The possibility of us receiving resistance was ever present. No doubt, our tank parked outside the home was reason to see who was in charge.

For them, the war was over when we arrived. As we entered this one home, I made certain our men understood that they were not to take liberties with the women or girls. Further, silverware and money were not to be taken. Actually, the order came from higher sources, so it was our job to cooperate.

The family seemed eager to accommodate us with fixing a meal. In addition, we ate a meal at the same table as the family in this one house. The wife was slender and looked frail and worn but very gentle. Her husband was a tall, slender gray haired person and they both knew some English.

We shared with our coffee and white bread. Our coffee was a real treat to the German families as they were using a barley drink. Our coffee made the meal for them and we enjoyed their brand of hot food and their very dark bread.

After our meal, the lady of the house allowed me to rest in the master bedroom. She recognized me as the sergeant in charge. I crawled in between two feather ticks, fully dressed with my feet sticking out the side of the bed. I fell asleep almost right away. I did not realize the hausfrau had removed my boots and set them by the bed. It may have been foolhardy to be exposed to a possible ambush, but I think we understood that these people could be considered friendly.

Time was short and after a two-hour rest, we prepared to leave. The man of the house told me that it was German soldiers who had abused his wife. As I left his door, he made a remarkable gesture with his hand under his chin as he said, "Cut their throats!"

INTERLUDE

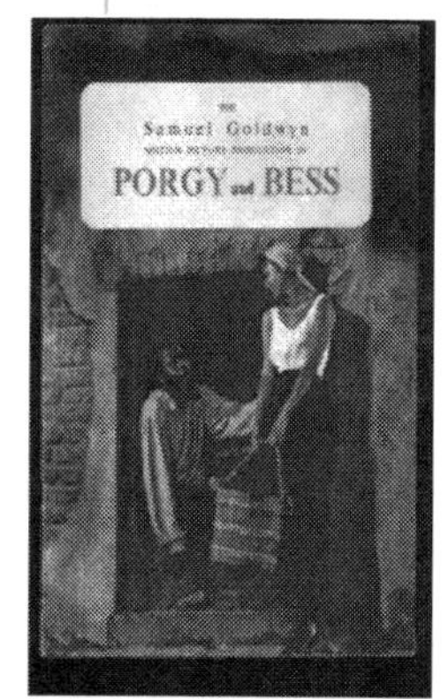

We were not in a position to challenge certain activity. I have mentioned that often so much of our activity was at night. It was surely to our advantage to have the cover of darkness for obvious reasons. This one night, we were not informed, but I believe the high command kept us 'in the dark' for their own reasons.

We were loaded in trucks for some mission. Sounds of war were always present. After a short ride we came to a strange looking configuration. The truck stopped and the order came to dismount. We were ushered to this strange place and unbeknown to us, canvas material was peeled back and we entered into a building. Once inside it all became clear. We had entered a theater.

The genius of certain military people proved the ability to come up with a real treat. The theater was so much like that back in the states, it look no time for us to settle in our seats. Someone had put the lights in shape, and after a short space of time, we were treated to a movie – namely PORGY AND BESS.

This was such a departure from our normal duties that I must confess that I forgot that I was in a war zone. Those of us who were blessed by this interlude will long remember the two hours.

BURNING HOUSES

Be it a war or not, I never felt the civilians were our enemies. Many towns in Germany were the provincial settings. It was common for our tanks to enter a town – softened by artillery and aerial bombs. On one occasion, we rolled into a town that was literally going up in smoke. Infantrymen were going house to house and our tanks stayed on main street moving through the town. Our job was to use heavy guns on stubborn resistance.

As we rolled through a village with houses burning I was grieved at seeing two older women standing outside their burning home – wringing their hands and pointing towards their burning home as if to say someone needed to be rescued. Firefighting equipment was truly provincial, and older men were dragging hoses around trying to hook up to some pumping unit. We could not help. As tanks rolled over the hoses, and cut them, it all seemed so futile.

We could hear rifle fire and some young girl about 16 years old was running in front of our tanks and suddenly fell. I am sure it was accidental, but not from our tank. As we moved on through the town, there was no way we could feel good about it. To me it was horrible. If that mess was considered winning the war, forget it.

I do not know what happened to the girl who fell. I hope that she was only wounded and survived; we do not know. We had no choice but to roll on through with ground troops following to secure the town. Of all the heart-searching things, I went through – this un-named town and the drama is ever etched in my mind.

THE MAYOR

When other tanks arrived, the sunset had put enemy artillery into a holding situation. It was another one of those periods when we just set up guards for the night and prepared for new orders.

I believe we were in an area called Bavaria. Small towns of 100-150 people were common. We loaded our tanks in daylight with ground troops that joined us. I suppose terminology may be a bit tiring, but our work was to flush out any enemy soldiers in small towns. We were told not to open fire but to move forward cautiously.

As we pushed on after leaving the burning town, we entered another town that was really spooky. As the lead tank, we moved forward into town that appeared to be deserted. There was not a soul in sight. It was early evening and with the sun setting, the windows all over town glared. It was truly a strange and eerie experience. As our tanks rumbled through the streets, we really expected some resistance. There was not a living creature – not even a cat or dog was seen. I recall only four tanks that were involved in this assignment. Our tank was always in the lead and by now, I had become assistant tank commander and had a front seat view of things to come.

We were almost at the opposite side of town when we came across something very unusual. It was a man-made ridge of earth that was similar to potato houses on farms back in the states. It was several feet in height and stretched out many feet. A door at the end nearest our tank suggested it to be a protective shelter but there was still no activity. Again, ours the lead tank came to a halt at one end of this strange configuration perhaps 50 feet from the door.

The eerie silence was broken when very slowly a door in this odd structure opened and a waving white flag on a stick was the first item to appear. Moments later the flag bearer, a middle aged woman emerged and she boldly approached our tank and knelt directly in front and bowed until her forehead nearly touched the ground.

When it was apparent that a platoon of tanks and a number of infantrymen would not harm her, a short, portly man emerged and joined her and the most unusual situation ever to expect unfolded before our eyes. The gentleman was her husband and approached our tank speaking perfect English. He explained he was the mayor of that town and was the engineering element behind all that transpired including the earthen protective safety shelter – a wooden framework with dirt covering.

The earth bunker emptied as the ecstatic town people emerged. I do not recall at any other point in my war experience a celebration that equaled that – even during combat days.

The mayor said he knew Americans well enough to prepare for them. He told the town people that if no one shot at the Americans, they would spare the town. The mayor reported that he once lived in St. Louis, Missouri in the USA for ten years and knew what to expect from Americans. If no shots were fired at the U.S. troops, they would hold their fire and spare the town. That was the only town that did not have even a window broken.

Our tank crew was invited to go to the mayor's home and the result was very rewarding. Food and all needs including lodging were eagerly met. Oddly, the mayor told us he once owned his home, but now it was the property of the government.

The following day before we prepared for our next move, the mayor took us to the school gymnasium where the mayor had instructed the town people to take every known firearm owned by civilians to the schoolhouse and lay them in order on the gym floor. It was his willingness to be cooperative. It was touching to see even children's toy pistols and water guns in the collection as such. I do not believe Americans took a one of the weapons.

This was, without a doubt, the most unusual experience for all of us tankers. The mayor had saved the town. It is regrettable that pictures and other considerations did not materialize. I believe that experience was a classic.

When we felt that experience with the Mayor was complete, it appeared our general tone was mutuality. We were careful not to give information that would jeopardize our orders from higher sources. The Mayor seemed to be at ease with us, but the town people avoided us. That could be expected, but we sensed great relief. This was an unusual case, but we believed we were fortunate to experience as we did with the sounds of war still all around us.

New orders were given in a method not shared with soldiers until the exact time to move on. The purpose may have been that change was ever a possibility. We learned to do as told, and if by any chance a mistake had been made, we were glad the responsibility was from a higher level of authority.

SCREAMING MIMI

After we left the Mayor's home, we felt that if the mayor was able to handle a situation as he did, the possibility could be that we could experience other times when resistance would be tapering off. The truth is our assignments often were in a wooded area. The protection of trees with ground troops was a natural for those we pursued, which also was to our benefit with tanks.

One early evening we were positioned to be in a ready mode – just waiting. The enemy knew we were there. The weapons used against us were artillery and mortars. The Germans had developed a mortar, which was truly a test of our morale. GIs nicknamed the mortar *screaming Mimi*. As these fell through the air, a shrieking, warbling sound was nerve shattering. Ground troops, especially needed to take cover as these explosive devices were made to explode above ground.

Tankers were in better shape than foot soldiers, but towards dusk, our assistant driver, Ivan was standing in his open hatch when the feared *Mimi* exploded nearby and caught our man. Ivan was removed and picked up by medics, but we never saw him again. Not sure if he was mortally wounded, but often someone like that would be back in action with another unit. That was the lot of a number who were not regulars in our outfit. There was a constant changing around of crewmembers. It never happened to me; I was never transferred.

LINCOLN HIGHWAY

More activity in the Black Forest called for the use of a few tanks. Some towns and highways were renamed by military headquarters for their own reasons. We were to establish positions along the ***Lincoln Highway***; the road was built up quite high. Our job was to dig our tank down – nearly out of sight, and only enough of the tank above ground to allow the big gun to sight down the road. A deep ditch at our selected spot was adequate without the need to do much digging. As our tank was adjusted into position, the officer in charge told us to fire at the first thing we saw coming down the road.

I was in charge of our tank when the officer was engaged elsewhere. I also took my turn operating the tank gun. It was a beautiful spring day and with the sun shining the thought of encountering anything was pulse quickening. Our boys felt like seasoned troops, a bit nonchalant about the order given. We sat there smoking cigarettes and cracking jokes to pass the time.

I sat at the controls and studied the terrain through the telescopic sight. Anticipating an encounter is pulse quickening. I am not sure if I was hoping for action. It was perhaps about an hour, as I stared into the sights of that 76 mm tank gun, I did detect movement several hundred yards ahead on that highway. It was some sort of troop carrier loaded with soldiers. Some sense told me to *hold it.*

As it approached our position, I had a high explosive shell in the breach-block. The cross hairs of our sights squarely fixed on that rig. My right toe just barely touching the firing trigger prepared for action. The vehicle was coming faster than I expected and a careful look as the steel helmets made me wait. They did not look like Nazi troops. They looked very round with a sort of dusty olive drab appearance.

Within moments, at what seemed to be excessive speed was an American Jeep streaking by loaded with American GIs. There was great relief on my part that the grinning soldiers – waving wildly in the familiar style of a GI – that suggested "all's well". They disappeared in the direction we had come from. If they weren't Americans then certainly I made a mistake. My question – how did that order originate and by whom?

This is one of the frustrations of being in charge. The front was not a clear line of demarcation. We may cringe to discover how often orders backfired. This is one of those times when it appeared that Divine intervention was the order of the day. My buddy Bob would have said that the situation was out of my hands. I was happy the GIs were spared an evil end. The road was in American control and we moved on to another assignment.

It seems fitting to report that often we seemed to have Divine Protection – even though in a true sense, many times we – or I didn't consciously offer a prayer. The report came through letters that prayer was offered from those at home.

AUTOBAHN

The Autobahn was truly a remarkable highway that was an example of German road building and engineering. It was built for high speed and occupied a good share of Germany that perhaps was, in general, a system of a two-lane roadway designed to keep traffic moving. Along with traffic was the discovery – perhaps part of the plan – that there was enough straight stretches to provide a landing and take-off for light planes. Planes could land on the highway and be backed into cutout areas in the woods and be ready for use. Some of this was in place, but we never saw any of it in use. The war was winding down and it was our experience to see equipment ready but not put into use.

Technically, we were out of action when in a convoy or relocating for other action. More territory opened up and our move to new assignments came more often. We heard of the Autobahn in Germany as a true super highway that could stand high speed.

Our mission complete we had orders to move to another location and this called for a rather extended drive down the famous Autobahn. Our tanks could attain 45 miles per hour on hard surface. When in transit, it was wise to "keep moving" as idle or stalled tanks make good targets.

We had the highway to ourselves – just tanks – with our tank leading the way. The hour of the day was early evening in late March or early April. The snow was gone and the highway was in excellent condition. The Autobahn was built for speed; hence, curves were gradual so that skidding wasn't a problem. So we kept on course in the effort to be on time to secure another highway.

Since I was normally the tank commander, our driver welcomed a change and I took over the controls. As we rolled along in the open country, we could see a number of places where trees were removed to create a place to have planes hidden and the highway was used as an airstrip.

We had no escort. As tankers, we were on our own. The country was somewhat hilly where we were and there were some streams to cross. As we rolled along, I believe I could speak for our crew – we felt secure and had 'no sweat'.

As we rolled along a gradual downhill grade, at what may have been maximum speed for the tank, to our consternation – about ¼ mile or so ahead of us suddenly there appeared a small man dressed in blue, wildly waving his arms for us to stop. He was not dressed in military clothing and he did not speak English. It is one of those situations where timing may have cost him his life. The thought hit me, "Who is this guy?" and that I could have just run over him, but he stood his ground. Using steering levers I brought the tank to a halt just a few feet from him, and then we could see his concern.

He was standing in front of a bombed out section of road that may have been created by retreating German forces. The road was too narrow to see from an oncoming vehicle. Standing on its nose was a small red car that would have been crushed by a tank falling on it had I not been able to stop.

It was not easy from a tank to see all that was involved where the little red car took a nosedive right into the water. However, a few feet ahead a bridge crossed a stream. How does one describe a scene like this? Remember, we were not in a position to loiter and check if someone was in that car – or if the man in blue was a friend or occupant. Wartime dictated our behavior. Tanks were following and we had to move on. There are times when we felt guilty not being able to help some situation, but the bridge was not available to cross the stream. As tankers, we had to be ready to take an alternate solution.

Unable to stick around and check further, we left the road and passed by driving the tank through the narrow stream. We were able to get back on the main highway. That was our lot; leave such matters to others. All of us had to realize the war takes its toll. As participants, we almost didn't feel guilty for our involvement as just soldiers. None of us including the victims in the little red car caused the problem. That was only a short trip until we reentered a wooded area and were able to see a remarkable display from a German fort.

THE GERMAN FORT

We entered a wooded area and came very close to the opposite side of the woods. In direct view, on an open hill, perhaps ¼ of a mile or less was a German fort with anti-aircraft guns pointing skyward. As tankers, we had nothing to do with what transpired but we became eyewitness to some action that beat anything seen in movies. Through the opening in the trees that morning we had a front seat look at a grueling air strike on the heavily armed German fortress.

Totally unrelated to what we were doing, we watched as wave after wave of American P-38 and P-51 attack planes rained heavy 50 caliber machine gun and 37 mm cannon slugs at the courageous Germans. German soldiers at the controls of anti-aircraft guns did not fare too well. They were exposed without protective shields and the results were deadly. How can one describe seeing a German soldier shot out of his position at an anti-aircraft gun and immediately replaced at the gun position with someone who dared to take a chance. We did not take liberties and go look, but we could certainly see that it took great courage for a soldier to go and replace a man who apparently was either killed or seriously wounded.

How our planes withstood the unbelievable volume of machine gun rounds and all pull away with no smoke trails or fire is a mystery. We could see tracers raining down and the same going up in return. We did not see one of our planes get lost. However, they did their mission and all quieted down. It made my bones tremble just to witness killings before our eyes.

We were not able to see the damage to the fort. All we knew was that people get hurt in such interchanges. Our only choice was to be ready for orders. I may mention that during combat situations, there is no provision for the U.S. Forces to jump in where no orders were given. Each organization had its own source of instructions. We did not remain to see the finale.

THE FIRST GERMAN JET

Some days the weather was beautiful. On a sunny day, when clouds are the fluffy white kind, I always felt it added something. Our position was on the south side of some German town. The report come through that German fighter jets were causing some concern.

Strafing – shooting machine guns from an airplane - is a devastating thing. Having seen the German fort being hit with the American planes, we now had to deal with fighter planes when it seemed we should have had no more sweat.

The one plane made several passes in this German village. Some of our men took shelter in basements. A concern was that bullets could enter basement windows. My memory reminds me that I was among those seeking shelter in a basement.

Heading back to our tank, we believed we should return fire at the jet. With its appearance in the east, it was easy to see the plane in mid afternoon.

I cranked up my tank gun, aiming at the jet and used tracer ammunition to establish position. That was almost humorous. The jet was moving so fast, our puny little 30 caliber was not even in the picture. Shooting at a moving target gives the impression that tracers are moving in a great curve.

Always near the military units, someone said, "Call the quad 50!" The menacing weapon was special air defense – mounting four 50-caliber machine guns at once, with the capacity of 1800 rounds per minute, with every fifth round a tracer. A wheeled transport rig, it was moved into position. The sounds were deafening while we watched intently as the gunner peppered the sky with a lethal barrage that met its mark. The last pass of that jet was his last. The smoke trail was a giveaway. With my own eyes, I saw the action. We were only a few feet from the gunner and the power displayed was awesome.

Though combat implies 'get him or he will get you', there remains the bone chilling reality that a human being was just subjected to a bitter experience. Enemy or not, I felt for the pilot. Was he killed? Did he survive? We saw the crippled plane flutter helplessly down through the clouds while our eyes were riveted to the sky – wondering – perhaps hoping. Relief certainly hit me as we witnessed the rewarding sight of a lone parachute emerging out of one of those fluffy, white clouds with its lone passenger while someone yelled, "There he is!"

QUAD 50

Our next stop was of new concerns. German planes were in the sky overhead. Tanks could survive strafing, but it was devastating to ground troops. We were positioned alongside a Quad 50.

The unbelievable firepower of the Quad 50 was felt on another strange episode. Bear in mind, we worked alongside of other units and at times were called on for special duty. From the position of our tank, we could target in on several emplacements. Even though it was past twilight, we were receiving an incessant harassment from rifle fire.

A lieutenant that I did not know entered our tank. He merely called me "soldier". Placing one hand on each shoulder as I sat in the gunner's seat, he was able to help me position the main tank gun by giving a tug in the correct direction. I could not see a thing, but when the big gun was positioned to his satisfaction, he gave the order to fire "high explosive".

I suppose we all feel better when we are on the offensive, but even when the report came back that my work did the job to a German bunker, the small arms fire continues to cause concern. Much of it was erratic, but people get hurt in such situations. We were to be in a holding position for the night.

An infantry officer nearby became irritated by the incoming shots from a woods to our south. I heard him say, "Get the Quad 50". Again, we were alongside the unit when the gunner let go with a terrifying blast at the woods spraying it from left to right – back and forth. It lasted perhaps only minutes. From then on, the woods quieted down. Only after sunrise could we see the havoc resulting from the feared Quad 50.

One thing tankers were not able to participate in was to inspect damage from attacks, but one look at the woods, even from our tanks, told the story. Trees were terribly scarred where bark was chipped off. If German soldiers were caught in the action, survivors were either picked up by ground troops, or retreated to safer terrain.

All of us had a feel of anticipation as the affairs of each day unfolded. I doubt if the average German soldier was fanatical as we heard was true of those exposed to jungle fighting. But, he had his work to do. Tank mines were a consideration, but we probably thought it would catch someone else.

MINES

The Germans were masters at dreaming up devastating devices to harm Americans. Cables were stretched across roads at a height that would catch Jeep drivers under the chin and some had their heads severed. The U.S. answer to that was to install a device on the jeeps that would cut the cable. I never saw one in action, but most jeeps were outfitted with cable cutters.

The use of mines has always been a part of war. Mines were of different styling. Tank mines were round and dug down in areas where tanks were expected. Earlier in my report, we had seen one of our tanks blasted on the road ahead of us.

Foot mines were of a total different shape. They were small and dug down very near the surface. Commonly, open fields were used for placing foot mines. There may not be any certain pattern to their placement. A small inconspicuous wire would detonate the mine. The entire purpose was to maim and not kill. A soldier with toes or a foot blown off needed help and thus take up the effort of one or two other soldiers. The philosophy of the military was that you could leave a dead man lie, but an injured one needed help. At times, when infantry soldiers were to cross a field, we were called to cross the field with our tanks. Foot mines did not damage tank tracks, but we could hear the popping sound. Soldiers could then walk where tank tracks had cleared a path.

At the time when we cleared a footpath for troops to move forward, there may not have been any particular duties for a tank and crew. However, we always were ready to move into some new assignment.

WAR STAGING AREAS

I believe that many people think a war goes as you see in the movies. Sure, there are explosions and rifle and machine gun fire, plus the sounds of artillery and a plane dropping bombs and all that – but even the enemy takes a break.

It may be worth telling that a war zone has different echelons or staging areas. Only about twenty percent of troops are at the front at one time. Behind this element would be the area taking orders for action. Next would be supply and organizational needs. Behind that would be hospital and in the stream of operations, we may find a "mix" of activity.

Even when we could hear gunfire, it did happen that the Red Cross would send out a truck with young girls to serve coffee and donuts – a truly welcome sight. The smell of perfume was quite a change from other war "odors" – exhaust fumes from tanks, sulfur smells from gunfire and all of us smelled strong of cigarette smoke. We were not allowed to light a cigarette after dark. A match strike would light up a face and make a great target.

I noticed a strange condition when we assembled for chow. Most of the time, we ate typical canned rations in our tanks. However, when the occasion of group chow was available, I noticed that seasoned men were always first in line. The green troops hesitated and went in afterwards.

When the lieutenant told us of lessons learned and more caution is taken, I have never figured out what that really meant. When the chow line got shorter and men were missing, who knows why?

I wish it were chronologically possible for me to give an account of episodes as they happened without being excessive. Bear in mind that soldiers were not necessarily informed of activity. We stood ready to do as told at any given time. Actual sequence of events may not be in order but I can be truthful that the different episodes are indelible in my mind. Every account I wish to comment on bears something unusual.

Since our job was to support infantry, it seemed natural that the tank units were required to take orders from infantry officers. The officers were often seasoned combat men and no doubt carried considerable authority. Some believed tanks could do anything. This may have been from the African Campaign.

Our unit experienced a full year in Europe, so we saw the seasons change. We did put up with snow and cold, but as tankers we could not complain, even though the tanks were designed for desert fighting. The air was drawn down through the hatches to cool the crew, and you can be sure that in cold weather, keeping our necks protected became each man's responsibility.

CASANOVA

One thing I have tried to avoid is speaking out against incompetent officers. Some may have been only a short time in training and needed experience. I shall not name one who was extremely handsome. His mode of dress smacked of a front line Casanova. When he gave an order to do something it bore authority; however, many fellows did not like him because of his arrogance.

After securing a small German village, we took over a neat one-story house. A petite young woman lived there. She was about thirty – thirty five years old. It surprises me that our men did not molest her. However, this handsome ne'er-do-well officer asked her if she had a liquor locker. She said “Yes”. He said, “I don’t trust our men." He further said, “If you have a key to your liquor, just let me keep it for you and it will be safe." She cheerfully handed him the key.

He also said she would have to leave since she was not allowed to stay with the men. She gathered up a few items and left the house. The officer watched her leave and when she was nearly out of sight, he gleefully said, “Hey guys – gather around. I have the key to her booze." Now you know the rest of the story. For your information, I have no idea what any of that foreign kick-a-pooh tasted like.

"MAY GOD HAVE MERCY
UPON MY ENEMIES,
BECAUSE I WON'T."
-GENERAL PATTON

PATTON

Road signs were changed to suit U.S. Army maps so we GIs had no idea where we were much of the time. We never stayed very long at one spot lest the enemy learn our habits. In the process of moving to a new location, we came across a sickening sight. The Germans had used horse-drawn wagons and artillery pieces, which I am sure was one of their pride and joy cavalry units. Many German soldiers had lost their lives along with the horses, but they had been removed before we got there.

According to reports, the famous General George Patton and his Third Armored Division along with air strikes annihilated the proud cavalry unit – stretched out for perhaps two or three miles along a winding country road. Here, on both sides of the road were perhaps as many as a hundred beautiful draft horses – dead – lying among wagons and other military equipment. The horses had been pushed into the ditch with Army dozers. All we could do was look and move on. What a grisly clean up job for perhaps German civilians.

Later, our tank battalion spent a lot of time cleaning up our tanks and paraded for General George Patton in Munich. I was a tank commander by then and was able to salute the general from my hatch. He stood on the sidewalk and we rolled close by in the street.

SGT. DONNELLY, EARL F.

Several men stuck out in my memory that left an image with me. Sergeant Donnelly, a good-natured fellow of average height and weight really took a lot of kidding about his very large nose. He was a good sergeant and had some remarkable responses to situations.

German soldiers seemed to be quite content to be captured by our troops. Perhaps much of the reason was that the older men had been either killed or replaced and the fanatic S.S. – or Storm Troopers – just were not used in the areas we secured.

Dozens of Germans were brought into our staging area. Two and a half ton trucks were lined up to haul them away. Our men were ordered to load the trucks. All the Germans were standing with no place to sit. Sergeant Donnelly asked one soldier "Got her loaded?" "Yep!" was the reply.

Sergeant Donnelly slid behind the wheel – started the engine – revved it up and dropped the clutch. The truck lurched forward about fifty feet and

Donnelly slammed the brakes. The entire load of men were forced forward leaving the back half of the space empty. "Now load it!" ordered the sergeant.

The last time I saw Donnelly was in the battle for Nuremberg. Always laughing or cheerful, he climbed on our tank, leaned in and showed his right hand – laughing as if it was funny. An enemy bullet had gone right through his hand, which was really a mess. That ended Donnelly's tour of combat duty. I never saw him again.

FOX HOLES & SLEEPING BAGS

Taking prisoners was not just for our men. As we moved on to new assignments, we came upon a very heart-wrenching sight. We took up a position near the edge of heavy woods. It appeared that a heavy enemy attack has routed our beloved comrades, but there were no bodies left behind. Dozens of foxholes were abandoned. Perhaps a truckload of equipment left in the dugouts included weapons, mess gear, personal belongings and dozens of Army blankets. As I mentioned earlier, there was no way for us to learn the facts.

To recover all this stuff would be nearly impossible but I saw a chance to help a need of my own. Army sleeping bags were minimal and tight. There was a reason they were called "mummy sacks". We believed it would be okay for some of us to make use of abandoned items. Some supply unit would have picked these things when there was a chance. I gathered together some of the O.D. blankets and made my own sleeping bag. That turned out to be a very welcome item and I was able to use it for a while. I became the envy of our crew with the special sack. Some other soldier must have liked it as well; I lost it to an unknown buddy. I did not resent him for that. All I had to do was make another one. I was lucky to find string and a sack needle for the job.

NUREMBERG

"The dominant desire of the Germans now, both troops and civilians, was to see the British and American armies sweep eastward as rapidly as possible to reach Berlin and occupy as much of the country as possible before the Soviets overcame the Oder line. Few of them were inclined to assist Hitler's purpose of obstruction by self-destruction. On March 19 (the eve of the Rhine crossing), Hitler had issued an order declaring that "the

battle should be conducted without consideration for our own population." His regional commissioners were instructed to destroy "all industrial plants, all the main electricity works, waterworks, gas works" together with "all food and clothing stores" in order to create "a desert" in the Allies' path. When his minister of war production, Albert Speer, protested against this drastic order, Hitler retorted: "If the war is lost, the German nation will also perish. So there is no need to consider what the people require for continued existence." Appalled at such callousness, Speer was shaken out of his loyalty to Hitler: he went behind Hitler's back to the army and industrial chiefs and persuaded them, without much difficulty, to evade executing Hitler's decree. The Americans and the British, driving eastward from the Rhine, met little opposition and reached the Elbe River 60 miles from Berlin, on April 11. There they halted."

Nuremberg is and was a very important German city. It was Hitler's pride and joy and referred to as his Queen City. We were called on to take care of several days of *pockets* holding out. Rifle and machine gun fire could be heard around the clock. However, as always happened, air strikes and days of artillery shelling preceded our involvement.

Some strange behavior of people (Germans) had us intrigued. I did not see it, but one of our men reported on old woman sitting in a rocking chair on a porch. She was not rocking all the time. It was believed when our men tried to secure some area, this old woman would rock back and forth and enemy response followed, when they moved towards their goal or target.

An infantry soldier believed she was involved in giving signals. Hard as it may seem, the order was given to get rid of her. Maybe it was a soldier dressed like a woman, but the report indicated that our men could move without enemy resistance after her demise.

Our tank was facing east on what may have been an important street. Our job was to be ready to fire our weapons on command. Actually, I hated the job. Who – or what – were we shooting at. I stood in the hatch of my tank and from out of the blue, a sharp rifle bullet missed me by inches. The crack of air as it passed by reminded me of the sound of an expert cracking a whip.

ONCE THE SHOW PLACE OF NAZI LAND

Adolph Hitler once called Nuremberg the most German of all cities. Adolph should see his city now. After our air corps and the RAF had given the Nazi birthplace a good going over tanks, TDs and infantry of the Third Division moved in. These tanks of 756th are moving toward Hitler Platz from the Castle. That nice wide path was cleared by a tank dozer from the 10th Engineers. - Third Signal Company Photo *(Dick had in his possession an actual newspaper clipping of the scene above and proudly claimed that HIS was the lead tank in the photo).*

I dropped in the tank and within seconds, one of our men, a young blonde fellow, jumped up and looked in the hatch – his body draped over the top of the tank. "Are you alright, Young?" I hollered, "Get out of there - they may get you!"

We entered a home where the occupants must have left hurriedly as the table was still set up and a meal only half eaten left to mold. A person could not help but feel sad for those caught in such situations. Our mission was to give support to the ground troops and often given a specific assignment to fire at certain buildings or bunkers with questionable uses.

Firing a tank gun in an apartment window was a direct order from our platoon officer. The distressing part was that there did not seem to be any reason for the strange order. However, it was wartime and whereas officers were considered to have the authority to make some decisions and the net results often are shocking.

My involvement was to follow orders and it was from my tank that the gun was used for this strange order. Who would have known that someone was trying to get a look at activity, and became the victim of his or her curiosity? We perhaps were not kept in the dark, but certainly we were not always informed and when something unusual took place, it was truly a puzzle.

These sorts of things were common and when the day wore on and some of the things we were called on to do were behind us, we truly did not know how seriously we hurt some people. The record book claims 18,000 civilians were killed in the total siege of the city.

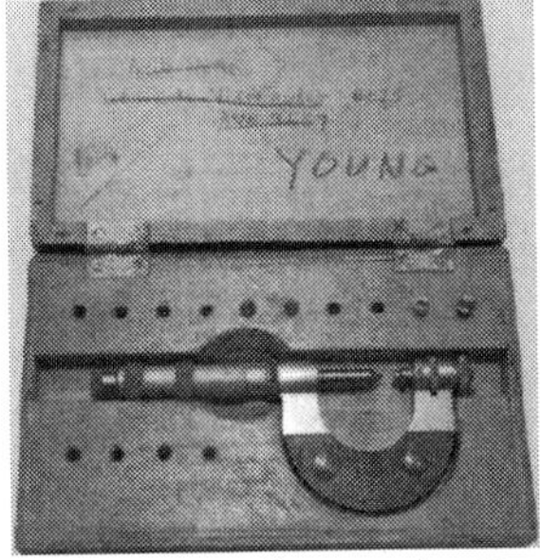

My inquisitive nature caused me to do something that was questionable. While in the city of Nuremberg, our tank was stationed a short way from an underground factory that was open and had no one guarding it. There was some daylight, but to get a good look, I dared to light a candle. I was intrigued at the machines that I was familiar with using. I did not ask for permission, but loaded my pockets with measuring tools. I am sure I would have drawn a strong disapproval from members of my family. War time does not seem to have rules for such matters.

The last day of Nuremberg, we edged forward on a street that adjoined large blocks of residential housing and apartments. We were stunned to see large numbers of civilian women, boys and girls and some elders pour into the street and surround our tank. I estimate over 100 people. They seemed ecstatic and the behavior must have truly been something they all shared in.

Nuremberg was liberated! How the signal was given is not known, but this huge, beleaguered city was now fully in Allied control. No more shots were fired.

CAMOUFLAGE

I regret that keeping track of our moves and dates escaped most of us. Names of towns and cities often had military changes for reasons known to the high command. However, for purposes of reporting our activities, I believe our involvement in daily routines is more for the interest it creates. Much of our activity was not of exciting nature.

Placing our tank in a wooded area near the Rhine River was for holding a position and it maybe had the effect of keeping enemy soldiers out of sight. American soldiers always had some activity that may not have been ordered by an officer. In this case, we tried to hide our tank. Since all our equipment had distinctive markings, we saw fit to use mud to smear over the white star and other identifying marks.

The day was dull. An unexpected visit by an infantry colonel who came to check up on our position caused some concern. He ordered that we get rid of the mud and clean the tank. I was only a corporal, but I tried to be courteous and took a chance. I said, “Sir, I believe the tank is quite well camouflaged." He did not answer me, but when he turned away, I was certain his ears were a bit red.

ON GUARD WITH HAND GRENADES

The so-called ***front*** was wherever we were stationed to perform some mission. It may be at some crossroads, farm place, river's edge, or deep woods. After crossing the Rhine River, we were set up in a heavy wooded area, which I believe was part of the Black Forest. Our job was to find enemy positions. As a lone tank, we had no special orders but to hold our position.

Normally, foot soldiers were a part of all operations. They rode on the tank and we felt that each had a role in protecting the other. Tankers were, for the most part, hidden in the tank, and the view of operations was limited to the telescope or open hatches if orders were to that effect. The average person believed that tanks were invincible, but an enemy soldier could mount the tank and drop a grenade inside killing the crew.

Night fell after the attack. It must be made clear that artillery and mortar attacks do not mean we were visible to the enemy, but scattered incoming rounds often found their mark.

A five-man crew, we were alone – no foot soldiers - on this particular assignment. When there were no troops to accompany us, we took turns standing guard outside the tank. We spread our tanks out in a better pattern for defense. When it was fully dark, it was inky dark in the woods. We had no specific orders what to do if we were attacked. Each had to stand for two hours before the next in line took his turn.

On this clear night, it was very dark with no moon. Tank engines were not running. No lighting cigarettes, or turning on any type of light. In standing guard, each man had his preference for protection. Firing a rifle or Tommy gun seemed questionable in pitch darkness.

When it was my turn to stand guard, I chose a rather unlikely weapon - two hand grenades. The thought of the firepower gave me a sense of security. I stood by a tree, holding one of these nubby configurations in each hand and hoped and prayed. If attacked, what would I do?

To throw one of them in the night – the "what-ifs" entered my mind. However, as pitch black as it was, I thought if I throw one, it might hit a tree and bounce back. The effective range of a grenade is perhaps less than 100 feet. There is about a ten-second delay when the grenade is armed until it explodes. I could not tell where friendly troops were dug in either. I just stood there – near enough to our tank to get back in if some emergency developed. All sorts of thoughts enter one's mind.

BATTLE PATROL IN BLACK FOREST

One of the most feared units were battle patrols. Men volunteered the night missions of traveling light with only a few items for combat. They used wire to choke their victims and knives to cut throats.

Every night was punctuated with sounds of heavy guns in the distance, but where we were, it was almost an eerie stillness. The rest of the crew was in the tank when suddenly in the stillness of the night, I heard twigs snapping and coming closer. That meant footsteps.

Proper procedure when on guard is to call out sharply, “Halt, who goes there?” which I did in my best military voice. No response. The sound of twigs snapping ended and everything was quiet. Whoever it was made no sounds other than what I first heard.

In the space of about ½ hour, I heard more twigs snapping. Again, I sounded off, “Halt, who goes there?” The answer was scary but welcome, and I was relieved to hear the clear unmistakable voice of an American – “GI battle patrol.” My next question was obvious. “Who was here only minutes ago?” The leader said, “It was a German Battle patrol we were tracking.”

There was little conversation to follow. We kept our voices low to keep from giving our position away. I could not see any of the men in the darkness, but they left after our brief interchange. Soon, all was quiet again.

I was replaced at the guard post, but it was so dark we could barely distinguish faces. My two grenades, warm from holding them in my bare hands, were properly returned to the grenade storage. That was the only time I ever used or considered grenades for protection. I sat in the gunner's seat 'til dawn, only to be greeted by the command, "Crank 'em up, we're moving out."

To reiterate some of the account of front line troops may seem indelicate, but the humor may be worth the risk. Still on guard in the wooded area, we always tried to keep up with our needs – opening rations, lighting cigarettes and just resting.

'Pop Lansdale' was next for guard duty. As he left the tank he said, "Hey guys. When you go to relieve yourself, go off a ways from the tank so the next guy won't step in it."

The comment was not answered, but the comedy of it all came about when Pop shortly re-entered the tank from the top hatch, his right foot bore the unwelcome news as he slipped. I was impressed that there was no "cussing" and after a bit of laughter and Pop, taking care of the problem, all was back to normal. The night wore on and at daybreak, we moved on to a new assignment. We were thankful that the night ended without any confrontation.

HEY, CAN I SEE YOUR KNIFE?

The men in battle patrols have a unique job. There are usually several fellows that are perhaps the most daring of service troops. They travel light. They may have a pistol, but more likely a knife. Equipment for survival may include wire – yes, wire – used for strangling the enemy without sound.

Reports are that Arabs (they were on our side) were very good for battle patrol duty. They excelled in the use of hand weapons and they spent hours sharpening their knives when in a rest mode. My friend, Bob Padgett, was intrigued at the behavior of the Arab soldiers. They preferred to sleep in hay in a barn rather than use a home, as was the habit of American soldiers. Bob was trying to find out why these men were a bit different and went to talk to some of them. Bob had heard that they were skilled in the use of knives. He asked to see one of the

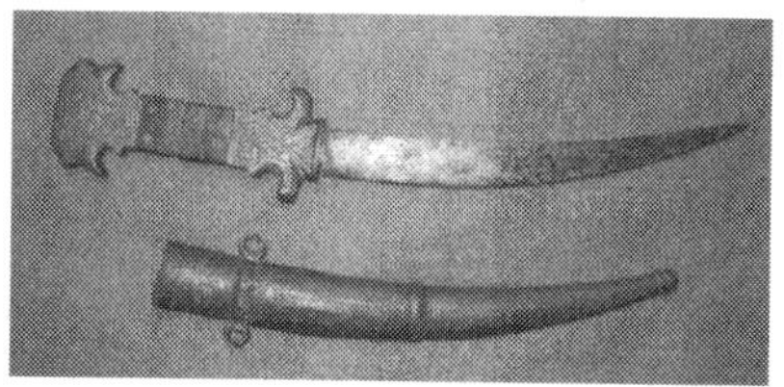

knives. He was told that the only time they take the knife out was to draw blood – or when spending time sharpening it.

Bob insisted that he would like to see a knife. The leader told him that the only way he would show it would be to cut Bob's finger a bit. Bob was only about twenty years old, but somewhat daring. Later, those of us who knew about the episode learned that the knives were special and VERY sharp indeed.

SLEEPING IN A HOG BARN

The title does not sound very impressive. However, we must remember that a soldier has a feeling in the back of his mind that his days in a combat zone are uncertain. No one has a guarantee that he will be around long. Who would choose to sleep in a hog barn? The Arabs sometimes chose to get some rest there. During this time of duty in Germany, it was during cold weather. If we found a way to get some rest there, we felt quite secure in that domestic arrangement. We did not know enough about hogs to make it a concern. Soldiers were, for the most part, equal to and ready to do whatever worked. Fresh hay or straw was the key to comfort. Such behavior was rare. After a brief rest, it was back to duty.

CROSSING THE RHINE RIVER

None of us knew that ahead of us was a dangerous piece of business. We had to cross the Rhine River at Worms, Germany. This was the city where Martin Luther did much of his studies in scripture. None of us really had any preconceived ideas of the job ahead of the actual crossing. The day was a sort of mix of partially cloudy skies and, in daylight, that river looked a mile wide. Combat engineers had created a heavy smoke screen, which prevented the enemy seeing us.

Imagine if you can the extreme weight of a 50 ton tank, fully loaded, crawling up on a rubber pontoon raft.

I must credit the Army engineers with one of the most carefully engineered operations we faced and the ingenious handling of what could have been a total flop. How often we, in the lead tank, were called on to sort of *test the waters*? It may have had some advantages to be in the lead, but often our job was a test of the preparations for some activity that was not explained. We were ordered to move our tank to the river's edge where docks were in use as most of us were accustomed to in the States. The distance across was not told, but it seemed to be several hundred feet.

Our tank was gingerly ushered to the riverbank, and this seemingly unwieldy craft was anchored until we cautiously drove our tank on it. I believe by that time, all of us were prepared for anything. Did these fellows know what they were doing? The floating platform must have been tested – who knows? Nevertheless, there we were – the crew of five inside the tank- as four outboard motors were started, one on each corner of the raft. I marveled at the crew operating the outboard motors hooked to that queasy raft. If combat is dangerous, what about these brave men – exposing themselves to a hazardous task?

As we edged into the water, we could hear anti-tank gun shots (not ours), as we slipped into a space of time that seemed an eternity. It felt like a marshmallow floating in a hot chocolate drink. We were being shot at the entire time in the water, but the many near misses reminded me that there was truly some "Great Power" looking after us. We knew that one stray round could puncture one of the raft floats with only disaster resulting. Sure, we prayed. What else? All I could see from the tank was through the large gun sight. The best way to describe it is like looking through a pipe about the size of a broomstick.

In one sense, we were protected by the tank armor, but the men on the motors were exposed to the enemy guns. The period of crossing perhaps seemed extra long, but we made it to the opposite side without incident. What a great relief to reach the opposite river bank – but all was <u>not</u> well.

Reaching the other shore created more trouble. The bank was fairly steep and loaded with rocks varying in size from baseballs to soccer balls. Very carefully, the raft was lined up with the exit maneuver, and who would know that the rocks would roll out under our tracks and prevent good traction. Our tank slipped back and damaged the pontoon craft enough so that getting help from other tanks was delayed for hours. We finally struggled up the bank by the driver using an angle approach. We all breathed easier when we reached level ground and made it to a wooded area.

The net result of the damaged raft was that we were alone all day until toward evening when three other tanks finally made a safe trip. It was somewhat revelatory of human nature. After a safe landing, the adrenaline flow subsided and we felt like old combat troops – a bit smug perhaps. I look back with a degree of disquiet when I realize that concern for our boys in the next tank was almost casual.

One thing that I have been pleased to report is that most of our tank officers were not aggressive to try some heroics. If the people back home could have seen us at times, they would have been either shocked or disgusted. I recall a day when I was sitting at my gun post while eating peanuts and reading a Lil' Abner comic book.

"DUNKED" IN A FORTY TON STEEL TRAP

Every day or night, we lined up for some kind of action or perhaps just sitting in a hold position at some crossroads. Setting up a roadblock was a common occurrence. After crossing the Rhine River, we moved on to a small town in Germany. Streets were unpaved and houses were very well built, mostly of stone.

One night in particular was clear with a welcome full noon. The air was crisp. The earlier evening involved refueling; a field-prepared meal from 'ten-in-one' rations; and time out for a smoke and brief rest before orientation for a night move. No action was anticipated. No enemy was in sight. Several friendly elements were on the trail ahead of us. Our mission was to establish a roadblock in territory already taken. Usually this consisted of one or two tanks and a platoon of infantry.

The advantage of moonlight made night travel easier. Many roads were graveled, appearing white in moonglow. Blackout lamps were not required and were not to be compared with nature's marvel.

As we rolled along, remnants of war dotted the countryside. A blown tank here, a burned truck there, crumbled walls and abandoned field gear, all pointing to the futility of whatever someone attempted to hold or gain.

At times, I took my turn driving just for a change. The tank steered with levers as used on a 'cat' tractor. The driver's seat is adjustable in height, the top position easiest to drive from. The clutch, designed for heavy gearing, depresses with the least effort from high seating. Also in this position, the driver's head is out of the hatch for a clearer view of his duties. When the seat is lowered for "button-up", one could hardly say the tank is comfortable. The shape and styling in a tank is not conducive to comfort. At best, the position is cramped for all. There is no back on the gunner's seat (at least not so of the vintage of the times), so one must make up for the lack some other way.

There was, however, one possibility that presented itself. We could stretch out under the receiver of the big gun. When convenient, I made use of the feature, albeit, I did at times look up at what must have been several hundred pounds of steel and calculate it falling on me. However, securely anchored on a trunnion, I quickly dispensed with the thought.

I may add here, that in any event, if Bob was uneasy, my rest was out. I made no use of the turret floor, because there was no resting. Bob's notions kept me seated straight away in the gunner's seat, where I could work if needed.

For a change, I had been driving and when I returned to the turret, Bob was making a clicking sound with his cheek. His heel thumped the floor, and a semi-rhythmic slapping of his knee told as much as words. Sensing trouble, he reminded me at intervals that <u>not</u> all was well. Here again, I may ask – what was on his mind? What evil device of the enemy lay in wait for tank number B 1?

Large sections of territory had been taken from a weary and shattered German army. The feeling that any day the war would end permeated every outfit. Token forces took entire companies and even battalions.

The Southern France Campaign, the Colmar Campaign, the crossing of the Rhine, and the Battle of Nuremberg **<u>were all behind us</u>**, yet Bob had contagious apprehension.

We pulled into a small town that gave the impression of peaceful, rural living. A small white church to the north stood as a mute reminder of unseen Powers. A few scattered tombstones near the church also gave a testimony as to the irrevocability of death.

There were no sounds of guns to punctuate the night. The pleasant 'face' of the moon gave occasional nostalgic nudges to remind of better days and memories cherished.

This paradox was almost torture as I caught myself sitting tensely, leaning forward, pressing the palms of my hands together and doing nothing but waiting – and praying softly. Bob took deep, heavy drags on his cigarette and from the greenish glow of the monitor on the radio I could see his face revealing concern.

A huge house to the right of the trail, sitting diagonal and facing northwest, became the new Command Post. The road we would block lay east of the house. Directly in front, perhaps fifty or sixty feet, was a very large tree, bare of leaves, yet presenting a heavy network of branches.

Under the tree and shadowed by the two-story house was some unidentified space surrounded by a white fence. It was a coincidence that we should be on the opposite side of the dwelling from the moon's light by preference and by necessity for the best position. The brilliance of the moon made the dark side of the house seem even darker; hence, some guesswork on our part. Curiosity brought an old German gentleman out of the new headquarters. Lt. Willette ("Willy") inquired of him about the fenced "area", which appeared to be a little longer and only a few inches wider than the tank.

The interpretation the lieutenant caught, led him to believe it was a dance floor, but who could tell what it was at night. At least it was provided with a heavy plank floor and was accessible through a small gate. Only a few minutes were needed to determine the best spot for the tank; right in the middle of the floor. The tree gave overhead protection from the air. No one could see the tank from the south, while the fence provided cover for the lower parts of the running gear.

Our new driver, "Salty", who had replaced Joe Torchia, waited for the inevitable order from Lt. Willette to "back her in". Lt. Willette directed the operation, slowly and carefully as space was limited. One end of the fence had to come down, but yielded easily to the 500 horsepower Ford engine. Timbers creaked and snapped as we edged backwards.

Not yet in position, an excited out-post runner reported, "Krauts are coming into town over the hill just south of here!" As I said before, we always were in direct cooperation with the infantry troops.

Bob was nervous. I looked at him from the gunner's seat. "What do you say, Bob?", I asked. "I don't like it, Young", was his cautious reply.

Our engine still running and everyone awake, we took little time to pull out, swing west around our command post and establish a firing position. Heavy machine gun fire spewed from our guns. Rounds of high explosives from the '76' were also hurled into the night. Infantrymen moved forward under the protection of tank fire as they joined in, their own rifles crackling defiance. The short, sharp action quickly dispersed the foe. Our orders came by intercom and we kept on until our supply was nearly exhausted before a ceasefire order was given. The officers were satisfied that our efforts paid off. A quick check relieved us to find all men from our units present and accounted for. To this day, I am thankful that the decision to unload a whole tank full of heavy shells at the Germans was not mine to make.

Smoking brass, still too hot to handle, covered the turret floor. Heavy sulfur fumes clung in the tank. Cigarettes were lit but tasted of gun smoke. Our ears felt the heavy concussion of tank guns and I could hardly hear for several days. Oddly, we were never given any kind of ear protection. We could have used cotton if any was available, but this is the lot of soldiers; do your best under circumstances. Waiting for further orders, someone opened a can of Planters peanuts to provide us with a bit of protein. Though loaded with chemicals, a cup of cold water relieved parched throats.

Using the radio directly to the rear of the gunner, Lt. Willette checked with sister tanks. Satisfied with the situation, he left the tank, carrying his steel helmet by one strap. With a sweep of his arm, he motioned to the driver to return to the roadblock position. Bob and I cleared the tank of empty shells. I thought Bob would be relieved that we beat off the enemy, not knowing how seriously we hurt them, but he remained uneasy. The conflict completed south of the big house did not satisfy Bob. He insisted that there was something he feared. It was spring and not too cold, but Bob stuck to his feelings. Only Providence knew our plight. I sat in my gunner's seat, shivering from anxiety and from the chill of an early March day.

Orders remained and the next thing was to return to our roadblock position at the same spot by the house with the fence. We were now back at the edge of the "dance floor", the lieutenant waiting alongside. The planks groaned and crunched under the forty odd tons of a General Sherman tank as the tank officer stood in front of the tank giving direction to the driver by using hand signals. Each man tried to get as comfortable as able for the balance of the night. I sat in my crouched position at the gun controls, trying to get accustomed to sitting up all night, waiting, watching and clinging to an unsettled feeling. I quit looking over at Bob who was quiet but had not given the "all clear".

Every cleat on the tracks could be felt as Salty moved still further into position. Joe Salvatore of Chicago slumped in his seat after announcing his retirement. Salty was tall and thin and quite the opposite of "Little Joe" who stood 5' 2".

The cracking of boards breaking was not sufficient warning. Our nostrils still filled with gun smoke, how could any of us guess without warning, we would crash through the "dance floor", plunging into an abyss of murky green water? Our tank dropped rear end first into a water reservoir. The tank continued to slip on down into eleven feet of water. I hit my head on the radio as I flew out of my seat. I was stunned.

A deluge poured into the hatch. The rear of the tank hit bottom first, as the tank tracks continued the backward momentum. Water quickly filled the tank as the front-end slid into the concrete pit.

The large main tank gun caught on the rim of this strange recess by the big house, wrecking the gun and forcing the receiver of the gun tight to the tank floor.

Bob, unhurt, scrambled to safety. As I dragged myself out, too groggy to know what had happened, I could hear him yelling, "Get Salty! Get Shorty!" I realized two men were still in that tank, but I could not move.

Lt. Willette, disregarding his own safety, jumped into the water bristling with twisted timbers only to find the drivers' hatches jammed shut by planks impinged under the tank gun. Working frantically he freed enough planks to open Salty's hatch, but no Salty.

I saw something that impressed me greatly. Going down into the tank, the lieutenant found Salty trying to get out the bottom escape hatch. Grabbing him by the seat of his trousers, Lt. Willette pulled him to safety, soaked, confused, blubbering and grateful for the rescue. Salty, with a wild mop of uncombed hair hanging in his face, tried to shake water out of his boots. Looking at Lt. Willette almost apologetically, he quipped, "I thought she flipped over Lt., and I tried to come out of the escape hatch. One more minute and I would have been drinking water."

Bob was trying to find Joe. The lieutenant tried Joe's hatch, also jammed shut. Seconds later, the high-pitched shrill voice of Joe could be heard, "Here I am, Lt.!" Joe had wiggled out through a hole in the turret basket and came out through the tank commanders' hatch. Had Joe been an inch taller or two pounds heavier, he may not have escaped.

Jubilant that all had endured the experience without a mark – except my head, which began to clear, and soaking wet in March, we laughed, joked, and stayed awake all night. We could not help but thank God we were all safe.

Bob was exuberant at the outcome. His sense of humor accentuated all conversation, which continued to speculate the fate of our fallen fortress. He said, "I knew it! We were in for something!"

I usually turned sideways after some action and stretched my legs out under the tank gun receiver. When Bob persisted that something was haywire, I sat straight up in my seat. As I said earlier, I was actually shivering, not so much from cold, but anticipation of Bob's report.

To this day, I believe that Bob's so-called *psychic* thought was, in truth, Providence, sparing me being pinned in a 50-ton coffin under the tank gun receiver. How often it has come to mind that Bob, showing concern, prompted my reaction to my benefit. Perhaps it would be more fitting to give the Lord the credit. Fortunately, there was no more contact with German soldiers, but we had to see another tank left to fate. Salvage was not possible.

The old man who lived in the big house was very receptive and gave us free use of his home. We all needed rest and some means to fix food. Ours was a total loss in the tank. The next several hours were spent in shedding our wet clothes and drying them before a very welcome fire in the fireplace.

Soon after daybreak, inquisitiveness bought many to witness a most unlikely situation. The reservoir, we learned (no reflection on "Gramps") was part of the village fire protection system. Water was pumped out with a hand pump unit requiring a six man team, with three men on each side. We were also amazed to see the close dimensions in all directions pertaining to tank length and width. Mere inches front, rear, and along the sides remained.

The **only** portion of the tank not in the hole was the big gun sticking out at a high angle. The four or so feet of the gun that projected in front of the tank had caught on the rim of the concrete wall dragging planks along with it.

Observing the main gun sticking out above the edge of the reservoir reminded me of how critical it was that I was not pinned under the receiver of the gun. At other times when we had finished some assignment, I would sit with my legs stretched out under the receiver of the gun and relax. Had I been in that position when the tank broke through, I may not have escaped, as the gun mount had broken and the result as noted – the receiver, which included the breechblock, was several hundred pounds and rested squarely on the tank floor.

The local pumping unit joined the operation and soon drained the pit. Our job was to salvage as much as possible from the storage compartments. Several prisoners of war were brought to the scene to start excavation of a slope to remove the tank.

The once proud unit looked, for the entire world, a helpless as an elephant in a pit, unable to free himself. Sooner than expected, our replacement tank rolled in the area, courtesy of headquarters and service company.

As we began the salvage operation, we were honored to have the famous General "Iron Mike" O'Daniels visit the site to inspect the unusual and rare oddity. He also gave a wordless account of why he held the fabulous nickname. Usually, a visit from a general is viewed with trepidation especially when his sonorous voice pinpointed one man.

"Who drove that tank in there?" he boomed, in a rather gruff voice.

Salty stepped forward and admitted sheepishly, "I did, Sir."

Everyone breathed easier at the general's reaction when he laughed heartily in a complete change of demeanor and jokingly said, "Bet you couldn't do that again!"

That broke formalities and as we all stood there waiting for our replacement to arrive, German artillery threw in a barrage that sent us scattering for cover, except Iron Mike, who stood as if oblivious to the condition. A close look at his face showed battle scars and a man of leadership qualities.

When the air had cleared, all worked to the common effort of salvage. As I worked in my own compartment, I could not help but notice the breech mechanism jammed to the floor. A feeling of chill and awe raced through my body as I looked at the spot where I had very often stretched out to relax. Here, but for the grace of God, could have been my body, pinned in a watery grave. The gun mounting had been wrecked as the tank dropped. I mused – what did Bob have to do with all this?

Our replacement tank loaded and ready for action arrived. I shall never forget looking back at the gray suited men swinging picks and the muzzle of the gun projecting out of the reservoir, reminding me, that instead of disaster, we had only been "dunked" in a forty ton steel trap. Lt. Willette was not yet aware he would receive the Soldiers Medal for saving Salty. Bob and I were inseparable as he continued his valued predictions. It was here Bob became a gunner and I became his tank commander. We remained together until we reached Salzburg, when Bob went home.

FIRST LIEUTENANT WILLIAM WILLETTE

I was a gunner in B Company of the 756th for Lt. Willette, the handsome, bronzed platoon leader who possessed an adventurous spirit, never allowing boredom to dampen his impetuousness.

Early spring of 1945 saw a rapidly changing front, as large elements of "Der Fuhrer's" army succumbed to powerful arms of the US Military machine. Infantrymen of the 3rd Division rode on our tanks as we pressed deep into enemy territory, "mopping up" as we advanced.

Lt. Willette also commanded the tank in which I was assigned. Frequently his duties as platoon leader took him away from the tank; the gunner then took command. Some decisions were to be made without the tank commander. This was my lot at times, and of course, there was no telling if the results were best for all, especially where it concerned the state of fellow men.

CAT AND MOUSE GAME – YOU MISSED!

Just to show how nonchalant we became, we were in view of forward observers from the German side. They called on artillery to harass us. A direct hit could do a lot of damage, but near misses were brushed off as 'so what?' We used the system of moving to prevent a direct line on our position. Being in a tank is a combination of experiences. It is clumsy, cold, cramped, and noisy. It is also your home on tracks, safe from small arms fire and relatively protected from mines and artillery shells.

Shortly after finding a spot for our tank, German artillery shells landed nearby. As the enemy bracketed in with successive rounds coming closer, we did the obvious. We moved a little ways. Shelling continued, but we were smart. As the bursts came close, we kept our cat and mouse game by moving far enough to throw the forward observers off. The actual artillery positions could be as much as five to ten miles away. Observers had to phone in their corrective adjustments.

Picture this – a crew of five tankers, alone on a piece of uncharted ground, ducking artillery shells, reading Li'l Abner cartoons, eating peanuts, smoking cigarettes, grabbing a wink and waiting for the next tank to appear.

We encountered practically no activity as night fell. I was always surprised to see how soon wayward tanks could reassemble. None of us were given any idea of what to expect, but stood ready to do as ordered. When a lieutenant mounted our tank, he may say something like "Crank 'em up at 5:45 and line up on the gravel road to your right." We were not told what we may encounter, but just follow orders. It seems reasonable that the first tank may hit the worst resistance while the possibility existed, the enemy learned to knock off the last tank, blocking escape for other tanks. Nothing was for sure.

As we moved into a holding position about 5:00 PM, everything seemed relatively calm until a mortar attack hit our position. The assistant driver was in the right hatch of the tank when he was hit and he dropped like lead, moaning with pain. It took very little time to evacuate him to the medics, but I never saw him again.

FORWARD? N0, BACK UP!

I sometimes feel that war stories sound fictitious especially when some rather odd behavior is required. I have felt that honest reporting is best and easier to relate.

Things were moving fast now. We had to push on towards larger targets. Again, preparing for action we were poised with four other tanks along a country road leading into a medium sized city. To our right was a steep bank along the road. To our left were open fields with scattered trees.

We did not know what to expect but the presence of our tanks might have prompted the enemy to prepare for an attack, as German anti-tank guns knew our approximate position. We learned of enemy anti-tank guns, but how close, we did not know. Anti-tank guns were not in full view.

A flash to our left signaled the inevitable. We were being fired at as we could hear the sound of distant guns. Four of our tanks were the target. They must have been armor-piercing slugs because they did not explode against the high bank. We were being fired at, but they missed.

Though there was a slight delay between rounds, our clever and enterprising young tankers invented a relay system that worked. Incoming slugs made a swishing sound in the air. Some of our brave men listened for each incoming round.

"They're getting closer, back up a bit," said one. Later, the order to run forward a hundred feet put the errant slugs behind us. Our tanks were kept running. The system of enemy gunners anticipating a target was to keep moving the action to the right or left hoping somewhere in there to get a hit. It may have been dumb luck, but not one of our tanks was hit as each used the ear-sound system to protect his tank.

Being fired at is not funny, but I often was intrigued by the behavior of GIs who in a remarkable short space of time became quite bold – or, perhaps, foolhardy. I should mention that the fellows who took upon themselves the dubious job of identifying sounds of the slugs were <u>outside</u> the tank. We escaped being hit, and perhaps the enemy gave up when it appeared nothing happened. The space of time for this unusual operation was perhaps shorter than it seemed, and we all concluded the enemy gunners could not see us, but Providence spared any of us being hit.

SLIDING INTO TOWN

In the daylight, shortly after sunrise, we prepared to rev up our tanks and streak into the town to secure it. Ahead of us was an overpass with the concrete highway passing under. The road curved entering the overpass.

Our tank had the new style steel cleat wide tracks. Who would have believed the tracks had become worn enough so all sharp edges were rounded over which we found had very little grip on the smooth pavement.

We were going at a fairly high speed for tanks – perhaps 45 miles per hour when we suddenly skidded on dry pavement, when entering the curve, as if we were on glare ice. The steering levers were useless in preventing our tank from going into a frightening spin, a really weird sensation. Bear in mind that the driver and assistant driver were able to see better than the crew in the turret. Our driver corrected the problem and we barreled on into the town with no further incident. I mention it as one of those things which become a part of soldiers' meeting emergencies as they arise.

Reports were often rumors; however, we believe the German anti-tank gunners were silenced by ground troops. Our skid in the town received no further gunfire. Often, our days were used to clean weapons, fix meals as able, gab about our affairs and just wait for the next night mission.

ROYAL TIGER

The war was winding down, and much of the territory secure, but infantry soldiers still dug foxholes for protection. It was evening when we set up our position and even though the tankers were relaxed, we could hear infantry soldiers, who were ordered to 'dig in' ahead of our tanks, chopping foxholes most of the night. Though spring approached, much of the ground was still frozen. Out in front of our tanks we saw infantrymen digging in for the night. I can still hear sounds of trench shovels – even steel helmets used as tools with which to dig. Some of the men had a small hatchet to chop into the rocky soil. We could hear the clanking sounds throughout the night.

There were country trails, gravel roads, built up high, which proved to be a benefit. Using daytime to travel to new locations, often our job was setting up roadblocks. We joined forces for cleanup and security in the battle for that city. We entered another woods with our tanks facing a country trail at about a 45-degree angle.

It seemed like a rather uneventful space of time. The night wore on. We rested but did not sleep. Night always seemed to have the tranquilizing effect when things were quiet. One of the other fellows sat in the gunner's seat while I stood in the hatch with my upper body exposed, on guard, to relieve another soldier. The tank commander was sleeping in my seat at the gun controls. I was still a gunner at this point.

A sense of security caught each of us. To our left our lieutenant was in tank number one with far less firepower - an old Radial engine tank with a 76 mm main gun. He was nearest the road. We were deeper in the woods feeling content, as we had no contact with the Germans. At least we thought so. When we set up a roadblock at a fork in the road, we happened to be tank number two with a 76 mm gun.

The road we were guarding was a high crowned road rising as much as two or three feet above flat ground. Little did we know that across that road, while American soldiers were digging in on one side of the road for protection, only a city block or two away, Germans were also digging in.

I stood in the tank hatch watching as daybreak brought the first streams of light into the woods. At early daybreak, to the right front, I heard some engine start up. It was not the destructive sound of our Sherman tanks. It made sounds unfamiliar to our tank troops. The American tanks had a much different sound than other engines. We had a Ford V8, 500 horsepower and we enjoyed the sound of these iron monsters. I woke the sergeant. Whatever the sound was, it started to move. A cluster of trees to our right prevented us from seeing what the sound of the engine would reveal.

Emerging from the cluster of trees to our right was one of the feared Royal Tiger tanks with the infamous 88 mm gun. The most feared combination of enemy war equipment was the 88 mm anti-tank gun mounted on a Royal Tiger tank.

I may have ignored it if his gun did not point at us, but the lieutenant started shooting at the monster tank, which meant we had to join in. Our tank commander was not accustomed to gunning, but since he was in the gunner's seat, we had to take a chance. In tank warfare the traditional shell was armor piercing (AP). Tank warfare is tricky. We were told to always have our gun loaded with AP, which we did. Several shots fired only ricocheted off the behemoth; all they would need to do is see us, and we would be smoke.

In the space of five minutes, we were not sure why, but we were stunned to see our lieutenant and his crew abandon their tank, running towards and then past our position heading for safety. Not to question him, we saw he had abandoned his post so we left our tank, thinking he would include us. The lieutenant shouted, "Get back in your tank! You have more fire power than we do!"

Embarrassing – yes, but always the lieutenant is in charge. That order was the closest to giving me the feeling that we would not survive the confrontation. I believed I could smell death in the air. It is the most acute feeling I ever had, that my time was up.

An old saying, discretion is the better part of valor, but they needed gunners and not philosophers. Hastily, we took our positions. The monster yellow-brown tank was heading towards the corner where the lieutenant had been. The difference in the tank guns meant it would not be wise to encounter the German tank crew. I had seen some of our tanks after an encounter with Tiger tanks and the results were deadly.

I took over the gun controls. We had no choice but to start shooting. Our 76 mm APs were useless against the armor on a Royal Tiger. We could see the slugs just bounce off without causing any damage.

Ground troops ahead of our tank were dug in, but as we fired our tank gun over their heads, the Lord knows it was a frightening experience and they scattered.

I saw the huge gun slowly turning towards us. Seeing that we had no effect against the German tank with the APs, I yelled "HE" (high explosive) to Bob Padgett, as the psychic gun loader took his place. The next shell Bob loaded was high explosive. The shells were designed to explode on contact and I was fortunate to get a direct hit with the first shell. The noise and dust was unreal. Repeatedly we fired. That action was enough to drive the Royal Tiger tank away. We believe the noise and the dust shield prevented **them** from seeing **us**.

It was reported that, as the Royal Tiger moved down the trail, other tanks from another unit converged on it and finished the job. The tank body was so thick it would be a miracle to penetrate its armor, but one experienced tanker told me to try to wreck their gun or tracks and disable the tank. We were told that the Germans believed that they should only go forward. Supposedly, there was little protection for the rear of the tank. Who could get close enough to learn the truth? I am glad we were ordered back in the tank. I feel better for it, plus the fact if we had not stirred up the HE storm, we may have been mowed down.

The episode with the big tank topped anything we had experienced. Considering all other combat experiences, I prayed harder during the Royal Tiger battle than at any other time. I had heard that there are no atheists in foxholes. We should make it known that tankers did not require prompting to pray.

As mentioned earlier, German soldiers had dug in on the opposite side of the road but did not provide a major confrontation. It appeared that there was a sense of relief on the part of the Germans that our men did not engage them in an exchange of rifle fire. Many of the German soldiers were very young. We were at the point in the war that caused large numbers of soldiers to surrender. I am not sure how the soldiers were kept, but the word must have reached those still engaged that Americans treated them with respect. Certain captured men proved to be very willing to work for U.S. forces.

Shortly after the action, my all time favorite soldier friend, Bob Padgett, was released from active duty ahead of me and shipped on home.

"WATCH" THOSE GERMANS

There may have been an advantage in us being constantly on the move. We had to be refueled and ready. Changing locations would keep the enemy busy keeping track of us. It appeared that confrontations were tapering off. News did not always find its way to those of us still at the front. However, we had some situations that were real eye openers. We all could see that Germany was fast turning into a grandiose hubbub. German soldiers were surrendering in large numbers.

We heard a strange sound nobody could interpret. One of our men saw a building on a hill similar to our garages back home and decided to check it out. This young fellow was somewhat daring. The building was near enough to our tank that we were available, if needed. Bob kicked the door and yelled, "Raus (out), you bastards!" Something he never expected; the door opened and two German soldiers came out. They seemed eager to surrender.

Four of our tanks were assembled on a road – just waiting for orders. The road we were parked on was some sort of hard surface and, looking back, the road curved to the left and was alongside a very steep bank – fifty to sixty feet high. We spent about two days in that position with no activity militarily speaking. At about 3:00 or 4:00 in the afternoon, we heard a very strange noise. It reminded me of horses clopping on a concrete highway. The noise was clear, but what created it was not.

The shock of it all, around the bend in the road, hidden by the high bank appeared two or three hundred German soldiers – all marching in cadence, no one talking, their steel cleat shoes all coming down to give the sounds we at first couldn't identify. Every man was in full uniform, without weapons marching in a column of three abreast. The amazing part; all had their hands clasped together over their heads, passing our point, moving on to some rendezvous – this obviously was a surrender technique.

Ironically, the apparent behavior that suggested surrender was something we as a crew had never experienced. Here we were, about fourteen men in tanks and this group came by without any apparent leader. We did not know their destination.

Had they turned on us, we could have been overwhelmed. Candidly, I believe they were relieved that they were free of further action. It was the largest number in surrender status I had seen. Had these been spirited fighting men? Who knows?

Often I heard GIs say, "I'm not a fighter – I'm a lover." Knowing men as I do, that expression had some interesting overtones.

Other Americans nearby were not of the tank crews. The behavior of some of them was very out of order. Bear in mind that all these Germans with their hands clasped on top of their heads, caused their sleeves to slip back.

With their arms bare, it was easy to see that most of them possessed a fine wristwatch.

One of the Americans dared to enter the column of Germans and help himself to wristwatches. A German soldier, who knew English, said in an accusing voice, "None of you Americans have watches!"

This ne'er-do-well soldier said mockingly, "Who you kidding, Buddy?" He pulled his sleeve back and displayed watches almost to his elbow.

This was a rude, very daring stunt that I was unable to correct. When I think of what could have transpired, I cringe to this day. I had no authority over him. When a situation like that takes place, there is no telling how the so-called enemy soldiers consider such behavior.

This may seem odd to report, but the episode went through my mind long after the last of the German column had passed. When such activity takes place, it throws our thought patterns out of order. It is not easy to consider such as normal.

HAIR THERE?

I have not said much about our food supply. The possibility of entering a home – either in France or in Germany – did provide a change of pace. If the home was abandoned, we would stoke up a fire. Sometimes in cases, we found eggs – a welcome change of diet. Nevertheless, for the most part, we were stuck with 'C' rations, which usually came in three average size cans per man per day. One was stew; one was beans while the third was some sort of hard biscuit we called 'dog biscuits' and a small can of cheese. Oh, yes. This was the can with the coveted paper napkin or towel.

The first time I opened cheese I found two long strands of auburn red hairs wrapped around the contents. Wax paper separated the cheese from the hair, so I carefully got rid of the hair, but my response to hair in my food caused my appetite to bend slightly away from eagerly devouring a needed portion of calories.

GIs have almost a weird set of standards regarding the females in their lives and I would not be able to report with dignity some comments my friends have made regarding their ladyloves and friends. However, it occurred to me that when men brought along reminders of home and wives and girlfriends, it included pictures, lockets and perhaps a lock of hair. I thought the red head hoped she would leave some lonesome soldier a reminder of home. Well after the third, fourth and fifth cans were opened and all had two red hairs wrapped around the cheese, I became suspicious. Surely the supply could not last.

I asked Salty, "Hey are you getting hair in your cheese can?" "Yeah", he said. "I don't mind. Maybe she's lonesome, too."

The next opening solved the mystery. I carefully examined the red objects and found they could be stretched to almost double their length. The key to the situation was the key. That is, the key that opened the can. It was designed to roll up a band around the center of the can. Inside the can was reddish shellac used for overseas food shipments. The metal band, as it was rolled, caused a shearing action on both edges; hence the red, mystery hair.

Our favorite food supply was the ten-in-one. Not bad if you could add onions. There was enough food to provide food for about ten men. Since I was a sergeant, I did not become involved in food fixing. Therefore, my memory is a little short to recall the basic foods provided. Sometimes a local meat market or potatoes provided us with a change, as we learned to improvise. The other less desirable was K Rations used mostly by scouts and individuals on missions while you carried food.

BEST EVER TOASTED CHEESE SANDWICH

Some experiences reported from Army days may sound a bit exaggerated. However, to a soldier there may be some times worth recalling concerning his involvement. Most of us have enjoyed the pleasure of smelling freshly baked bread. When our field kitchens saw fit to surprise us with a couple slices of the kind of bread Grandma used to make, that was special.

Some of the fellows ate their treat right away, but I guarded mine and proceeded to look for some of the cheese so common to the military. I took the time to make a toasted cheese sandwich. Some of them wanted a bite, but we were all with only two slices. Dare I say that mine turned out to be one of the best – ever?! I believe some of my buddies wished they had done the same thing.

V-E DAY – MAY 8, 1945

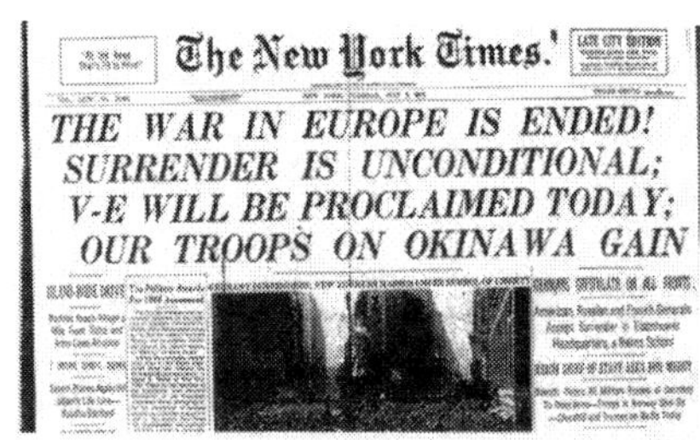

The New York Times.

THE WAR IN EUROPE IS ENDED!
SURRENDER IS UNCONDITIONAL;
V-E WILL BE PROCLAIMED TODAY;
OUR TROOPS ON OKINAWA GAIN

There came the day when we learned that Germany was in total surrender, May 8, 1945.

The response on the part of combat vets was no doubt varied. I cannot think of a better word than "relieved".

I wish it possible to record the sounds of church bells ringing simultaneously all over Europe. Soldiers were allowed to fire their weapons in the air to celebrate. Some were not sure if we had some sort of confrontation to address. However, we who were still in our tanks could look out and see men walking around as if unconcerned, and we knew that there was not some attack to consider.

That caused everyone to feel upbeat and that included the German people and the men held in prison camps scattered over the country. Looking back, we knew there would be major adjustments to consider. Enemy troops were not free, and to our good fortune, they had become quite easy to quarter and work with.

We were all treated to a time of relaxing and for a time, escape routine duties. We were able to take hot showers and receive a better meal. When I turned in my clothing that I wore all winter – yes, not even a change of underwear – the garments were waxy and cold.

I wore double clothing in cold months and even up to the time of showers. I turned in everything at this shower point and was a bit puzzled to receive only singles of all I turned in. However, to my surprise the allowed amount of clothing was very comfortable.

Since the GIs had nothing to do with post combat assignments, all we could do was wait for the next order of the day. Chances are very strong that, had the war continued, it may have spread into Austria. United States Army units occupied a large portion of Austria. We were also confronted by Russian troops who had a role to play in WWII. These, too, were very evident in Austria. It is my opinion that there was a marked degree of competition between American and Russian troops.

FINAL TANK CLEANUP AND INSPECTION

Surrender was not a total condition that gave us freedoms, as we would experience in peace times. There was still a lot of work to do and training continued. The exact date when tanks were no longer in use for combat purposes was a sort of sketchy time. Moving to a new holding position in Linz, Austria may have had reasons not shared with the troops. As enlisted men, we simply obeyed orders.

Salzburg provided considerable interest for the adventurous. One bit of business had us questioning headquarters. We were directed to line up our tanks and point our guns toward some mountains. The reason for the operations seemed strange, but we were told to fire all remaining shells in our tanks; using a certain mountain for the impact area.

To me it was just another part of the entire spectrum of war zone activity. All tanks were called in for a final cleanup and inspection before going into storage. After the tanks were emptied, our job was to clean them up; spread tarps on the ground to make a temporary method of checking equipment. Everything relating to tanks, other than ammunition was lined up for inspection and checked for shortages. That included fire extinguishers; bore cleaning equipment, grenades, machine guns, belts, grease guns and anything tanks require for a full complement of gear. Our tank was short some things but all we had to do was list it as a combat loss and there were no further questions.

During my combat experience, I had some narrow escapes, but losing a tank was only a temporary condition. I have used some of the latest as well as some of the older war-scarred models. We had to settle for whatever was available.

The last tank my crew and I experienced was an old white model with less firepower. We had changed tanks so many times I lost track. At one time, we had a great Pershing tank with a 90 mm gun. As it turned out, the last tank we had was a "beater". It was okay, with much war-related problems.

Our work was cut out for us and I was fortunate to have four young men who were eager to perform. As luck was with us, these men were relatively small in stature and that is a factor in crawling around in tight places. They could crawl around in the engine compartment and wherever – cleaning and scrubbing.

Hardly did I dare even think that when the inspecting team went through all the checklist of entries that my little old white tank would receive top rating. The top prize was a thirty-day furlough of sightseeing in England.

Even though I was the sergeant in charge of the tank, we all worked together in the cleanup. How could I reward my crew? It seemed that a hand shake and a pat on the back was sufficient. Most people seem to thrive on participating in a winning cause.

In a few days, all things were put together, and it cost me nothing. All I had to do was get my uniform out of storage and prepare for a ship ride across the English Channel. All paperwork was taken care of, and I just needed to be there on time.

LONDON

A backward glance tells me that posterity would have enjoyed some of the details had matters been more carefully recorded. That may well be the lot of service men in general. Had I planned the trip, much detail would have been the 'norm'.

London was certainly in the news back in the 1940s. How could a service man react to a gift of adventure? I was not looking for any particular experience, but be alert to matters as they developed. It was necessary that I had some form of money; learn the exchange rates as well as other details.

Experienced seamen carried out the trip across the Channel. It was late spring of 1945 and the weather as could be expected. Here again, as recipients of a cordial atmosphere, from Southampton and up to London, we just absorbed the goodwill and experienced remarkable acceptance by all those we encountered.

GIs trying to stick together did not prove anything. I had been teamed up with another sergeant, it took very little time for that to just fade away, and he chose not to stay with me. Apparently, seeking some adventure in another country was a factor.

Part of London had the title of "Piccadilly". The fact is that the exposure to Piccadilly was a revelation. Here was a part of London known for its shops, stores and residences.

This part of London was also called "Piccadilly Circus". A circular part of the street was in general created to aid in keeping traffic moving, with no stop signs. Cars could enter and leave without the use of stop signs. However, careful driving would be the order of the day.

During wartime with the major shortage of gasoline, Piccadilly served another function. It appeared to be a favorite gathering point for service members. The area became so loaded with people at night that you could not drive a car through there at all. May I add that hundreds of beautiful females dressed very fancy were also a part of the growing crowd in the evening hours? Many were there to offer their 'services' to the military men. If a man was not inclined to accept, then he just kept walking around.

I do not remember what factors caused me to be there. I was married and had two children. My sense of duty prompted me to ignore the "offers" so freely available from the many young beautiful women.

As I was walking around, I observed a middle-aged lady sitting at a small table, set aside from the general crowd, holding a sign WOULD YOU WISH TO VISIT A BRITISH HOME? I noticed that I was the only soldier who had considered her offer.

I gave it some thought. What could I expect? I stopped to talk to her and one of her first questions was, "What would you like? Would you like to be where there are children?" I told her that I had two children, but I do not think so.

She said, "Well, I think I have just the place for you." She suggested a young woman living with her mother in a part of London called Stratham Hill, which was quite set aside from where I was standing.

I had one week to spend in London. I was given the address of a young woman named Ivonne Watkins, Stratham Hill, London Southwest 2, England. The taxi driver knew just where to go. In a reasonable space of time, I was shown to the apartment door of Ivonne and her mother Marie, who was a war widow.

I was welcomed in and the custom was first to be seated and I was served a cup of their tea. Conversation was a bit awkward at first. After a space of time, I was shown my room and a place to drop my duffel bag.

Ivonne was a young and dignified blonde-haired woman, about 20 years old. She had learned to know much about Americans. I never met him, but Ivonne told of some young man from the States that she was quite interested in. His home was in Iowa.

I had no idea that the woman at the table near Piccadilly was part of an organization, similar to the USO. The young women were encouraged to conduct themselves appropriately. Their main work was to give tour guides through their famous city.

Ivonne was very skilled in her assignment. I saw massive government buildings and homes of famous people. Not having a notebook handy, I have to depend on memory for giving a sketch of experiences.

Ivonne seemed to have a keen interest in the escalators throughout the city. I believe it was reported that in certain parts of London, escalators were up to five levels. As I write this account, I have no record of the system that dates back to the 1940s.

I was interested in hearing their language. Using the same words we all use, there were times when it was difficult to catch some thoughts because of their foreign (to me) accent.

One day we visited a ballpark. I am embarrassed to report that I was way out beyond the playing area and in a moment of lack of paying attention, I was hit in the head with a long fly ball. The Army cap we were required to wear was a truly great help in absorbing that sort of a surprise. Entering a baseball stadium in the middle of the sixth inning was a bit embarrassing. My lady companion asked a man in our row, "What is the score?" "Nothing to nothing," he said. "Oh, good," was the unexpected reply. "Then we haven't missed a thing!"

Some may feel that my experience in London was rather limited. I felt subject to the extent of Ivonne's directions as a guide. I accepted her offer as experienced in matters that may be of interest to an American soldier. One thing I did was be alert to eating places that had a Yankee setting.

Somehow, it appeared mutual that we did not attend bars and liquor places. I had no knowledge of the use of their form of currency, but it appeared in general, that the needs were taken care of for the short time I spent in London.

I never met any of the Watkins family or friends. As wartime created many shortages, we all learned to get along with less and make use of the time in walking many miles.

The days slipped by so fast that it seemed there was much more to experience. The day came when the visit was over and Ivonne accompanied me to the ship. I recall standing in line to get back on board ship, with no regrets. I chose, as a married man, to behave myself and not go home ashamed.

The ship took me back to the same port in France where I had first arrived in Europe. I enjoyed other sightseeing in France and the remainder of my thirty-day furlough was sightseeing on the mainland of Germany. Much of the rubble left by the war had been cleared but the scars of war were still evident.

It appeared that each country had its own culture. I do not recall seeing women looking after cattle in France, although my reach into France was limited. I was only passing through and had to be alert to my connection back to Germany.

This part of Germany was very well kept – getting closer to Austria. Since I was a first sergeant, I'd gained a little bit of authority – not enough to be able to take off and do what I felt like, but what I took the liberty to do. Being in uniform, I was able to catch a ride in a jeep or even borrow one for myself to get around. It seemed there was always a place for me to bunk in. I found places where other GIs would assemble – perhaps a café – and was directed to other places to see.

So many towns and roadways had been renamed for military needs. None of that prevented those assigned to getting men on leave back to their headquarters. The ever-present shuffling of outfits in Germany seemed quite natural. My return found elements moved to new locations and in some cases, the scenic beauty was a great pleasure.

When I got back, the outfits had switched around so much there was a change in the whole structure of things in Germany. It was hard to keep track of it. I found my unit near the Austrian border and properties abandoned by German officers. When I returned to my outfit, my commanding officer accused me of being AWOL (absent without official leave) and I thought, "Well prosecute me then." He had a kind of a grin on his face as if to say, well, you are an old combat man and you have earned the right.

Ivonne and her mother learned of my address in Germany and I was truly surprised in a few days to receive a package with an aluminum container with what may have been their favorite wine. The time came for our move into Austria and I had no further contact with Ivonne and her mother.

AFTER V-E DAY

Actually, during combat experiences, we were often moved to a new front on some of the fickle railroads using the 40 and 8 rail cars. That meant forty men or eight horses per car. You can believe that when forty men are in one car and the door closed, you can expect almost anything.

It is thought that soldiers express their needs quite well. That is true, but often we had to put up with some condition where no one took charge and a put a stop to it. At this point, we were all veterans not subject to somebody giving orders.

I smoked in those days and being a smoker myself, I would have no excuse to ask others to "cool it". However, here is the stickler; somebody wanted to heat up some canned rations. They built a fire in the rail car with scrap pieces of wood. Without ventilation, it was not long and the air became intolerable.

Maybe it hit me differently, but I needed some air. Our trip was relatively short, but the smoky freight car put us all to the test. I found a jagged hole in the floor about the size of a banana. I lay down on the floor – face down – right over that spot so I could breathe. The time came when the need for a fire was over and a can of heated beans improved the mood.

Judy Sweetheart, I know you can't read this so Mommy will have to read it to you. I got the nice box of cookies and candy and they were very good. You have a pretty smart Mommy who can do all those things. You give Mommy a big hug and kiss for Daddy because he can't. Don't climb too high on the windmill because you might fall and get hurt. Someday soon Daddy is coming home to see you and Dickie and Mommy. Love always, Daddy

(DeLoris told story of Judy climbing a windmill ladder while visiting at a neighboring farm. Since none of the men wanted to climb up to get her, DeLoris climbed up herself to rescue her young daughter, about age 3).

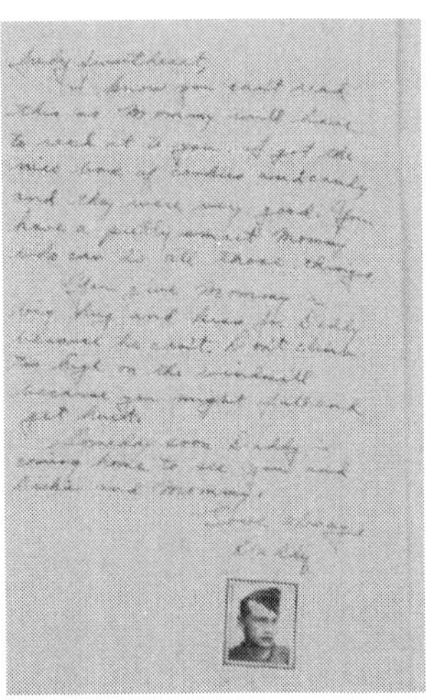

CLEAN LATRINE

Returning to my outfit in Germany was rather routine. In fact our constant moving around was very much a part of our Army life and it was looked at as an obligation to be ready for some special orders.

Using tanks for warfare was over. Our main duty was to prepare tanks for storage and possible release to some other need. Some duties with tanks became rather questionable. We were subject to taking orders from higher sources; hence, to question or resist was not for troops.

Austria was a beautiful part of Europe – practically escaping the war and cities were intact. Our latest assignment was occupation in assigned areas and did not include tanks. I would have difficulty to name locations, as identifying certain areas was hidden in military maps that service men did not have access to. However, some of the outlying parts of Germany had little scars of the war, and much of the scenery was extremely beautiful.

Before we actually established quarters in Austria, we shifted in temporary locations until the desired arrangements could be made. We all had to be ready to accept any form of transportation available. The famed GMC ten wheeled Army trucks was the mode of moving men and equipment. It also afforded us the relatively quick movement to new locations. We moved along a route known only to the high command, but some things were very acceptable.

Depending on who was in charge, we had to learn to adjust. Rations served in narrow cardboard boxes did not bear any rules as to when to use. The desire on the part of soldiers was to travel light. The solution was to not be burdened with lugging excess things and that included dry rations.

The answer if you are short of containers, eat the meals, which is what I did. After being loaded in a truck for a new assignment, we were so packed in we had people sitting on our legs and rising up was not to be.

We never knew where or how far we were going. Soon, my poor judgment caught up with me and I got very sick. How could a person throw up from such a cramped position? I was able to twist my body to find the outer edge of the truck and my memory does NOT leave good thoughts. I was fortunate not to involve anybody, but I am surprised to have survived such an experience.

There was no competition between outfits, but we all took the assigned bunking as adequate and none of us felt like asking for more comfort. Finding training stations used by German officers, we began to have a great update in conveniences. We were not told who occupied some places before we were assigned. It just so happened that officers in charge merely did the best they could and sometimes we received bunking that was very well put together, which appeared to be quarters for German troops and possibly officers.

We found the abandoned army quarters of the German officers in Wolfgang to be quite comfortable. We were able to fix our own bunks and return to a semblance of order. Bunks were better than sleeping in a tank. It would have been difficult for us to keep track of the locations, but the Germans were able to provide for their own use some of the better buildings. There was however, a distinct lack of engineering in German latrines.

There were many mixed duties in the spring and perhaps the advent of warm weather was a benefit that created an unwelcome problem. Perhaps I should say that the warm spring weather aided in correcting this unwelcome problem. The latrine used by the Germans perhaps was victimized by the warm weather; how it happened is not important.

My outfit was assigned to a unit that was two levels. The upper level was prepared for bunk space and the lower level for latrine. When I went to the latrine, there were four individual stalls where the toilet bowls were plugged to overflowing making them useless. I could hardly believe men would allow that condition to prevail. The building was a fairly decent place but the problem needed immediate attention.

By some stroke of luck, there happened to be running water. I looked around this men's room; I found a broomstick and jammed it into the toilet, while I started the water running at the same time. Working with the broomstick and other equipment found in washrooms I was able to free up the first clogged bowl and proceeded to clean up the entire stall.

The temperature in May seemed to help and it worked so well I went after stall number two. After about an hour or more, I had all four toilets working again. Oddly, I had no offer for help, so I worked alone, even though I could have asked for help, but I did not object.

When I was nearly finished with the job though, I had a visitor. He was our own company first sergeant. He asked, "Who told you to do this?" I said, "Nobody, but when I want to use a toilet, I like it clean."

The remark following that was much unexpected as he informed me that based on my performance, I would become the next first sergeant of the company. That was a major jump from buck sergeant to first sergeant. My reaction could be expected; I was stunned. I was pleased, but in those days, a job wished on one unexpectedly is more *caught* than *taught.*

One interesting instance occurred when I was given my set of first sergeant patches. Some fellow who perhaps wished to keep me straight asked, "Are you going to use those stripes?" I detected a bit of resentment, but I said, "If I won't be able to use them, I will take a scissors and cut them into PFC stripes."

Word has been received by Mrs. Richard E. Young, Baker, that her husband has been promoted to the rank of sergeant. He is in Austria. Sergeant Young was formerly with the Seventh army but has been placed in the Third army since V-E day. He was with one of the divisions that crossed the Rhine, and was a tank commander in his group. He has returned to his outfit in Austria, after a week's furlough in England, and will now be in the army of occupation. Sergeant Young has been in the service for 14 months, and has served seven months overseas. Mrs. Young is the former Deloris Butenhoff.

After that, I heard no more comments. I was about 24 years old and a good share of the fellows was younger. I will say I never tried to pull my rank on any situation.

For the record, I only held three ratings after being a lance corporal. I went from lance corporal, to corporal, then to buck sergeant (I skipped staff and tech sergeant) and last to first sergeant. That was my favorite rating.

WOLFGANG, AUSTRIA

After my return from England, the actual process was rather involved. With all the separate units to be relocated, the officers in charge of the various units were required to work together. As a service member, I had no authority but work with orders as presented. We could not choose where we would have preferred, but often had some challenges and surprises.

There were training areas used by Germans and often, it seemed were afforded some unique situations. In America, we would have considered the places we were stationed as highly desirable campgrounds near small lakes and streams. It appeared that such areas were not touched by fighting forces. Lawns were mowed and, in general, the surroundings reminded me of vacation places. Buildings were neat and well kept.

So much of the area was extremely beautiful around small lakes. One place where we settled into comfortable quarters, built of natural lumber, was at a very scenic lake near Wolfgang in Austria. Our guys were ecstatic and made good use of the dock and boat or tennis court or whatever our predecessors left behind.

I had time on my hands, which prompted me to fill a need. The barracks were okay, but there were no clothing hangers. My mechanical background led me to a fairly large coil of heavy galvanized wire. With the use of some heavy pliers and cutting tools, I was able to shape together a number of coat hangers. That helped to make our new living quarters more acceptable.

As I recall, our squad or platoon was in the range of twelve men. I tried to follow some sense of a cooperative spirit and, as I was a buck sergeant, at that time, I was the leader of that group. The one bunkhouse had bed space on the second floor and was quite acceptable. I got the general impression that whoever was assigned had some sense of order.

I did not try to use my authority, but the fellows all took a bunk in an area where they were together. One Army bed set aside near the head of the stairway where some other GI or perhaps a German had preferred quarters seemed natural for the squad leader.

Since we were all created with a sense of enjoying certain amenities, there were a number of pin-up pictures around the barracks. I may have been accused of looking for favoritism, but some of the items tacked on the walls by solders left a definite impression of soldiers' interests.

It just so happened that at the head of my bunk someone had created a pencil drawing of a totally nude female. Whoever this artist was is not known – perhaps the work of some GI, but this artwork, about three feet tall, stayed right where it was. Dare I say it – whoever took the time to create such a drawing – did an excellent job.

For the record, I never would have put it there. Common decency perhaps should have prompted me to remove the drawing, but to live in the presence of two dozen other men and deny them the privilege of a glance did not enter my thoughts.

Our stay in that bunkhouse was limited to a few days, but military personnel seemed to be of predictable nature. The standard procedure for any garrison living always called for an inspection by a company officer. One morning about 10:00 AM, after breakfast, we had a visit from the inspecting officer, and each man had to stand at attention by his bunk. I believe he was a first lieutenant and appeared to be a good-natured fellow. The officer moved from one man to the other as we were standing by our bunks at attention, making comments as he felt warranted.

When he stopped by my bunk, he stared so long at the penciled sketch that I became jittery. He did not utter a word but finally, his curiosity satisfied, he turned to me with what appeared to be a slight grin and said, "What is your gun number Sergeant?" My thoughts were totally jammed by the officer's demeanor so that I could only answer, "I don't remember."

I detected a slight grin as he turned to leave and in a typical military manner he said, "Carry on" and nothing further followed the interchange. I do not need to explain my relief. The lieutenant left and I must admit that for a space of time, I was sort of wondering what the fellows were thinking.

My sense of responsibility perhaps should have destroyed the sketch, but I also estimated the reaction from me getting rid of the sketch would have also caused a reaction like – "Hey, what's with you, Sarge?" Some of those matters seemed to be natural for a military unit. Every man had his own characteristics and I doubt if two of us were alike. The pencil sketch remained for the few days we had left in these particular barracks, before we moved into Austria. Our short stay in Wolfgang was like a short vacation. Next on the agenda was finding an area where training could continue. I do not believe the affairs of our unit are worth commenting about as it turned out to be the normal procedures in loading up and moving to our new assignment.

The war with Japan was still requiring additional troops and equipment. With our duties technically completed in Europe, it was with mixed emotion that we continued with infantry training, believing we may find out about our next move to the Orient.

AUSTRIA

We were at this stage just entering Austria, a beautiful country with a lot of culture. Fortunately, Austria was not caught in heavy military activity. The holding camps were for captured military men who were retained for questioning and rehabilitation. I believe the city we first experienced was Linz. Germans were not exactly in prison, but detained within fenced areas. They could easily have broken out, but they seemed to sense that some form of control was acceptable. In fact, they almost seemed anxious to be among those selected for special duty. These men did not wear military clothing, but none of us found it necessary to determine if they were, in fact, ex-soldiers. Their conduct suggested no problems. We found many skilled men that were eager to be called out for duty with American camps, and, I feel, the association was a healing factor.

Sometimes it is not easy to second-guess what is going on, but I had gained the rank of first sergeant and I had certain duties, which gave the Germans some hint of my authority. Laying out a workload was fairly easy, as many of the men we used had carpentry skills, which was to our benefit. Their work period was regulated and as I reflect back on this time, I do not recall that it appeared necessary – ever – to hint that anyone getting out of order would be in trouble.

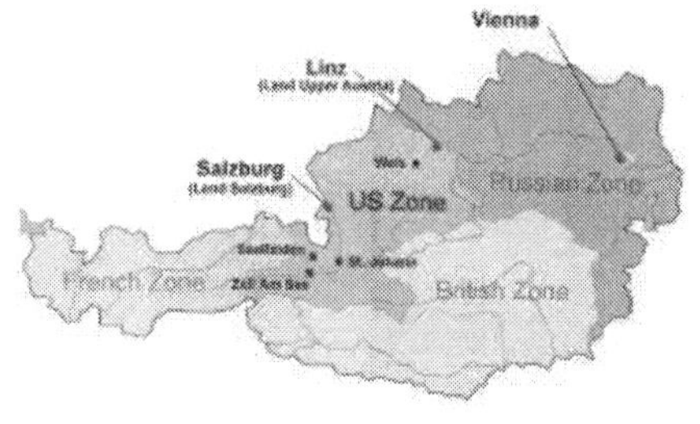

From where we were working, it appeared to be about one half to three quarters of a mile back to their compound. There were about a dozen men, and it became my job to escort them back. I kept my 45 side arm in its holster and I sensed that the entire group desired to cooperate. As an added thought, the smell of new cut wood was a pleasure and I have a good memory of that time.

After V-E Day, our movements took us into Austria, where, from our observation, there were few, if any, scars of the war. It was a beautiful city in a beautiful country. As we entered Linz, Austria, a forerunner delegation had selected areas for troops to be quartered; these being conveniently on the outer edge of the famous city of Salzburg.

However, we were by title the 756th Tank Battalion, most of our activity was on the company level. Sections of the city were set aside for different companies and broken down into platoons. As Company B, we required several private homes for bunk space and the owners had to vacate for our benefit. I was surprised to see how many homes were heavy built of stone and masonry, which perhaps was either for traditional styling or even safer against attack. The house chosen for my platoon was an average home, similar enough to our America that we could settle in quickly. None of us had a large amount of clothing and personal items to require that much extra space. How the people occupying these homes reacted to being asked to leave was not shared with the troops. We left that to the officers in charge. We were part of the occupation forces, thinking ourselves fortunate to be in scenic Austria.

As platoon sergeant, it appeared to me that soldiers in general were predictable. If the home was built with average design, it was expected that the men would attempt to be agreeable in either selecting bunk space, but none appeared to demand preferred treatment. We all learned to adjust to conditions, which I believe were a dramatic change from combat experience.

Salzburg is the famous home of Mozart. It was my privilege to be able to go to an ornate theater and see a popular opera – The Barber of Seville. My interests were different from many of the men. I was married with two children. I liked music and played chess for hours. Bars and beer halls were not for me.

Outside my bedroom window, I could see a tremendous castle. I would have enjoyed visiting it, but military regulations were intact and the possibility of being caught in some explosive device or even an ambush was still to be considered.

A number of weeks after V-E Day, we had the totally and unexpected report that though the German forces were surrendered, news of a pocket holding out was delivered to our battalion. Why they chose Company B to clear out the "holed up" Germans, I am not sure, but the thought hit me – people get hurt playing these games. I wondered, "Has my luck run out?" Several times in my memory bank, I seemed to have escaped real problems, and I trust I have sensed Divine protection, yet I feel it is NOT because I was special, but truly blessed.

A bit of anxiety hit us, as the strength of the enemy is not known. Maybe here were some fanatics with a dose of their brand of retaliation.

How does one gracefully word himself when by a twist of fate, we were told that a change of orders sent a platoon of light tanks to do the job. I am a bit ashamed to recall that I was not worried about *them.* From reports at the time, the resistance was minimal and the "Krauts" surrendered pronto.

Since soldier boys are not free to do their own thing, even after fighting ceased, training continued with rifles, bazookas, machine guns, physical training, and whatever our commanding officer deemed necessary.

GIs as such are quite innovative and to be fair, the credit should go to the executive officers. We were fortunate to be near a lumber company that provided adequate space for an assembly hall. This also became our mess hall after a number of tables resembling picnic tables were built by our troops.

GERMAN COIN NECKLACES

The back engraved - Styre Austria 1945
Love Daddy & Styre Austria 1945 Love Dick

Dick related the following information about the necklaces with the names engraved on them. He found a German coin on the side of the road and then added his own coin to have the necklaces made while in Austria after combat ended. He called the man a 'craftsman' - not a jeweler - and was highly complimentary of the work done. He related that cigarettes were a highly desired commodity and he believed he traded a couple of packs of cigarettes for the necklaces.

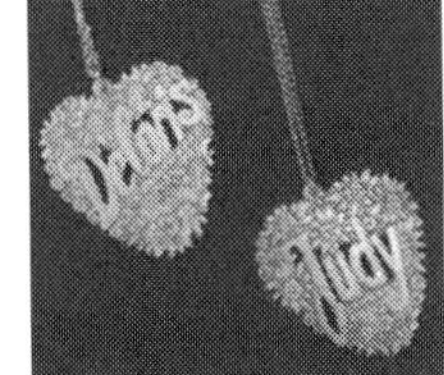

HEY SARGE –DUCK!

One of the puzzling aspects of human makeup is that men can sit around in a casual arrangement and swap stories with ease. The day came when we assembled in the converted lumber yard building mess hall to hear, once more, the dos and don'ts of submachine gun – sometimes called a "grease gun" - use. The standing rule with the submachine gun was *never* load a clip when the bolt is retracted. The corporal chosen to give the lecture was standing at the front end of the hall. Now, as he was facing his buddies as if to give a speech, he was frightfully nervous.

As their platoon sergeant, I was standing in the rear of the room and I could see the soldier was very uneasy while he proceeded to tell the well-known lingo. I thought I was making him nervous so I walked out of the building.

I doubt if I was ten seconds on the outside when this soldier did as he was telling ***not*** to do and a hail of bullets passed through the assembly of men, hitting several and sent one to the hospital. Any holes in the end wall where I was standing could very well have included me. The number of narrow escapes in my tour of duty really made me think.

Aug 16 - 1945 - Austria
Dear Judy, How are you my little sweetheart? Your mommy sent a cute little picture of you and Dickie and I have it here to look at all the time. Aren't you proud of your little brother? Your old Daddy is so anxious to come home. I miss you and Dickie and Mommy. When Daddy comes home we will all go for a vacation and have lots of fun. Thank you so much for the nice box of goodies. Daddy is going to try and bring along something real nice for you and Dickie. Bye for now.
Yours, Daddy

Richard Charles Young (Dickie) Judith Ann Young

1945

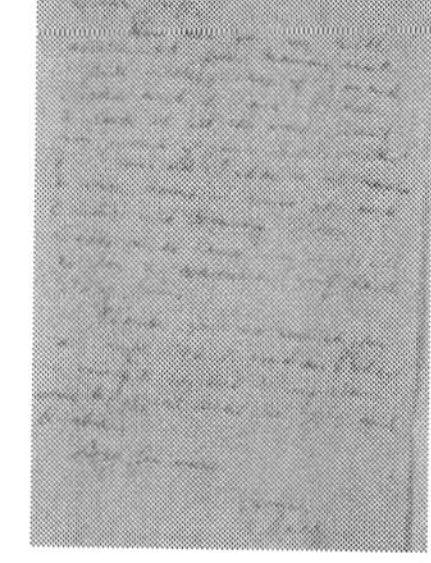

MOUNTAIN CLIMBING IN AUSTRIA

Mountains looming in the distance gave rise to believe we could get rid of excess ammunition. The so-called shooting part of the war was over. However, tank activity had some strange requirements that I take the liberty to place on the powers that be. Moreover, that we did, by firing the extra ammunition into the mountains.

Later on when some of us wanted to try a new sport – namely mountain climbing - in Austria, it was a tempting activity. A couple of other fellows were interested in expending some energy, so we started up the grassy area by pulling ourselves up by grasping twigs along the way. Interestingly enough, mountain dwellers had taken flat stones and made steps all the way to the top. We ran across the steps that allowed us to finish the climb. We were relieved to notice there was no evidence that our last use of tank guns bore any bad news.

But, to our distress, we found there were people living in the mountains, above the timberline – not a tree was in sight. The very friendly people who lived there were willing to share some of their brand of good things to eat. I could not help but notice that the women who lived there had legs so muscular that they looked like nail kegs. Our time was limited, so returning to our unit was next. The climb was a neat adventure.

A HONEY OF A TREAT

To deviate a bit from the routines of activity, I never ceased to be amused by the behavior of young soldiers. The weather was such that outside my bedroom window there was an apricot tree bearing fruit, which could be picked from the window. How a sequence of events could lead up to a seemingly off-the-wall feat, it is hard to describe.

The home where we were staying had a small shed outside the back door. One of the guys was poking around in the shed and found a wooden bucket. It was about half full of some substance and covered over with a heavy layer of dust.

This enterprising soldier scraped off the dust, which covered a sort of grainy looking substance. Dipping his finger in the strange element, he first smelled of it and then tasted it. "That's honey," he said.

Wishing to do a favor for his buddies, he picked some apricots and proceeded to cook up some sauce using the honey in place of sugar.

As platoon sergeant, I avoided some of this type of activity but a number of the guys were willing to have a helping. All I can report is that the Ex-Lax company never came close to accomplishing what the honey-apricot sauce did.

Someone in our reassembled outfit, who had served a short time in Africa, got hold of a monkey, called "Monk", that became a sort of mascot. The fellows thought the honey-apricot sauce would be a good treat for Monk. He ate it with interest. However, the laxative also did its work for Monk. He managed to leave his mess all over the hand railing in the house we stayed in, as he climbed about. **That** was not a pleasant experience. Some other tricks the fellows taught Monk are probably best left untold. Personally, I had very little interest in the monkey.

TRAINING FOR THE ORIENT

I do not recall the location by name nor could I even pinpoint it on a map, but one day, when our unit was in a wooded area taking instructions on close-in fighting, we had a visitor: an infantry major.

He was grinning and seemed to be in a good mood. Clasping his hand in a sort of victory gesture, he announced, "I have great news! They dropped an atom bomb in Hiroshima, Japan and killed 300,000 people." That was

August 6, 1945. My stomach actually cramped at the devastating report. If the major was pleased, he proved to be a true military man, intent on the destructible forces that, from his standpoint, win wars.

THE NEW FIRST SERGEANT

Shortly before veterans received the notice that we were to prepare for our trip back to the USA, there was a different first sergeant assigned to our unit. It appeared that those of us who had served during the fighting were given special treatment and relieved of most duties. A bed was made for me in the kitchen in a house used for special duties. It was like a "first" for me as I felt that, when in uniform and having the title, we were obliged to take care of the function of the office.

I recall looking out in the yard towards evening and seeing my replacement talking to a group of men. I did not make it any of my concern to investigate. I had no idea if he had the title before coming to our unit or if he was a veteran.

LEAVING EUROPE – RETURNING HOME

Most of us were accustomed to the various methods of transportation. It was always our lot to receive orders that were made known to us shortly before the need. So it may be assumed that one of the characteristics of soldiers was to create some rumors that were his form of a good joke.

When replacement forces had made major changes in military units, servicemen were anticipating the day to receive orders for the return to the USA.

There were mixed emotions, and it may seem strange that a few single men chose to stay in Europe. For those returning, it may be assumed that many were combat hardened veterans and braced against taking orders. Because of my rating of first sergeant, I was subject to some who no longer felt comfortable in taking orders. I heard one outspoken soldier say clearly that no “blankety-blank” first sergeant was ever going to tell him what to do again!

As we prepared to enter a ship (I do not recall the name of the ship), there was a mixture of servicemen from various units. We were not told that it was a very small ship not made for military use, and rumors were that the ship was overloaded.

All this took place in January of 1946. There may be some issues that many of us felt were not important enough to record in our memories. One of the matters I regret is that I did not keep a running account of the voyage. There may be some resistance to that thought, but most of us were tired and wished to be free of commitment. That tells something about the nature of servicemen. We took orders over the intercom, and the orders were limited to the exact needs of the hour.

How we were quartered was not our concern. Our rank did not appear to be a factor. We soon learned that bunk space was tight, and the fact that the ship was overcrowded, we had to make the best of it. Rumors were that the number aboard the ship designed to carry 300 – 400 actually had closer to 1200 soldiers. Rumors were so much a part of military units that we had to be accustomed to the practice.

There were gamblers aboard, and card games were the norm. Not wishing to enter into card games, I had saved $1200 and had that strapped to my waist under my clothing. No one knew about it. Another soldier about my age named Brody had about $1400 he had saved. He also was careful – to a point.

There were card games where thousands of dollars were passed around. I heard figures, which seemed unreal. I kept quiet about my savings, and Brody seemed content for a while. However, after days out on the trackless ocean, he got restless and was talked into joining some games.

True gamblers are smart about their practice, and it took very little time for Brody to lose it all. I believe he was a single man, and I gave him $50 to find some way to get home.

The number of days aboard ship was regulated by the weather, and it is worth telling that we were subject to some violent weather. Some of the windows in the galley were three-quarter inch glass. When windows that thick are smashed, it causes great concern. The fact that we survived the storm is a miracle. We were told not to go out on deck. It appeared to be more of a suggestion than an order.

I disobeyed and went out on deck. That turned out to be a scary experience. The ship tilted so far I was nearly washed away. One of the facts regarding ocean-going vessels is the extremely large waves and swells. When they hit the ship, there is no way to anticipate the results. There were two days when fixing meals was not possible. Coffee making also was not available. At best, we could only expect dry rations. For the most part, about all we could do on board ship was to look after personal needs. Passing other ships in open waters was practically unknown.

Sometimes it has occurred to me that my first sergeant rating was affective only in the unit where I was afforded the rating. If one was not in charge, he did not feel as a comrade among other men.

Be that as it may, we had to endure the trip home on a very small ship and if there were officers aboard, they did not mingle with the servicemen as we were a mixture of returning veterans from various outfits. It was common for service men to express their discontent with routine activity.

The mess hall had stainless steel fixed counters and they were for standing only, to have a meal. The counters were across the width of the ship and when the ship tilted in rough weather eating became a chore. Sometimes events may be humorous. Consider a mess hall filling with enlisted men who were passing a point to pick a meal from a master kitchen and took it to stand by a fixed counter.

If a sudden large wave hit the ship, the mess hall caught us all off guard and our plate of food slid away in front of some of the other men. Hanging on to the plate was not an option, as we had to hang on for our own good. When the ship tilted the other way, each one had to try to identify his own plate of food returning.

By now, I am sure the reader has realized that this was not a pleasure cruise. However, we all endured the trip home and all of us being veterans and accustomed to matters of fact took each item as natural part of a serviceman's responsibilities.

We all looked forward to the news that we were nearing the good old USA. When the skyline of New York came into view, I am sure there were mixed emotions. We were only a few weeks from the rigors of the combat zone. I do not recall a lot of cheering or noisy behavior of the men aboard ship. There was a mix of servicemen aboard where chatting about war experiences did not appear to be a factor.

Seeing the skyline of New York to many of us was a very emotional experience. As I recall, entering the harbor, seeing the Statue of Liberty so gripped me that I was unable to speak. My throat actually hurt from emotion. Perhaps many of us were thanking the Lord for deliverance from the war zone.

Returning to the USA did not mean that we were free to do our own thing. We had to follow military rules until we had some paperwork to free us to return to our loved ones.

I was discharged from active duty in Company B, 756th Tank Battalion. My separation took place at Camp McCoy, Wisconsin on January 25, 1946. I returned to Barnesville, Minnesota, where my wife and two children were living with my wife's parents. We packed up and moved to Grand Forks, North Dakota. The house that my parents purchased in the 1930s was given an additional entrance and some remodeling was done. That entrance led to the upper floor apartment that we occupied for twenty-plus years. It was a blessing to be close to my parents and to have their Godly influence on my family.

Upon returning from the war, I found it easy to get a job as the need for skilled workers was ever present. Nevertheless, the luxury of a massive factory was not to be, such as the Minneapolis Moline Tractor Company, I worked in before the war. I took a job in a very small, smoky welding shop that had minimal machinery. At least I was home.

Judy, Dick and "Dickie" 1946

At present (age 90), I am lacking any written account of the camps we passed through before meeting family members. There was a distinct shortage of hotel and motel rooms and we were fortunate to be able to attain a room or rooms.

I believe Army camps are the natural points to consider for the paperwork on returning veterans. I doubt that an accurate record of camps used to process veterans would be of any value, but I recall Camp Kilmar, New Jersey, as one of the processing centers.

This may sound a bit indifferent, but I believe that most veterans were hoping to find an open phone or a hotel room for meeting loved ones or friends. I have seen some men hang on a phone for an extended period of time, hoping to get through.

Pictures have always been a natural source of communications, and I had waiting for me a new son, whom they named after me. In the event I could not return home, DeLoris had learned to adjust to the facts of war. She was able to meet me in a small hotel room. That was quite an experience after being apart for over a year.

Anticipating meeting my children, and especially a son, who had to realize that I WAS part of the family added to the excitement. But, settling down after war took a space of time. I anticipated returning to Minneapolis to gain back my employment at Minneapolis Moline.

Dick wrote these verses in September, 2009- Age 90

Some other entries I believe are worth telling
The procedures included a tour of Ft. Snelling.
The various camps all had duties to perform
And some one may say they are all part of the norm.

The medics came by and said "now bare your arm
The shot you'll receive will do you no harm"!
It may sting a little but that goes away
And the hurting is gone by the end of the day.

You're all being prepared for a trip overseas
The end results will all be something that surely will please.
Now stop for a moment and take a quick glance
Included will be a time spent in beautiful France.

London, of course, is part of the text
Including that city is coming up next.
This outline is short but now quite complete
There is not much left I need to repeat.

The major matter of course was the war
And telling much more would just be a bore.
That's all I can offer in this short space of time.
And now it's a blessing to complete all in rhyme.

These verses were written by Dick in the fall of 2009, (age 90)

I, among others had received a call
That I should report soon to our City Hall.

Our nation was engaged then in a shooting war.
It became very certain it would reach my door.

Where do we all go from here, I may ask?
So much is involved in this unending task.

It had become my duty to be open when ready,
It suggested I remain alert, calm and steady.

I recall being sent to Ft. Knox, Kentucky
At that point, I considered myself very lucky.

I received an assignment as a Lance Corporal
It became obvious I should remain on the ball.

I was not an officer with a leadership role
We all worked together in reaching our goal.

Our task was to take part in an unwelcome war
And return as able to those we adore.

To work with different branches of service was my lot
The armored division was the one that I got.

To say it in another way, we also called it tanks.
There was just no way I could say, "No thanks".

The following verses were written by Dick in July & August, 2010 - nearly age 91.

Many men had received the call
To make his appearance at the City Hall.

The news came through of WWII
Now each should learn what he must do.

You may be the age to join the troops
Provision has been made for substantial groups.

Mostly men, we all worked in teams
Surely a great decision it seems.

None could follow his own inclination.
We were all headed for the same destination.

We all hope to endure the trip overseas.
No one could do just as he pleases.

We packed our bags and boarded the train
Any attempt to escape, it was all in vain.

We all were sent to a town overseas.
And no one was able to do as he please.

The training we received proved to be a great blessing
It was certain to remind us what may not be just guessing.

Our first assignment, we were all sent to France.
All this was different, we could see at a glance.

The buildings and clothing were different from ours
The towns were not covered with many tall towers.

Entering Germany was next on the list
The powers-that-be made sure no one was missed.

It all turned out in a wonderful way
That we would all be thankful as felt to this day.

The last thing I can't overlook
Is the beauty of Austria to include in our book.

And finally over, the return to our home
And making quite certain not given to roam.

Robert (Bob) Padgett became a close friend to Dick as they served together during WWII. After Bob was discharged from the Army, he married Jean Hemrich and together they farmed and had dairy cows. After his discharge from the Army, he was severely injured in a motorcycle accident. He told his family - years later - that the day of the accident, he remembered looking up at the truck that had just hit him and he said he saw Jesus sitting there looking at him and saying "You didn't keep your promise to me".

That promise was that he would go to church when he returned home from the war. Bob related to his family that he made that promise to God, when during the war, they got trapped in a basement somewhere in Germany. The Germans were upstairs and they could hear them talking and he just knew at that point they would all be killed.

That was when he prayed to return home safely. He lived through the rest of the war with the comfort of Psalm 27, his favorite. One of his six children, Bonnie Huff, said he was a hard working man dedicated to his family and church. She also said her dad had a lot of respect for Dick and looked up to him during the war.

CONGRESSIONAL RECOGNITION:

IN RECOGNITION OF

THE 50TH ANNIVERSARY OF THE 756TH TANK BATTALION,

WORLD WAR II (House of Representatives - May 30, 1991)

[Page: H3731]

The SPEAKER pro tempore. Under a previous order of the House, the gentlewoman from Maryland [Mrs. Morella] is recognized for 60 minutes.

- Mrs. MORELLA. Mr. Speaker, I rise today in recognition of the 50th anniversary of the 756th Tank Battalion which was activated on June 1, 1941, at Ft. Lewis, WA.

- The 756th was mobilized with only 5 Regular Army officers and approximately 50 Regular Army enlisted men. The remainder of the battalion--whose authorized strength was 800--included approximately 35 Reserve officers and 730 enlisted men who were volunteers and draftees from 43 States. The average age of these men, when they were sent overseas for the invasion of North Africa, was 22.

- The battalion was engaged in combat almost continuously for 26 of the 32 months that it was overseas--from October 1942 until the end of World War II in May 1945. The 756th fought in North Africa, Italy, France, Germany, and Austria, amassing six campaign streamers to their colors. It was attached to one of the finest divisions in the U.S. Army--the U.S. 3d Infantry Division--for most of their operations. The other attachments for combat operations included the 36th, 45th, 85th, 88th, and 103rd United States Division and the French 2d Armored Division.

- The 756th's mission was to engage and destroy the enemy and to liberate occupied territory. The battalion accounted for thousands of enemy casualties and itself suffered 640 casualties. Of these, 111 were killed, the remainder were wounded, missing in action, or became prisoners of war. The authorized officer strength was 40; of these officers, 14 were killed, 17 were wounded, 3 were missing in action, and 2 became prisoners of war. Seventeen noncommissioned officers were promoted to second lieutenants on the battlefield.

- The 34th Division and this battalion hammered on Cassino, the gate to the Lira Valley, for more than 30 days. The 756th was awarded the United States Presidential Citation and the French Croix de Guerre. Many members of the battalion were decorated, including two who received the Congressional Medals of Honor.

- The battalion was the first wave to hit the beaches of southern France, using DD tanks that floated in water. From D-day in southern France on August 15, 1944, until the end of the war on May 8, 1945, the battalion was continuously in combat action except for one 10-day period after the devastating Colmar Pocket battle. After Colmar, the battalion, attached to the 3d Infantry Division, participated in the successful siege of the Siegfried Line and the capture of Nuremberg, Munich, and Berchtesgaden. It was stationed in Salzburg, Austria, at the end of World War II. The battalion traveled approximately 5,000 miles--from Casablanca to Salzburg.

- In the opinion of knowledgeable military officers, the 756th was one of, if not the outstanding separate tank battalion in the U.S. Army during World War II.

- The 756th tank monument will be put in the Fort Knox Museum on September 21 this year. I congratulate all the brave men who were part of the 756th and recognize the great sacrifices which they and their families have made over the decades.

POETRY

SEASONS GREETINGS

1962-1963

We thought we would give a "copy letter" a try this year to keep each on our mailing list posted on our activities.

Since a year ago, the expected amount of normal days followed New Years, but as spring approached, the old house hunting urge cropped up and after looking at short and tall, long and low, new and old, we settled on an old home next to Dad Young that needed much repair and had no basement. However, the price was right so we bought; and then the fun began. We tore off the old shack entry to the West and the front porch, and made several necessary temporary frame strengthening repairs. The house was raised 24 inches and we, I mean us, dug the basement with tractor, slusher, cable and muscle. So as not to forget those who put in the hard effort, Dad Young, Dick, Jr. and Dick, Sr., with the help of 3 or 4 men from working associates did the job; and no one can estimate how large a pile of earth can come out of a basement excavation. So that this letter does not become cluttered with constructions details, we will summarize and mention that the new basement is in, and several major remodeling operations have put the house in a 'weathered-in' condition. But, the bulk of interior remodeling and redecorating is left to be done. From the exterior, the house appears livable, but the inside - OUCH!

What with the building program, the lake property was neglected. We went, I believe about 4 times. The first time was to open up, and clean out the cobwebs. The second trip was to rake leaves and prepare for a family party. The third trip WAS the party and the fourth - to close up for the season. Oh well, it was a change at least.

Judy is now engaged, but we don't know the date of the wedding. We don't think Judy knows either. Mike speaks of a tour in service, however, it is only talk. Judy is in her second year at the University and works part time in a department store.

Dick, Jr. is a senior in high school and just loves it - we mean the girls and the hallway jargon. Per chance he graduates, he becomes owner of a 1954 Chevrolet that had been a school purpose maintenance run-about used by Dick, Sr.

Dave is four, and is learning fast. He plays with mostly older children, and we witnessed a fist fight in which Dave was involved. (P.S. - he was NOT the loser, at least not in that one).

Dee is her usual self, knee deep in home activities. There is not another wife who tackles a wider variety of homemakers ideas. She is a hat maker, chair upholsterer, seamstress and gardener. Some in the family envy her 'green thumb'. On top of all this, she was the major drafts lady for the house remodeling, and Father had to admit it was a fine job.

Dick, Sr., had a few changes in the program. A jam packed summer included moving the school office to a new location and setting up a new department, namely a supply warehouse. Also, a new school maintenance shop was established, which took a sizeable amount of time and planning.

On the civic side, a new training center for mentally handicapped was established and someone thought Dick, Sr. was qualified to be Chairman of the Board. Needless to say, the organization should bring some folk a happier way of life.

This only hits a few highlights in our domain, but we trust it has brought us a little closer in the domestic sketch.

May this special season bring you and yours much happiness, and may the Peace on Earth, Good Will to Men, instituted by the Babe in the manger be yours also.

The Dick Youngs

MERRY CHRISTMAS 1972 HAPPY NEW YEAR 1973

Dear -

We weren't so very certain 'bout our letter for this year
It seems that Annie Landers doesn't like that form of cheer.
At least she gave the hint that people do get awfully bored
At hearing all the family chat from notes in diaries stored.

But really now, we do believe, from everything that's said
The readers of such letters haven't very much to dread
The central theme is usually a favorable report,
Although, that very thing is what will cause a few to snort.

It's daughter this, and sonny that, - and Dad and Mother, too
They all somehow get in the act to share the ballyhoo.
But that's about the only way we hear from many kin,
So we're consoled a little that the letter's not a SIN.

We must admit we're tempted to let averybody know
That WE'VE got kids and LIKE to tell of when they come and go.
So - hold your hats, and settle back - We'll try to do this quick
A verse apiece is all you need to see what makes them tick.

Judy and Mike and their two boys have moved to Illinois.
Mike manages that OSCO Store so he's their fair haired boy.
Aurora's quite a thriving place (we'd say that anyway)
Because it's where our daughter plans to settle down and stay.

Our oldest son, Dick Jr. - Lorna, Jeff and Brian too
Just hold the fort where they are at - it's all that they can do
They took the plunge and bought themselves a modest little home
So all expenses now are theirs and they're not free to roam.

Our youngest son - at age 14, the one that we named Dave
Is quite a boy at hunting rocks and other things to save.
He's tallest in the family now - it doesn't bother him
It's handy for an outdoor man to be quite tall and slim.

There's not much new from Dick and Dee to enter here in print.
Just keeping up with daily chores is all that we will hint.
If anything develops that we think you ought to hear,
You'll no doubt learn it anyway, or find it out next year.
A few lines back we lightly touched upon that small word SIN

What earthly good would Christmas be if JESUS hadn't been
The ONLY one that GOD would send, to break captivity -
And loose the bands of sin and woe, to set HIS people free.

Amazing Grace - we sing so oft, and have we really thought
The love of GOD through JESUS is a thing that can't be bought?
The Bible simply bids us come and let HIM be our LORD
So let us all be thankful we can find HIM through HIS WORD.

P. S. The welcome mat is always out at our house.
The Youngs - Dick, DeLoris and Dave

CHRISTMAS 1975

FROM - Dick, DeLoris and Dave Young

I can't believe Christmas is so near again.
Perhaps it DOES come to our minds now and then.
In my way of thinking I'm not nearly ready-
I ought to get hold of myself and be steady.

The whirlwind pace of the last 12 months
has my head spinning - I feel like a dunce
that I didn't accomplish the things I had planned
and many a project un-done and un-manned.

The banister didn't get hung on the wall.
I fear my wife thinks I'm not on the ball.
She's had minor surgery done on her feet
so she thought the railing would be rather neat.

If she fell down the stairway, some Government clown,
would stop at our house and my name he'd take down.
And then there's the slippery condition outside.
The porch needs some carpeting with a tough hide.

Our lives have become so involved with demands
from an out-fit called 'OSHA' - we throw up our hands
and say in despair - "Brother, what is the use?"
I 'spose we'll just have to accept this abuse.

But now as I think of it, maybe they're right.
We ought to comply and not be so up-tight.
The safety devices would be for OUR good
if only this whole thing were quite understood.

Well, now that I've gotten that off of my chest.
I figure some nice things to say would be best.
The kids are all fine and each doing his 'thing'
Since all have left home we just wait for a 'ring.'

Judy and Mike live a distance from here.
They're still in Aurora - we wish it were near.
Scotty & Dan are as peppy as ever
and come up with things that really are clever.

Lorna and Dick are now most energetic.
Their newest adventure is almost like - hectic.
Their Citizens Band Radio is going all the time.
According to them - the whole thing's just sub-lime.

I must include Brian and Jeff in this poem.
Most of their pastime is centered 'round home.
They play with their pets and watch color TV
and now and then come to see Grandma and me.

Dave is a senior at Hill-Crest this year.
He's safe and he's sound so we've nothing to fear.
The kids there all think their lives really quite 'norm.'
It isn't so bad living in at the dorm.

It's really no secret our Mom had a fall.
Of course Father Young was right there on the ball.
It didn't take long and the ambulance came.
We all felt so bad but there's no one to blame.

Mom's hip was broken and had to be fixed.
For her to be walking around now is 'nixed.'
But time is a healer and we'll wait and see.
It may be quite soon - on her feet she will be.

There's much I could write about in-laws, et-al,
but I'm afraid that would take me til fall.
I'd better get on with the rest of this rhyme
and finish this message while I've got the time.

I did mention Christmas a little before.
The best part of course CAN'T be bought in a store.
The tinsel and glitter is all very nice,
and candles sweet smelling of perfume and spice.

But Wise Men and shepherds of old traveled far
as they looking Eastward followed the Star.
They came to the manger and found the young Child
as the prophets fore-told He was gentle and mild.

And then there assembled a Heavenly Throng
and raising their voices echoed the Song
God in His infinite Wisdom and Love
Sent US His Son from His throne up above.

SEASONS GREETINGS 1976

I'll just try to cram in a limited space
a few of the facts from our lives crazy pace
The truth of it is there's so much to relate
and we really prefer to keep everything straight.

I always believe I should start in the Spring
to carefully jot down about each little thing
that happens to families and friends every day
and then in a letter have something to say.

But here it is - only a few days to go
and I'm only starting - which proves I am slow.
Believe me it wasn't intended that way
so we'll move right along without further delay.

Mom and Dad Young have put in quite a year
waiting for Mom's hip to heal - the poor dear.
But time moves along and they both feel much better.
I thought I should tell it the first in this letter.

The old home is sold and that DID bring a tear.
But when all's said and done there's nothing to fear.
It's a cute little place where the folks now reside.
That's just what Dad wanted - to be by Mom's side.

Judy and Mike brought the family much joy
when back in July, Jude delivered a boy. [Paul]
It really was thrilling to Scottie and Dan
as they both like to play with the new little man.

Dick Jr. and Lorna are building this year.
With these crazy prices one wonders - "Oh, Dear"
But Jeffy and Brian are quite satisfied
and what happens in life - just take it in stride.

Dave is a graduate - and working - you know.
His plans for the future develop quite slow.
A young lady too, in his life just a friend
But one never knows where a friendship will end!

Dee and I carry on rather routine in style.
And not too exciting - but once in a while
we get in our car and go somewhere to dine.
(I'm hoping my wife thinks the idea is fine).

I wish I had more space to talk about friends
as I'm nearing the point where this letter ends.
But maybe next year I'II give that a try.
And that won't be long as we see the time fly.

Just ponder a moment with me if you will
and reflect on the night when all was quite still
When there in a manger in Old Bethlehem
was the birth of a Savior who came for all men.

Now may we rejoice as we pick up the phrase
and chorus our voices in Heavenly Praise.
Before I sign off may WE say - Loud and Clear
a most Blessed Christmas and Happy New Year.

CHRISTMAS 1977

My thoughts again have turned to rhyme-
And somehow I won't take the time
To fill you with a bunch of chatter
About so much that doesn't matter.

A few short verses out to do
To let you know we all came through
A really hectic, busy year
That went so fast we say, "Oh, dear."

So much we planned did NOT get done,
And yet we had some time for fun.
A busy schedule is a blessing
Even though at times it's pressing.

Our business place is going strong
And active days are NEVER long.
We're fortunate to have a crew
Where each one knows just what to do.

So with those thoughts, I'd like to say
With the Advent season on the way-
We're drawing near the time of year
When holidays are filled with cheer.

And mingles with the glitter part
We'd like to think in every heart
Springs forth the joy of faith and love
That's given so freely from above.

In Bethlehem so far away
In a crude old stable filled with hay,
Our Savior lay in manger still
As God, His great work did fulfill.

SEASON'S GREETINGS TO FAMILY
AND FRIENDS FROM:
Dick, Dee, & Dave Young

CHRISTMAS 1978 GREETINGS

Well, here it is December first,
and I declare, I'm at my worst
It seems I haven't had the time
to just sit down and make up rhyme.

My wife keeps at me during the year
to jot down things I see and hear
That some-how we convey to friends
these newsy little odds and ends.

The kids in school & weddings too
or taking trips to see things new.
There's always something to report
including how WE hold the fort.

Our family's now reduced to 'two'!
as Dave and Beth have said, "I do".
They're settling down in their own place
little home with 'just right' space.

Dick and Lorna - next in line
with their two boys are doing fine.
They spend their year like all the rest
and do the thing that suits them best.

Jude and Mike in Illinois
are quite content with their three boys.
They're active in their church and school
and are very busy as a rule.

There's no real point in saying more
or you will think me just a bore.
To cover all things great and small
would drive some people up the wall.

In change of thought I'd like to say
that since we're nearing Christmas Day,
It is that magic time of year
that little children hold most dear.

They really feel each special part
of everything that stirs their heart,
Of toys or things that bring them mirth
or Christmas Eve and JESUS birth.

So let us take the time, and pause
to think of not just Santa Claus
But each become once more a child
and think on HIM in a manger mild.

MERRY CHRISTMAS HAPPY NEW YEAR

CHRISTMAS GREETINGS TO FAMILY AND FRIENDS 1979

We thought we'd use our Christmas poem
To tell about our newest home.
It happened sometime during the year
When Judy said - "We're moving here".

Now this was Judy's little plan
To twist the arm of Mike - her man
And get him thinking of a change
And find a home that's in their range.

Then Mike said - "0kay, let us buy
Your folks old home - if not too high".
And that's exactly what they did
When giving us a worthy bid.

Now Dee & I were pleased you see
To find someplace where we would be.
We're not complaining you should know
We're glad to see our city grow.

With Jude and family back in town
We think it's really done up brown.
The family circle then complete
And surely - we all think it's neat.

Our other kids are near you know
The distance isn't far to go.
It's easy now to get together
In almost any kind of weather.

For you to find our NEW address
We'll fix it so it's not a guess.
Just check this map & you will know
To visit us - just where to go.

CHRISTMAS 1980

Well, what do you know, it's time again
To take up paper and ball point pen -
And let all our friends and family know
Just how everyone in the Clan doth grow.

Or, maybe you would rather let that be
That I not be sounding so boastfully.
Of course, now, it wouldn't be right to blurt
A whole bunch of gossip to somebody's hurt-

So - back to the system that still meets the test
Where everything said is only the best.
But, really, I'm stumped and haven't the space
To cover each newsworthy item with grace.

There are a few things that just have to be told
As we see each day how our lives do un-fold.
DeLoris and I found our heads in a whirl
As David and Beth became parents of a GIRL.

Judy was first born and then up to now -
It's boys - only - born in our family somehow.
Boys are OK. but we think it quite nice
That baby Michelle April has broken the ice.

I could go on with a whole lot of chatter
And fill up a page 'bout things that don't matter.
But Dee & I feel that we should let you know
Our children and grand kids set our hearts aglow.

Speaking of births - it's near 2000 years
When wise men and shepherds all allayed their fears -
And went to the manger to see THAT young child
A heavenly messenger - tender and mild.

Bringing salvation so full and so free
The best part of all it includes you and me.
With that, I'll sign off & say with good cheer-
A most blessed Christmas and Happy New Year.

Dick & Dee Young

DECEMBER 1981

Dear Family & Friends:

For perhaps a dozen or more years I have been helping my wife with Christmas letters by writing poetry. Some of your generous comments about my nonsense poems has prompted me to make an attempt every year to do it - at least - once more. Most of you know that my intent was two-fold. First, I tried to make a few remarks about family members using the old logic that "many a truth is said in jest", and second that the beautiful story of Jesus birth be included in some small way.

Somehow, my abilities to put this year's affairs into rhyme haven't clicked. Maybe - before this letter ends, something will develop.

But - it has been a 'something else' year. Our business has had some dramatic moments with certain of our major customers going bankrupt (owing us). The tight money squeeze is epidemic. (We're eating though.)

Then, Happiness and Sadness. Kirsten Joy, Judy & Mike's first girl was born on July 10th. That is also her brother Paul's birthday. Then Dad Young became ill and entered the hospital before he could see his new great-granddaughter. He passed away on July 24th at age 89. Mother Young was also 89 when she passed away a year and a half earlier. Cherished thoughts about Dad and Mom include their devout lives and their devotion to their children.

Elaborating on problems is out of character with the holidays and festive times of the year. But permit me to indulge a few thoughts about DeLoris. She has suffered a great deal this year with a very sore right arm. Most of the problem seemed to be centered in the upper arm, like bursitis. She has had surgery on her feet. She was hospitalized early in November with some lower back ailment which made it nearly impossible for her to walk. She gave in to being wheeled in a wheel chair. It appears to be a ruptured disc and nerve troubles. As I write this letter (Nov 27) she is down in bed trying to ease the aches that prevail.

In October our children planned a beautiful 40th wedding celebration for us. Family & friends came from all over to help with the festivities. Dee's illness has prevented her from responding to the many beautiful anniversary cards, so she asked that I squeeze in a thought here that says - Thank you - to all who gave cards, gifts and flowers, and that is from both Dee & me. We really appreciate each of you.

One real hardship on Dee is this; Michelle April, Dave's & Beth's little girl - age 1-1/2 and Kirsten Joy are the first two granddaughters. Sewing for these two and lugging them around may contribute to Dee's back trouble, so she may have to guard that. Bragging about little girls follows having five grandsons. Boasting would reverse if it had been the other way.

I get a kick out of te1ling people that I have four grandsons working for me. It builds me up a bit when they show doubt regarding that.

Paul - Judy & Mike's third son, has the really tough role. Picture this - Jeff & Brian, Dick and Lorna's two - and Scott & Dan, Judy & Mike's first two - all teenagers with football, cars and dates in their thinking. Then Paul - age five, sandwiched between four young men and two little girls. He'll survive it though. I haven't room here to tell you why but I'll venture one thought. He cherishes those two little girls and champions for them at every turn. Heaven help the 'wise guy' who tampers with "Shelly" or "Kirie".

The Bible says that children are an heritage of the Lord. Dee and I love them all.

How fitting that our Lord who admonishes us to be as little children -in faith, made His appearance as a Babe in the manger. His maturing to manhood, leading and teaching, all the way to the cross, His burial and resurrection ought to make us really stop and think that the Christ-Child and His life sums up our every need and hope. May He bless and keep you this Blessed Holiday Season and always

.

MERRY CHRISTMAS AND HAPPY NEW YEAR

P. S.

I am adding this extra note to inform everyone that on Dec. 3, at 6:50 P.M., DeLoris had surgery on her lower back and was in surgery until 9:45. She left intensive care at about 11 P.M. It is about 12:05 at this writing, and not wishing to dramatize matters, I can say briefly that this was major surgery, and Dee is extremely uncomfortable. She can not drink any liquids and can't move.

She had fragmented bones in the area of the surgery, and the Doctor said that he didn't see that on the X-ray. It was by accident that he found the sharp piece of bone that was actually penetrating a nerve. He said that her pains were real and really bad.

We appreciate the concerns and prayers each has offered, and no doubt by the time you receive this message, Dee will bc in much better condition.

CHRISTMAS 1982

This snowy, lovely, time of year
That young and old alike hold dear
Will once again it's magic cast
And bring reminders of the past.

The scurrying to shop and store
Where counters bulge with gifts galore
And every shopper has a list
While making certain no one's missed.

Nostalgic scent of Evergreen
That graces many homes serene
Will somehow play it's special part
To quicken every human heart.

Little children filled with glee
Take note of things placed 'neath the tree
In hopes to get an early look
At a train, a doll, a game, or book.

And oldsters too, are not left out
But also join the fun - no doubt.
A bit more patient, though they be,
Still view the scene expectantly.

This warm and cheery Christmas theme
Reminds us of another scene.
In Bethlehem so long ago
As hearts then, too, were set aglow.

The infant Jesus then appeared
And though so many hearts had feared,
A peace and quiet settled down
Oe'r man & beast in Bethlehem town.

Could you and I in this OUR day
Receive HIM in our hearts to stay?
May this joyful time of year
Bless each of you that we hold Dear
.
MERRY CHRISTMAS & HAPPY NEW YEAR

Dick & DeLoris Young

MERRY CHRISTMAS 1983

My wife announced the other day
The Christmas season's under way
And there's no time that's any better
for me to start my Christmas letter.

Now what's a fellow going to say
that may just help to make your day?
The weather always makes a topic
from way up North down to the tropic.

Or, commonly a person chatters
at length about his family matters.
We like to do a little braggin'
It surely beats a bunch of naggin'

The grand kids now are five and two
To understand THAT, here's a clue
It's five young men who first appeared
And then two girls our hearts endeared.

The first was Jeff, then Scott, then Dan
And Brian was the fourth young man.
Paul appeared a few years late
But he's the fifth at any rate.

We all had hoped for a little girl
Of course we knew she'd be a Pearl.
Michelle April came in May
Her birthday is the second day.

But we're not through with babies yet
There came one more who' s now the pet.
The latest one is Kirsten Joy
Her brothers treat her like a toy.

ALL our kids are doing O.K.
We see them nearly every day
We're glad when someone 'just drops by'
If only it's to just say "Hi".

Now Christmas is the time of year
we think of all we hold so dear
It doesn't end with just our kin
But let's remember the crowded Inn.

The prophets told it long ago
that weary hearts would be aglow,
The news spread fast to bring HIM fame
When the long awaited Savior came.

The lowly manger - bed of hay
Was where the infant JESUS lay.
A peaceful calm then settled down
O'er all who dwel1ed in Bethlehem town.

Let's remember while we may
that this most blessed Christmas day
Still holds in Nineteen Eighty Three
It's meaning meant for you and me.

WE WANT TO WISH ALL OUR FRIENDS AND FAMILY MEMBERS A WONDERFUL CHRISTMAS AND A HAPPY AND PROSPEROUS NEW YEAR.

Dick and DeLoris Young

HOLIDAY GREETINGS 1984

From: Our House
Grand Forks, ND

Christmas poems are lots'a fun
especially writing on the run.
It's hard to sit and think one through.
There's always so much else to do.

You have to make it interesting
and give your poem a little "zing".
Twelve months surely are enough
to come up with all kinds of stuff.

My wife has told me through the year
to write down things I see and hear.
The kids would be a perfect source
for thoughts and comments we'd endorse.

Our kids have children of their own.
Who knows, some day they too may groan
at hearing mischief their kids did,
that o'er the years was carefully hid.

We maybe haven't heard all yet,
of things that really make you sweat.
The daring things they did when young.
We say, for that, we'd have been hung.

Like riding bikes on river ice,
and things they wouldn't dare do twice,
like putting mice in teacher's drawers,
just to hear her holler 'Horrors'.

Of course, you know it's all in fun,
and who would want a weak-kneed son
that couldn't tell HIS kids some day,
of silly things he did at play?

Now daughters are another story,
they avoid the stuff that's gory.
Their world's full of other joys
like fantasizing over boys.

Kids or grandkids are the same.
the only difference is the name.
We love them more and more each day.
Believe me, that's the only way.

But now I'm getting off the track.
I'd better try and get things back
in true perspective for the season.
As you will see, there is a reason.

There's not another time of year,
that everybody holds so dear.
Men stand together; voices ring
as choruses glad carols sing.

If we could capture all year through,
the Saviors love for me and you,
with banners honoring Him unfurled,
We'd see a whole lot different world.

MERRY CHRISTMAS AND A VERY HAPPY NEW YEAR

Dick & DeLoris Young

1985 CHRISTMAS LETTER

A poem, this year, I'll have to skip
To tell you all about our trip.
I've really had an awful time
To put together thoughts in rhyme.
So I'll just write, if that's OK
To tell you how we spent each day.

It was 14 years since Dee and I had taken a recognizable vacation. Last time was in 1971, when daughter Judy and family lived in New Hampshire. Dave was 13 then, and it was also his last extended trip before his courtship and marriage.

In 1985, I was nominated to be a delegate to our church convention at the conference ground in Warm Beach - near Everette, Washington. One of the delegates from Minnesota learned of a pleasure cruise to Alaska that was due to leave two days after convention. But first, let me interject some background.

Briefly, it must be observed by anyone running his own business, that often, it is the other way around; the business runs the proprietor. It's hard to get away. Time, however, has decreed that, without pressure from anyone, our 3 children, Judy, Dick Jr., and Dave are all employed, full time in the family business - plus our four 18 - 20 year old grandsons, who work summers and part time. Dee, too, had worked for 17 or more years but gave it up when her feet could not take concrete floors. Dave, our youngest, has never worked anywhere else, except to shovel snow for the neighbors a couple of winters.

Do you get the picture? Here is old Gramps in his 66th year, still working a 7:00 A.M. to 6:00 P.M. day; while surrounded with competent help, including the crew, and the kids all said it is time for Mom and Dad to get away for a while. Why not take the cruise?

The trip to the convention was pleasant. We took Judy and Mike's van, which added to our travel comforts. We had normal stops for refueling, eats and lodging. We stopped at friends and family as time permitted. Scenery was exciting.

Convention days were sunny and beautiful. As could be expected, the pleasure of being among friends and feeling the blessings that flowed from the many meetings, we were in just the right frame of mind to put cares aside and take the pleasure cruise.

Our good friends, Pastor Tom Nordtvedt and his wife Matilda, who now live in Everette, took us to Seattle where we boarded the bus to Vancouver, B.C. where the 27,000 ton ship was docked.

The ship, named STAR DANCER, was a beauty. Almost a carbon copy of the famed Love Boat. For anyone who had never been on an ocean liner - it is quite an experience. For me, I had already been a total of 65 days on board troop ships during WWII and the Korean Conflict, so boarding STAR DANCER was quite an experience for me, too. Luxury, to be fully understood does not only mean refinements of a ship or building or vehicle, but the treatment received. Actually, Dee and I didn't have to do a thing. I fully believe, except for modesty, that the stewards would have given us a bath, and tucked us in for the night.

The ten decks, accessible by either stairs or elevators, were literally outfitted with almost every form of entertainment and convenience that one could expect. There were open decks for observation. For those who may not desire the windy days, hundreds of chairs and lounges were available on closed decks with plenty of windows to take in the sights and watch for marine life, other ships, or wild life in the mountains as we often passed by in close range. Goats cavorted over craggy rocks at dizzying heights.

The cruise price covered every need including meals. The dining hall was no place for dieters. Every meal included a variety that sometimes made a selection difficult. If you were in doubt and could not make an easy choice, you would not be denied if you asked for some of each entree. We were assigned a given table where we were seated for each meal. The purpose was because the waiters and busboys - mostly foreign - could learn of our tastes and desires. Six of us at our round table were served by 2 young men, one French and the other Italian. There were 14 languages or ethnic groups on board in the crew of over 400.

There were bars and pubs, theaters and dance halls, casinos, and teen clubs. Entertainment was 1st class and even shopping was available on board. The gift shop was very expensive. Though alcoholic beverages were easily obtained, there was no pressure from the waiters to drink. If one wished to be in a pub just to hear the music, a waiter would ask if drink was desired, and if not, he would lay a napkin or coaster on the table which signified he had been there, and would not ask the question again.

The ships swimming pool was enclosed, but the giant canopy covering could be rolled back and expose the pool on sunny days. The pool area was also a health center where organized activity occupied mid morning hours. Next to the pool area was a weightlifting and exercise room. The ship's captain, from Sweden, mingled freely with passengers. We saw him engaged in ping-pong with some youngsters.

Slot machines were very busy, but only at certain times of the day. (No, we didn't try even one quarter). We saw one lady get $300.00 worth of silver dollars, which is quite a purse-full, but she turned them in for green backs.

Other ship activity included snack bars, pianos for passenger use, late night buffet lunch and I guess I could go on and on. There were no pool tables though. (Too easy to cheat when the ship lurched).

Picture taking was epidemic. We stopped at Juneau, Skagway, Haines and Ketchican. Except for Haines, we could leave the ship and walk around the towns. Novelty shops appear to be the main business in most water-front towns.

All of the ships course was through inland waterways. We visited the glaciers and were thrilled to see large chunks of the bluish glacier crash into the water when the ships whistle was blown. We could feel the vibrations of the whistle as we stood on the observation decks.

The most memorable day was the trip to the Misty Fiords. Normally, a mist hangs about 10 feet above the water, but the day was superlative, clear, bright and pleasant. The channel was so narrow in places that we could see wild life in towering mountains on either side of the ship. I believe more pictures were taken that day than any other. I was able to get one picture that shows the ship as if it were nestled in the mountains, and no water in sight. At the same sight we spotted a huge Alaskan brown bear on the port side about 4:00 PM. He put on quite a show eating lush greens (some sort of swamp grass).

We also watched as they lowered a life boat loaded with about 15 persons who went salmon fishing in the fiords. That became our evening meal. Deeelicious!!

The STAR DANCER is one of the tallest ships afloat. It was completely outfitted in France for the SUNDANCE FLEET at a cost of $140,000,000. It was the replacement ship for one that sunk exactly one year earlier on July 4th, when it snapped on a jagged rock in the night. The ship did not go all the way down but a 70 foot gash in the hull caused it to list at 45 degrees and the swamping of the lower decks cause a loss of all the vehicles in the hold, but not one life was lost. (The ship can be opened from the stern with very large drop doors so that literally hundreds of cars and busses can be driven in the hold).

Approximately 1,600 persons were aboard at the time of the accident, and of that number - 138 returned to be on board the new ship for the anniversary of the mishap. They took it so calmly that it put everyone at ease who may have wondered where that rock was. The town where passengers were taken to, after the collision, had made ready for the 4th voyage by the new ship. We were told to watch to the port side for the fireworks that were set off when the captain blew the whistle. It was quite a sight at 11:00 PM over the water.

Those of you who receive a picture of Dee and me, are seeing our cabin with a beautiful bouquet from our children. Needless to say - it was inscribed - BON VOYAGE. The cabin was comfortable and nearly in the center of the ship. that, by the way, is the best place to be for passenger comfort. It affords the least movement of the ship. Radio, television, air conditioning and compact built-ins made the quarters attractive and pleasant. Fresh fruit was placed in the room every day. It is a good thing we were only a week aboard that vessel or we would have been spoiled rotten.

We disembarked just 7 days after boarding STAR DANCER - a most memorable voyage. Our bus was waiting for our return to Seattle and the continuance of our trip. While in Seattle we visited friends who took us to the famed Space Needle. The 660 foot accent was breathtaking. The visit is free - if you eat, so guess what? We ate our noon meal in the rotating dining hall. It makes a full turn during an average meal time. (We heard it is scary during an earth-quake, the way the entire structure sways).

I hope I haven't lost my readers by now. Anyway, the weather turned HOT, HOT, and our next few days were spent trying to keep cool and visit more friends and relatives. We stayed with sister Vera and family in Oregon, then a leisurely trip through Oregon and the Lava Beds; then on through Idaho. We were able to visit the Mormon Tabernacle in Salt Lake City. We traveled through Wyoming and were only a few days ahead of the big flood which hit Cheyenne. We also missed a devastating tornado in Nebraska shortly before we got there.

We visited friends in Nebraska, relatives in Iowa, and finally made contact with Dick, Jr. and Lorna in Minneapolis. We mixed a bit of business with pleasure in our old home town, but took two more days before returning home.

We were greeted in our driveway with a huge sign that stretched across the front of our garage - WELCOME HOME MOM AND DAD. We were gone 38 days altogether. It sounds a bit different when we say 5-1/2 weeks. In any case, it has been a trip to remember and we must thank our kids for organizing our longest vacation - ever.

Dee and I want to wish each of you a very Merry Christmas and a prosperous New Year. The Christmas season that honors the birth of ONE who has changed the course of history. May our Savior who came as a Babe in the manger, bless you and yours this season and always.

Our love to all,
Dick and Dee

DECEMBER 1986

Dear Family and Friends,

The poetry is for fun, but there may be some of you who would like to hear a bit of news, good or otherwise. Generally, the year was routine, but Dee's health has been a major consideration. Those who know her and see her may say she looks OK, and does not appear to have any big problem.
DeLoris had a mild stroke on June 24, 1986. Call it mild, or light, she was in the United Hospital Intensive Care Unit for four days. It was a blood clot on the right side of her head, above her ear, pressing on her brain, and from her own words "the pain was nearly intolerable".

In November, 1985, Dee was hospitalized with a condition called, Fibrositis. It affects muscles, especially in the legs. That came close to spoiling her Christmas last year.

Then in March, 1986, she was back in the hospital with more fibrositis problems and had to take it easy. June 24th was the stroke, which called for eight more days in the hospital, and then in September, she was in the Fargo, St. Luke's Hospital four days for other follow up work.

Many visits to the Grand Forks Clinic, and two clinics in Fargo, have not found what is causing pain in her left arm and other parts of her body, on the left side. Doctors are not all agreed as to whether or not it was a stroke.
On the brighter side, pain or not, DeLoris had two large fellowship parties at our home. They were back to back - Friday, December 19, and Saturday December 20, with approximately twenty-five at each party. Dee had decorated the house in her inimitable way that gives the impression of Fairy Land.

In other news, Dick, at the age of 67, has seen fit to apply for social security. That, however, does not necessarily suggest loafing around. It will provide extra time to be of assistance to Dee, and also to pursue some hobby work.

With more time away from the factory, (an option) travel is also a consideration. So, a nearly new van has been purchased to make travel more comfortable. It is a Dodge Conversion Van, which seats seven or sleeps two.

Our kids are still all nearby, as the three are full-time employed in the family business. Judy, Dick Jr., and Dave are, in fact, the official management team, and the four grandsons; Jeff, Brian, Scott, and Dan all work at the shop summers, and off days from the University of North Dakota.

Dave, Beth, and girls, Shelly and Jenny, have moved five miles west of Thompson, ND.

Dick Jr., Lorna, Jeff and Brian, also live in Thompson. They like it there. They say that locking doors is not necessary, but since their dog Jocko has taken the long journey, they may start locking up.

Judy, Mike, and family continue their life style at the old address in Riverside park. Scott, Dan, Paul, and Kirie have a wide range of personal activities, and Dan's girlfriend, Patty, almost seems like a family member. I guess it comes closer when she calls the senior citizens, Grandpa and Grandma.

I believe when the typist sees this long list of entries, she may sigh if it calls for page two. With that, Dee and I say, the best to everyone this season, and may the Babe in Bethlehem be near and dear to each of you now and always.

Season's Greetings!

DICK AND DEE

DECEMBER 1986

My letter this year is an Ann Landers special,
don't look for much news from our house.
You won't learn a thing that's going on around here,
but please, don't think me a louse.

My clipboard was loaded with newsworthy notes,
but I won't burden you now.
If there's anything urgent and not revealed here,
you surely will find out, somehow.

Of course, you all realize it's all said in fun,
and Annie, no doubt, is our friend.
She's trying to be helpful, and trusts our excesses
won't see us lose friends in the end.

There is, though, a message that's told and retold,
that comes up afresh every year.
Millions are touched by the comforting news,
that young and old, 'alike, hold so dear.

Our Savior had come as the prophet foretold,
and was laid in a manger of hay.
His work, Just begun in Old Bethlehem town,
is extended to all, yet today.

Oh come, let us adore Him!
A Blessed Christmas and Happy New Year

Dick & DeLoris Young

DECEMBER 1987

My wife has been a'prodding
while I sit around at home.
She says I should get busy
on my year end Christmas poem.

It isn't all that easy
just to sit and start to write-
A little "snag" in just one verse
may cost you half the night.

One tries to sound intelligent
and not run off the track-
But lose just one small train of thought-
you may not get it back.

This really wasn't meant to be
some literary lesson-
But let you know my inner thoughts
instead of 'keep you guessin' .

I've always tried to say in verse
some truths that do occur-
And strive - alas - to keep it where
your thoughts won't be a blur.

But now, I just can't cover
every little family matter-
So bear with me - a wee bit more-
as I conclude this chatter.

There's something 'bout this time of year
that I would like to mention-
There is not one day in 3-6-5
that gets so much attention.

The evergreens and tinsel
bring delight to young and old-
and best of all - you guessed it folks-
the story that is told.

That Jesus came to earth as one
who's just like you and me-
In human form our Lord appeared,
He came to set us free.

Let's honor Him this Christmas time
as well as through the year-
And He will be our guide in life
in all that we hold dear.

MERRY CHRISTMAS AND HAPPY NEW YEAR from

Dick & Deloris Young

DECEMBER 1989

Dear Family and Friends,

No poem this year. Haven't got time. This year will be a major change for us because we sold our home on 17th Ave. S. We will be moving to a patio home.

How about this - we are leaving a six (6) bedroom house - with four (4) baths - nearly 4500 sq. ft. of living space (includes basement and game room), three (3) car garage, a Quonset 32' x 40' with upstairs and 1-1/4 acres of property that claims to have 100 trees.

The patio home is about 1/3 the floor space of the old home - and except for keeping the inside clean and livable, we will have NO outdoor work. But don't feel sorry for us that we are losing a "spread".

This fall, we hired four (4) high school kids to rake leaves, and after a combined effort of 36 hours - they filled 87 bags of leaves. But leaves continued to fall. Dee was amused, though, to find that a stiff south wind cleaned our yard - and promptly deposited the leaves - elsewhere. Oh well, whoever got them can have them.

After a snow storm, I could expect to spend 2 1/2 to 3 hours blowing snow. During the summer, mowing and bagging grass took 8 hours each time.

Hey, it's been fun. But remember, old Dick is now 70 and Dee is not far behind. Though we could go on and continue the work cycle, I believe it is best if Dee does not have to drag around 500 ft. of garden hose to water every area of her yard - plus all her other gardening.

The important thing now is to let each one know about the move, and a little map to help locate the new address. The correct address is High Plains Ct., Grand Forks, ND 58201. Now to get there, you will need to travel south on Cherry Street. Though the patio home is in approximately the 4200 block on Cherry Street, the number on the home is 605 -visible from Cherry St. If you can find Central Plains Ct., our new place is right off the east end of the street.

When we look at the turmoil all over the world, it is comforting to know that we have ONE who is the hope of the world, and all who accept the

"Babe in the manger" as Lord and Savior, have found what the true meaning of Christmas is.

MERRY CHRISTMAS & HAPPY NEW YEAR

Dick and DeLoris Young

DECEMBER 13, 1990

Dear Family and Friends,

Our Christmas poem has become somewhat traditional - intended for fun - and rather benign except for the last line or two. There are some things which enter our lives which may be only a sketchy report to many and perhaps not known to others.

It is exactly one year since we moved from the country setting home on 1-1/4 acres. Our patio home is less than one-half the space - but - no stairs to climb - no snow to shovel, or lawn to mow. The 2 car garage is heated, and we do have a medium sized fenced in - private patio that may have created a problem for

She loves flowers, and she fixed the patio up soooo nice - and really beautiful. Even our granddaughters commented on flowers around the front of the house as "the nicest on our street".

Sometime in June, 1990, Dee was beginning to experience congestion and severe coughing which has been diagnosed as allergy related. Several trips to various clinics have all pointed to a number of things to avoid - plants, flowers, perfumes, cigarette smoke, exhaust fumes, and last but not least - dozens of common foods which most of us eat without a whit of concern. At present, Dee is on a liquid diet, and looks longingly at foods she loves, as the rest of us chow down. She is taking special treatment and hopes for a cure soon.

Sadness, too, entered Dee's family. Her sister, Grace, passed away on Nov. 6, 1990. She was 1-1/2 years younger than Dee. Dee's mom reached 91 on Sept. 27, 1990. Grace had been so close to Mom Butenhoff as the two lived in separate apartments (same building) in Barnesville, MN. Everyone is really surprised at how independent the 91 year old lady has become since Grace is not there to look after her.

About our kids - Judy and Mike are very busy in their work, plus church activity. Mike is head usher, and from reports we receive, he is much appreciated. The two older boys, Dan & Scott work at the shop - plus Patty, Dan's wife. Left at home are Paul and Kirie. And as youngsters go, they are knee deep in activity - mostly school related. Judy has to be an all purpose mom.

Dick, Jr. & Lorna have great interest in boats and lake property at Fergus Falls, MN. Dick is an avid boat re-builder, and when he is done - they (the boats) look great. Some are vintage crafts. A valuable hobby. Lorna and DeLoris have a mutual problem - namely allergy. Lorna's experience covers more time, and offered some worthy advice to DeLoris. Their son, Jeff, is very busy at the shop as chief expediter on new work. Brian is at UND with employment plus being busy with studies.

Dave and Beth go hunting together. Their daughters, Shelly, 10 and Jenny, 6 tend Sam, their dog, four cats and two bunnies. Along with other family church activity, Beth has been helping out with Child Evangelism Fellowship meetings. It is very good for youngsters learning the Gospel. Shelly won blue ribbons at the fair with 4H entries. Jenny, the youngest in our family holds her own - no matter what, & loves to sing - on key.

What about Dick Sr.? Busy, yes. I go to work every day as a matter of habit and sometimes have a list of things to do that grows more than shrinks. And I bowl, sing in the choir, play the NEW church organ, eat garlic - (but use the odorless kind on Sunday) and I am fortunate that I can enjoy all foods. I am trying to get Dee cured so we can TRAVEL. More next year.

Our love to all and again we wish each a
VERY MERRY CHRISTMAS &
HAPPY NEW YEAR

Dick and DeLoris Young

CHRISTMAS 1990

A BIT OF NONSENSE (Plus a thought)

Every year I try to write a poem I hope is clever -
And when I see what month it is, I know it's now or never.
Looking back eleven months to bring you up to date -
We can't be sure it's interesting, or how it all would rate.

Can moving be exciting that it's worth a line or two?
Or trading in a car so we could own a van that's blue?
Well, that's the way it is, you see - there's two things on the list -
Now - let me see, is there some news I probably have missed?

Oh yes - we should avoid the tendency to talk about our health -
But when it's good one really feels it's better than just wealth.
Dee has suffered quite a bit with allergy this year -
We've tried a lot of things we hoped would help her out - poor dear.

She's not about to let it get her down - you can be sure -
But there are times - some elements one simply must endure.
I could go on, and fill another page or two - no doubt -
But I don't wish to bore you here and maybe wear you out.

We're in that special season that's so dear to everyone
Because our God saw fit to send to earth His only Son.
That special news should melt the heart of all who love the Lord
And may our Savior be the one that's everywhere adored.

MERRY CHRISTMAS & A HAPPY NEW YEAR

Dick & DeLoris Young

NOTES FROM 1991

Most of you are aware that we sold our oversized home on 17th Ave South in December of 1989, after enjoying the extra space for 10 years. This 13 room house with six (6) bedrooms, four (4) baths, a special music room, a large basement game room and 1-1/4 acres of lawn to care for became a heavy work load for DeLoris. My work included extra buildings on the property, which required considerable care and upkeep. Added to that was snow removal and other yard work which called for trimming trees and helping (a little) in Dee's garden. DeLoris took it upon herself to keep gardens and flower beds in super condition. She constantly dragged several hundred feet of garden hose to the far corners of the property to aid the dry conditions, plus watering raspberry and strawberry beds as well as her garden.

Several advised us we would have trouble to sell oversized property. It was almost like a farmstead right in town. We estimated the possibility of going on living there, but on December 1st, the first party who had seen our property for sale surprised us with an early decision and asked for occupancy in two (2) weeks. It was quite a challenge to move in 14 days and store many extra household items we collected over the years. Over half of our belongings had to go into storage.

Renting in December is no picnic. We almost had to settle for what there was, but we did find a patio home on Cherry Street in South Grand Forks which became our temporary dwelling since December of 1989. We rented, knowing something else would develop in time. Though the two (2) bedroom dwelling had certain comforts - including a heated, attached garage and lawn care provided; it was actually less than 1/3 the space we enjoyed in the larger home. It was difficult for Dee to see many of her favorite pieces of furniture and knick-knacks put in storage.

Well - in May of 1991, as I drove home one day - I thought - what a boring trip to travel the same street, every day, and become accustomed to the same buildings, turns and stop signs. Without any special plan in mind, I simply turned down a different street, and there it was a "for sale" sign that caught my eye, a one (1) story home on Walnut Street.

It didn't take us long to check with our Realtor. The thing that caught my attention was the large family room which - at one time - was the two car garage. Here we would have plenty of room for our piano in the converted space. (Another garage was built on the back of the property).

Our grand piano, in the patio home living-room, was about as welcome - in the limited space - as an elephant. I felt reluctant to play because it interfered with Tele-viewing and other family activity.

The rest of the house purchase is perhaps academic - but except for some redecorating and certain updates, the new home is generous enough for our living, and is a good place for grandkids to come and have space for fun times.

Enclosed is a photo of the Walnut Street home which in reality faces 28th Avenue S., but it is a corner lot and has a detached garage in back.

Dee and I are very much aware that lengthy letters take time to read, so I better not extend this much further. Work and getting on with our lives continues routinely. However, 1991 has been a hard year for DeLoris with an extended stretch of spending time at clinics to determine the best course of action which seemed to be Allergy related problems. At this writing, she appears to have a better understanding of how to control the symptoms.

Along with all other brief comments on several points of interest, how can I forget that by the time most of you receive this message, Dee and I will have celebrated our 50th Wedding Anniversary on October 26th.

Whereas, we had been made aware that there were plans for an open house at the Holiday Inn in Grand Forks (we weren't included in actual planning) that too will be history by the time this message reaches you.

We would like to travel next year. (How many years have we been saying THAT?) If you live a distance from North Dakota, we may be thinking of finding your place.

Best wishes to all in the coming year.

Dick & DeLoris Young

CHRISTMAS 1991

The gold's and brown's of fall are gone
and winter winds increase -
December's such a favorite month
with promises of Peace.

While shoppers jostle through the stores
and cover many miles
The Seasons fellowship prevails
as faces all are smiles.

We talk to those we haven't met
and share a thought or two -
It happens all so casually,
it's just the thing to do.

Surely, there's a reason for this
festive time of year
It's truly felt by everyone,
for each that we hold dear.

It happened in Old Bethlehem
in a manger filled with hay -
The greatest blessing of all time
is felt down to this day.

The Savior's birth as long foretold
brings hope to everyone
As God had promised in His Word,
He sent His only Son.

Let's honor Him this Christmas time
and throughout all the year
We can have full confidence
that we have naught to fear.

MERRY CHRISTMAS & HAPPY NEW YEAR

Dick & Dee Young

Richard and DeLoris Young - 1996 - Grand Forks, North Dakota

YEAR END LETTER - 1997

Dear Family & Friends,

Every year since 1962, the idea hits me about in November to write some poetry with a little nonsense- plus reflections on Christmas and the reason for the season.

This year has been one we all hope can be put to rest after experiencing the worst disaster - ever- to hit Grand Forks & East Grand Forks, the great April flood of the Century. Composing a poem did not seem fitting after that - so - give me a year.

Knowing we could expect something, I checked with City Hall and they told me at our address that we didn't have to be concerned as we were several blocks from the river. However, at 3:00 AM, on April 19, 1997 - we were awakened by sirens and police in the street ordering us to get out of our house and leave town. We were told to take a pillow and blanket and a change of clothing.

And then - the horror of it all - the dikes broke and all the feverish effort to save our Cities was lost. Five feet of river water - more than ever before topped the previous flood crest of 49 feet and went to 54 plus feet.

DeLoris seems to remember that we were told we could return the next day, but the fact is, we stayed at our son's (Dave & Beth) in Thompson for a full 27 days before we could return home. All we could do was to clean out debris between curfew hours.

Electricity and water was off - furnaces were shot, sewers were plugged, gas service was off and it was a very smelly basement receiving a full 73 inches of sewer back-up of sludge and murky water.

We marvel at our Mayor, Pat Owens who was in office only a few months before ice storms - blizzards and then the flood which created a real dilemma for her. But she proved to be equal to it all.

It is worth telling that Pat prayed that God would spare lives and none be lost by the savage elements.

There isn't room here to tell of all the other problems in our family as some had worse problems than we did.

I could write more, but at this late date in November, Grand Forks to the outside world appears to be well on the road to recovery. Many basements need a lot of work as does ours, but we all have been impressed by the volunteer work from church groups from many states in this great Nation of ours.

We have seen a great "bonding" from the flood, and though many of our major churches suffered great property loss, the true Spirit has kept the denominations intact as some of the churches - who were able - shared space and made time for worshippers to get together.

As the magic of Christmas comes closer, the enthusiasm of shoppers has picked up - and little by little many have decorated outdoors in old traditions.

May the "BABE" in Bethlehem truly be with you and yours this season as HE, who never changes, blesses each one now and through the year.

Dick & Dee Young

CHRISTMAS 1998

To write a poem is really fun
But one must have his work all done.
Well, maybe there's some snow to blow
Or have some special place to go.

But all in all, you need the time -
To think about some "catchy rhyme".
The things we work with every day
Should 'spark' some thought for us to say.

But, really that could be quite drab
It it's only just a bunch of 'gab'.
Now, it doesn't have to be delirious
But, perhaps it should be somewhat serious.

What's important at this time of year?
When things about us we hold dear.
As shoppers flock to every store
Where shelves are filled with things galore.

Amid this spread of gift and toys -
The things which capture girls and boys.
We sense another yuletide theme
And this is not some passing dream.

The magic of this special Season
Truly helps us see the reason.
Throngs proceed to Bethlehem
To see what God hath wrought for men.

There - in a manger filled with hay
The Baby Jesus came to stay.
Inviting all to come and see
What the Lord has done for you and me.

Merry Christmas & Happy New Year

Dick and Dee Young

1999 CHRISTMAS SEASON letter from Dick & Dee Young

Dear Family & Friends,

The Christmas poem has been our greeting since 1962. The poem this year is different, in fact, I have been told that it isn't very "Christmasy". The thoughts came to me and I decided to put them in print.

It's been a while since we have given a family sketch, and some things took place in 1999 which have prompted me to give a run-down on the clan.

Judy, our 1st born, married Mike McNamee of Grand Forks. Their children by birth order, Scott, Dan, Paul & Kirsten. Scott married Katrina (Kitt) Cooper from California, and they have a daughter, Arielle, born Aug 9, 1999.

Dan married Patricia Bonnet from Streeter, ND. They have two daughters, Rachael 4, and Megan 1-1/2.

Paul married Amy Jo Stoltz from Lindstrom, MN. Their wedding was Aug. 23, 1999. They live in Blaine, MN. Paul is employed at Honeywell.

Kirsten attends Northwestern College in Saint Paul, MN, and this is her first year.

Dan & Scott are employed at Young Mfg Co. Patricia also worked in the factory until Rachael was born.

Dick Jr. was born while I was in Germany. I was loading ammunition in our tank when I received the telegram. He married Lorna Zenner from Sheyenne, ND. They have two sons, Jeff & Brian. Brian married a girl from Switzerland named Noemi (pronounced No-aim-ee). They live in Portland, OR where Brian is employed at INTEL. Noemi is in linguistics and music.

Jeff married Cyndi Koehn from New York Mills, MN. Aug 28, 1999. Their home is in Fergus Falls, MN.

Dick, Jr. and Jeff operate a Laser Shop in Fergus Falls, MN. Lorna has a busy schedule working with antiques.

Our son, Dave attended Hillcrest Academy where he met his wife to be - Beth Sundby from Colfax, Wisconsin. They have two daughters, Michelle (Shelly) and Jenny. Both girls are still in school. Shelly, her 2nd year of College and Jennifer a sophomore in high school. Beth is employed in a Day Care in Grand Forks.

Dave and his sister, Judy are both employed at Young Mfg., Inc. Dave & I flew to Germany a year ago to look at Laser machines. Dave saw fit to order a German built Laser. It is the latest piece of equipment to be added to our tool & die shop.

In other matters, DeLoris had foot surgery in June of 1999. She has had a total of 18 surgeries in our 58 years of marriage. She has been battling pain for many years and hoping that she will not need more surgeries. Bone problems have been with her a long time. It is worth reporting that Dee ran machinery for 17 years in our factory.

Old Dick has joined the '80' club Sept 27, 1999, but friends keep calling him "Young" man, so he just keeps going to work.

It is our wish that the Spirit of the Season will not diminish as the world celebrates the birth of the Christ Child. It is also our prayer that each will feel the love and warmth- generated by this- the GREATEST event in history.

MERRY CHRISTMAS & HAPPY NEW YEAR TO ALL

CHRISTMAS LETTER 1999
Dick & Dee Young

At Christmas, the favorite time of the year
When thoughts turn again to those we hold dear.
We all like to give a glowing report
And yet there are things we really should sort.

We hear so much about Y2K
It almost seems that it's here to stay.
And what's this problem all about?
It's fully man-made, there's no doubt.

Reflecting back on the "good old days"
Our problems then were just a "haze".
We did our chores and went to church.
A place where we could share our hurts.

Technology now invades the scene
And all is truly NOT serene.
All our lives are an open book.
And what's to get us off the hook?

A modern day marvel is the Internet.
For which so many will go in debt.
And men go forth to join the 'link'
That brings us together - so we think.

Now Y2K suggests a great change
And no-one knows how far it will range.
Will computers and Internet solve it at all?
Consider another on whom we may call.

In a lonely old stable with hay for a bed
Our Savior - Lord Jesus laid down His sweet head.
The Angels attended in a heavenly throng-
The air then was filled with a beautiful song.

God's greatest gift ever - given to man
Was from the beginning His eternal plan.
With great anticipation we face a new year
But by faith in our Savior - we have naught to fear.

CHRISTMAS 2000

This snowy, lovely, time of year
That young and old alike hold dear.
Will once again it's magic cast
And bring reminders of the past.

The scurrying to shop and store
Where counters bulge with gifts galore.
And every shopper has a list
While making certain no one's missed.

Nostalgic scent of evergreen
That graces many homes serene.
Will somehow play it's special part
To quicken every human heart.

Little children filled with glee
Take note of things placed 'neath the tree.
In hopes to get an early look
At a train, a doll, a game, or book.

And oldsters too, are not left out
But also join the fun - no doubt.
A bit more patient, though they be,
Still view the scene expectantly.

This warm and cheery Christmas theme
Reminds us of another scene.
In Bethlehem so long ago
As hearts then, too, were set aglow.

The infant Jesus then appeared
And though so many hearts had feared,
A peace and quiet settled down
Oe'r man and beast in Bethlehem town.

Could you and I in this OUR day
Receive HIM in our hearts to stay?
May this joyful time of year
Bless each of you that we hold dear.

MERRY CHRISTMAS HAPPY NEW YEAR

Dick & DeLoris Young

DECEMBER 2001

This year ending two thousand one
Suggests our work has just begun.

No one thought three months ago
New York would suffer such a blow.

It happened with uncanny speed
'Twas not expected - no indeed.

Our Nation watched in disbelief
And millions prayed to see relief.

Out of the blue two planes joined in
Accomplishing a terrible sin.

The hijack crew believed their deed
Was a worthy gesture of their creed.

Now if that act was not enough
Two planes further did their stuff

The one took on the Pentagon
The other lost out on its run.

It has been asked, "Now where was God
When all this evil hit our sod"?

He was at work, we can be sure
It's certain His Word has the cure.

We ALL are born to make a choice
And surely, we should hear His voice.

The best we all can do is Pray
That God would guide us every day.

GOD BLESS AMERICA

Dick Young

CHRISTMAS 2001

Dear Family and Friends,

The gold's and browns of fall are gone
And winter winds increase.
We enter in that time of year
With promises of peace.

It's evergreens and tinsel
Mixed with ornaments galore.
We marvel at the spread of gifts
We see in every store.

Little children all are eager
As they glance beneath the tree.
Surely - they are thinking
I wonder what's for me?

Grown-ups too are not left out
They truly set the pace.
As everything at Christmas time
Is always done with grace.

May we take some time to think
Of those who truly hurt.
The tragedy New York has felt
Makes ALL to be alert.

This blessed Season each one finds
Brings comfort every year.
May well become the needed time
To conquer every fear.

May all of us reflect once more
What God has truly done.
He saw fit to send to earth
His one and only Son.

Let's honor Him this Christmas time
And throughout all the year.
We can have full confidence
That we have naught to fear.

MERRY CHRISTMAS & HAPPY NEW YEAR

Dick and Dee Young

YEAR END LETTER - 2001

Dear Family & Friends

Christmas time for 2001 will certainly be a time of reflection for millions. The traditional anticipation of the joyous season has been punctuated with the tragedy in New York.

As we in our own families prepare for Christmas- we must consider prayerfully the needs of the victims and families in this soul searching time frame.

Each of us in our own walk have changes which affect our lives. For the Dick & Dee household, major changes have taken place since March 2-01. By way of explanation, Dee's health problems have been a factor for many years. Her numerous surgeries have caused much pain, and added to that, she has suffered 4 strokes- the first in June of 1986.

The flood in 1997 was very difficult for Dee as she worked very hard to clean up the items salvaged from the basement. A typical farm girl, she put away the plastic gloves recommended for clean-up work, and went after the job without concern for her own well being.

Since then, she has commented often that she is unable at times to keep her balance and is afraid of falling. She blacked out and fell outside by the front door about 2 years ago and bumped her head on a concrete step. Several months later, she lost her footing by the back door and fell forward causing damage to both shoulders. Surgery was required for repairs.

Dee's last stroke was in Oct of 2000. Christmas for 2000 was not the kind of holiday season as in times past.

On Friday, Mar 2 - 2001, Dee's energy level was low and she fell 3 times without warning. Luckily she did not break any bones. I watched her closely until March 5 when she was taken to the hospital for observation.

The Doctor kept her for three days to help build up her system, but on March 8 - 2001, he found it necessary to enter Dee into assisted care living where nursing is available. The doctor informed both of us that old Dick at age 82 would not be able to care for Dee 24 hours a day.

Dee seems to think that the stay in nursing is only temporary, and in time we should be able to put things back together. But when you receive this message, our home will have been sold and both of us are living in Parkwood Place where nursing is available in one end of the building and apartments in the other end. Actually, Parkwood is very large and spread out. The hallways to Dee's room must be at least 2 city blocks from my apt.

I am trying to not make this dramatic, but a practical approach to the very thing which happens to many families, as I am finding out. The advantage is that the only thing I need to be concerned about is to pay the rent. All needs are taken care of - no taxes - no heat bill - no repairs- and one real bonus is a heated garage under the building where I can keep both vehicles. If there was anything Dee hated was to get in a cold car. The thing we need to live with is - how to keep the car warm when it is out of the garage for a while. I think I know the answer - stay in the building.

With these thoughts, I want to wish everyone a very Merry Christmas and a Happy New Year. May we reflect again on the REASON FOR THE SEASON.

The birth of the Christ Child stands as the greatest event - ever.

DICK & DEE YOUNG

CHRISTMAS 2002

It's really true that 9-11
Is mentioned everywhere.
And surely. we can see from THAT,
Our people truly care.

New York has risen from the dust -
Courageous, loyal, strong.
Of course, they still are searching
To determine what went wrong.

The enterprising workers
finding in the rubble pile -
A metal cross to prove that God
Had been there all the while.

When evil things disrupt the scene,
And terror sets the pace,
A backward glance reminds us,
Someone cares and gives us Grace.

We like to think of Christmas
As the favorite time of year-
A special time for everyone
To put aside their fear.

And what could be more fitting,
Than our God to find a way-
That a Savior would be born to all,
In a lowly bed of hay?

We praise the Lord this special day
For His great gift of love-
A blessing we can surely feel-
Was showered from above.

Merry Christmas & Happy New Year

YEAR END NOTES - FOR CHRISTMAS - 2002

Dear family and friends,

Most of our family members and friends are aware of DeLoris's health needs, so I won't elaborate. But she is in comfortable living in the Parkwood Inn here in Grand Forks.

The Parkwood Inn is actually the nursing part of the Parkwood complex. The nursing part is one story as the residents are not able to use elevators.

Parkwood Place is quite spread with the apartments covering several long hallways with elevators to the 3rd floor. Residents are able to take care of their own needs including cooking and laundry. For those who prefer to take meals in the main cafeteria, wholesome meals are available.

Since I, too, live in the apartment area, I choose as many others to fix light snacks but use local restaurants for main meals. There are no set rules.

We have a nice chapel with organ and piano. Several residents have a piano. I was able to have our grand brought in on the main floor. (It was not for the elevator, so I am satisfied).

A long heated garage is in the basement. I was able to have space for two vehicles, but that costs $70.00 a month. But the advantage of the security plus a temperature of 70 plus degrees year around - it is worth it. I don't have space for a lengthy rundown on family matters, but the family in general is in good health.

My sister, Vera, passed away this last fall at age 84. She was in poor health for several years.

Dee and I now have 6 great-grandchildren, and the reports are in that three more are on the way. We welcome these little ones as gifts of the Lord.

Jenny Young, our youngest granddaughter is in her first year of college. We are happy that she chose a Christian college in Canada near Winnipeg. The name of the college is Providence. This is a little over 100 miles from Grand Forks, ND.

Old Dick still goes to the shop every day and welcomes a little challenge now and then.

Again, we wish each of you the Lord's best and trust the year ahead is a blessing to all.

MERRY CHRISTMAS & HAPPY NEW YEAR

Dick and Dee

CHRISTMAS 2003

By starting a poem the first of May
Gives time to think of things to say.
Let's see - what's first now on the list
I'm trusting nothing will be missed.

America was bound once more
to settle matters with a war.
Many believed it ought not be
But to solve our problems peacefully.

Now who can judge a subtle foe
we all believed would strike first blow?
It seems that's really what he did
by the act of keeping matters hid.

The 9-11, a treacherous act
is surely felt to be a pact
by those who wished to set us straight
with destructive actions born of hate.

There surely is a better way
and we're all looking for the day
when men in every walk in life
will gladly work at ending strife.

Again we reach that time of year
when thoughts RETURN to Christmas cheer.
The tinsel and lights help make the day,
and scenes where shepherds kneel to pray.

It's all a part of human trait
where children, men and women wait
in line to purchase gifts so rare
for those with whom they wish to share.

Let's pause and think a moment here
as festive days are drawing near -
the gift of all that tops the list
is one that's very often missed.

The trains and dolls and skates and clothes
and things to warm the ears and nose
are wrapped and given to those we love
with a warmth that's born of things above.

But most of all, the day will stand
as one that's in God's mighty Hand.
He gave the greatest gift of all,
our Savior in a manger stall.

With these thoughts, we wish to send our warmest greetings to all.

A MERRY CHRISTMAS, AND A HAPPY NEW YEAR!

The Dick Young's

2003 - YEAR END LETTER

To: Family and Friends   From - Dick Young

For a number of years, I have added thoughts to include with my Christmas poem. The idea of a poem came to me in 1962, and I have tried to come up with a new theme and not lose the flavor of the 'reason for the season'.

Most of you know that DeLoris's health has been a major problem, especially in the last 3 years. A number of strokes and her frequent falls caused her doctor to arrange for her living in assisted care. The first was Tufte Manor in March 25, 2001.

Next was Parkwood Place, June 1, 2001 where Dee could have nursing care 24 hours a day. We sold our home and I was able to move into the north end of Parkwood in the apartment area on July 1, 2001. We were separated by about 2 full city blocks, but I was able to see Dee every day, and the indoor walk was good for me.

On Sept 22, 2003, DeLoris fell face first into her chest of drawers. She was hospitalized for X-rays and observation. Her doctor determined that she could no longer live in the Parkwood Apt which was only considered assisted living.

Dee is now living in Valley Memorial Elder Care - full time. She is well taken care of and I will keep you posted.

Generally speaking, our families are doing quite well. I wish to keep my remarks on a single sheet, so there won't be lengthy explanations. Most activity of concern will surface in time.

We are pleased to report on the number of great-grandchildren we have been blessed with. It would take a full sheet to cover all the great- grand kids, and to which family, but at this writing, I will mention that we now have 10 great-grand kids.

The latest is a boy born to Nomi & Brian Young who live in Hillsboro, OR. They live farther away than any other of our families. Brian is the son of Dick and Lorna Young who live in Fergus Falls, MN. The name of the new-comer is - Calder Giacun Young - born Nov. 19, 2003. I believe the names have something to do with Swiss heritage. Nomi is from Switzerland.

Again, I have run out of room, but I trust this Season will bring great joy as we celebrate JESUS birth.

Merry Christmas and Happy New Year.

Dick and Dee Young

CHRISTMAS 2004

The seasons roll along with speed
And there is much to do indeed.
We reach that special time of year
That young and old alike hold dear.

The tinsel and the evergreen
A part of every Christmas scene
Has been tradition over time
And reaches into every clime.

Our natures like to think the best
But often we must meet the test.
There are times when things turn grim
To find an answer seems quite slim.

Our troops in danger over seas
And none can do just as they please.
They're under orders to perform
The many tasks that aren't the "norm".

We are aware of their many cares
And may we keep them in our prayers.
Their families, too, deserve the same,
Our Lord knows everyone by name.

We look now for a change of scene
And trusting all will be serene.
Kids and grown-ups join the fun
And what comes next fits every one.

There comes at times a clarion call
To make our way to our favorite mall.
And just as we had hoped to find
A wealth of gifts of every kind.

Giving gifts is a heartfelt pleasure
And to someone it becomes a treasure.
Our Lord knows the human heart
And this season plays a vital part.

In Bethlehem so long ago
A precious gift set hearts aglow.
Our Savior born in a bed of hay
In God's great plan - He's here to stay.

This truly wondrous gift of love
Is our heritage - sent from above.
May it keep us throughout the year
As we share with those we hold dear.

MERRY CHRISTMAS and A HAPPY NEW YEAR

DICK YOUNG

DeLoris passed from this earth to her heavenly home on 1/12/2004

CHRISTMAS SEASON 2005

When a certain time of year arrives
Something happens to bless our lives.
We all truly sense the reason -
We're getting closer to the season.

When stores get busy at a pace
That makes us think they're in a race.
Shelves are filled to overflowing
As happy faces all are glowing.

Shopping carts get in the act -
And they are needed for a fact.
Most are loaded to the hilt,
We all are happy they were built.

There are other matters we should share
-We want to show we really care.
That in this special time of year
We remember those that we hold dear.

Our Heavenly Father took the lead
To show to ALL His Love indeed.
The Baby Jesus, born in the hay
Will bless who seek Him every day.

May we now in heartfelt love-
Honor Him sent from above.
He promised He would never leave us
That is the gift from our loving Jesus.

Dick Young, Sr.

CHRISTMAS 2006

October gives us a wake-up call
Sending a message that now it's fall.
Most enjoy the time of year
When festive days are drawing near.

Tradition plays a vital part
in stirring up the human heart.
And now we begin our shopping list,
Trusting that no-one will be missed.

The Grand-kids have enriched our days
in ever so many special ways.
We hear from them throughout the year
And every contact we hold dear.

Now ponder a moment if you will
and reflect on the night when all was still
When there in a manger in Old Bethlehem
was the birth of a Savior who came for all men.

Now may we rejoice as we pick up the phrase
And chorus our voices in Heavenly Praise.
Before I sign off may we say - LOUD and CLEAR
A most Blessed Christmas and Happy New Year!

Dick Young, Sr.

CHRISTMAS 2007

When looking for the time to write a poem
May work the best to just stay home.
I could pull up a chair to rest my feet
Making an effort some line not repeat.

Great-grand kids add so much to our joy -
We surely are happy for each girl and boy.
The energy each has is something to see.
There's no other way we'd want it to be.

The boys all have an inquisitive mind,
And they dream up ideas of every kind.
We say - boys will be boys. How about the girls?
Where so much attention is spent on their curls.

We try to be alert to the mood of the day
Avoiding the matters that cause us dismay.
The Spirit we look for at this time of year
Keeps us in step with the things we hold dear.

Stores are all crowded with shoppers galore
Hoping to add to their list a bit more.
We wouldn't wish to change the tradition.
It appears to be part of everyone's mission.

What more could we ask when we ponder once more -
A marvelous message awaits all in store.
There in old Bethlehem was a blessed event
When God in His wisdom - a Son He had sent.

Writing a poem for Christmas occurred to me in 1962. Since then, I have tried to come up with a poem every year. I may have a copy of my first one somewhere, but the intent was to have some light-hearted verses and finish with a few words emphasizing - the Reason for the Season.

Merry Christmas everyone.

Dick Young

Richard Charles Young, David Carl Young
Richard Emory Young, Judith Ann McNamee
2008 Grand Forks, North Dakota

CHRISTMAS 2008

There comes a certain time of year
When everyone that we hold dear -
Alerts us to consider again
It's time to take up paper and pen.

Many times we need a hint
What's best for us to put in print
Grandkids give us a special treat -
Their brand of input can't be beat.

What can you can expect from a growing boy
His behavior is meant to bring us joy.
The girls will add in their own special way -
Their interests that keep them busy all day.

The changing times keep us guessing it seems
And has an effect on our personal dreams.
We wish for the best for each one in need -
And Christmas has proven the time - yes, indeed.

We all are aware of the troops overseas
Unable to do just as they please.
Facing danger in so many ways
Creating the unwelcome and anxious days.

Changing our thought patterns just for a bit
Wishing for something to make a big "hit".
Stores will be crowded and all over flow
To usher the Season including the snow.

It adds to the beauty for all to enjoy -
A most pleasant time for each girl and boy.
Now ponder a bit for this special season -
When we feel in our hearts that there is a reason.

The birth of our Savior in a crude bed of hay -
He won't forsake us - He's here to stay.
It's all part of our God's priceless treasure -
For all to experience - and That without measure.

Merry Christmas and Happy New Year

Dick Young

CHRISTMAS 2009

To my family and friends,

You may have heard by now that I celebrated my 90th birthday on September 27th. It was wonderful to have so many family members and friends stop by to see me and I've really enjoyed reading all the cards I received. Thank you all for coming and for your warm greetings.

It's been a tradition of mine to compose a new poem each Christmas season. Last year I made the move to an assisted living facility. It is nice here, but like most people I do miss living on my own. My balance has become poor when standing and walking and my legs are weak from lack of use.

I can't complain though. The staff helps me get to the dining room for my meals and my room is small enough that I can make it around fine with my walker. I had cataract surgery on my left eye in June and I am pleased to report that my vision is much improved. I hope you enjoy this year's poem and my wish is for all of you is for you to have a wonderful Christmas season.

To write a new poem is always a pleasure
As we enter the thoughts we can treasure.
It's always a challenge to find a new thought
And it's normally something that cannot be bought.

It's best to converse about just things that matter.
And not carry on with much useless chatter.
Some of our responsibilities are truly not work.
Still, even simple duties we dare not shirk.

Our times are quite filled with many events.
Including the advent of a new president.
When we look around and consider our days
There is so much activity, life seems like a haze.

We've been at war and seem unsure why.
And it causes us all to heave a big sigh.
But inaction can't settle the problems at hand.
We've learned early on we should take a stand.

Now once again it's that time of year
When our thoughts turn 'round to those we hold dear.
We are fast approaching that wonderful season
When our Savior arrived for a very good reason.

He came as a child to show us the way.
May we honor Him greatly for this special day!
The Father sent Jesus from Heaven above.
And He willingly came, His heart filled with love.

We can trust in his Word, the truth of it stands!
The wonder of Christ is known in most lands.
May your Christmas be blessed & your New Year be better.
I pray you stay well 'til next season's letter.

Dick Young

CHRISTMAS POEM - 2010

When we get a notion to create a new poem
Maybe it's best if we just stay at home.
Pull up a chair and just rest tired feet
Trusting some thought that you won't repeat.

A fresh blanket of snow now covers the ground
Hiding ALL problems that somehow abound.
We're all very thankful for this time of year
Truly, we all have nothing to fear.

Little children are always at ease
And, they are happy to do as they please.
The grand kids especially give us great joy
And that includes every little girl and boy.

The tinsel and the evergreen.
A part of every Christmas scene.
Wrapping gifts includes pleasant days
And thanks to all including praise.

December is always a favorite time of the year.
It's natural our thoughts include those we hold dear.
We like to consider that there IS a reason
We're preparing to enter a great special season.

Our Savior has promised He'd be near at our side
We're thankful when we truly can in Him abide.

Merry Christmas, Dick Young

2010 GREETINGS

To everyone, this is Judy, Dick's daughter, writing for him:

Dad lives in a bright, one bedroom second floor apartment in Wheatland Terrace, an assisted living facility, built after the 1997 flood. There are a number of activities to participate in, but Dad seems to enjoy musical events the most - in particular the piano. He spends most of his time watching TV, reading and snoozing. He uses his walker with wheels to sometimes roam the halls. However, he prefers going down to his meals in his wheelchair. Since Dad hasn't driven for a couple of years, he enjoys an occasional ride to see sights he has forgotten about.

A few times this year, Dad and I were joined by his brother Rol and his daughter, my cousin, Jane for a meal at a local restaurant. It was fun for Jane and me to listen to the reminiscing between the two brothers about the days when they were younger, before moving to Grand Forks in the late 1930's.

In September, Dad had his 91st birthday and we enjoyed birthday cake and ice cream with other residents, some of whom were also celebrating September birthdays. Dad wrote a little poem and he read it at the party when he was handed a microphone. It follows:

Turning ninety-one is really kind of fun
You can just sit back and watch the work get done.
Everybody pitches in and does his little bit
Hoping what he adds will somehow make a hit.

Many of you know that Dad started writing his WWII memories many years ago. In fact, I found something he wrote in the 1960's. He had written many pages of memories in notebooks and on slips of paper - sometimes even the back of a placemat while sitting in a restaurant. Maybe 3 -4 years ago, I asked Dad if I could take all those written reports home with me and get them typed on the computer. It made the process of taking a story written in notebooks at different times, with several years between the entries, a bit easier to try and mesh them into one account. I'm not proficient in editing, so it became a challenge to find the best in each account and write it as one story, since Dad used different words and often had more information in one account than the other one.

When I started the project, I thought it would be something we could staple together and share it with family and friends. Little did I realize that those memories will now be published in a book. A true joy was when the original handwritten poem, "A Soldier Muses", by Dick, at the German war front in 1945 was found in his files.

Perhaps a highlight this year was the time in June when Joy Bliss and her husband Gay Dybwad, formerly from this area, now living in New Mexico, met with Dad to continue the process of getting those memories into print. Another meeting with them in September brought the project closer to publication.

Dick's family has grown over the years. Besides Judy, Dick, Dave, and their spouses, he now has eight grandchildren and eighteen great-grandchildren. I'm sure Dick would love a chance to visit with each one of you, but since that isn't possible, I send you good wishes from him for a wonderful, God-filled year.

Judy McNamee

This year would be the last one, for the letters and poems, to be sent to family and friends from Dick, and DeLoris - before she passed away in 2004.

Following are a few miscellaneous poems written by Dick.

Oct 24-2003

Thirty eight years ago in June, 1965, my parents, Herbert and Alta celebrated their 50th wedding anniversary. I do not recall if I was asked to prepare a poem, or if I chose to do so, but as I have been going through my papers to thin out extra items, I found a copy of a poem that I wrote. It is old and turning a bit brown with age, but here is a copy.

TO HONOR THE "50th" OF HERBERT AND ALTA YOUNG

In 1915 the courtship began
As Herbert liked Alta, and after her ran.
He chased her with vigor 'til SHE caught him-
To escape from it all was exceedingly slim.

The romance grew in a little church choir
Where "strive for perfection" was Herb's desire.
Poor Alta was hurt as he scolded a bit
And this was the time when Dan Cupid had hit.

Herb was so sorry, he made up his mind
That from that time on he would try to be kind.
He promised her then he would ask for her hand
And set out to look for a nice wedding band.

They were married and moved to the Bland farm nearby.
There this happy couple proceeded to try
To put all the buildings in best of repair
And worked side by side all their effort to share.

In due course of time a small stranger appeared.
To this new baby the household was geared.
'Twas Vera who came as the first one of four.
She still was too young to know there would be more.

But time keeps on marching and out of the blue
The second was born and the count went to two.
Son Dickie took over and Sis was dismayed
To note that to him ALL attention was paid.

So Dad went into conference with Mother to see
That something be done to increase it to three.
Now four year old Vera thought SHE heard a hen
When to her amazement arrived brother Ben.

Lest we forget that by now Dad had moved
To some new location that all had approved.
The quaint little Bland farm no longer was able
To feed all the mouths at the H. E. Young table.

For Grandma decided to live with her son
And joined in the chores as well as the fun.
Though Grandma was given her own private room,
She spent most her time with the dish pan and broom.

The Epple farm now was the place of abode
With white house and orchard not far from the road.
The cattle and horses were Dad's main delight
With good old dog Shep so alert day and night.

Mom kept herself busy throughout all the day,
And took special care of her children at play.
Her schedule included the gathering of eggs
And the churning of butter in large wooden kegs.

However, the stay at the farm was to end.
The date for departure was just 'round the bend.
The auction caused father to feel rather blue.
Many things sold then were still good as new.

The question remains in their minds even yet-
If moving to town was to be their best bet.
But why should there be even one little tear
When they really knew there was nothing to fear?

In the town of Anoka the family did settle.
Mother and Dad displayed courage and mettle
To arrange their affairs to a new way of life
A cooperative venture for husband and wife.

Dad took right a hold of an oil truck route
And made every effort to squelch any doubt
That he would give up when the going was rough
For he's just the kind that would really hang tough.

So many changes would always take place
In our family living to keep up the pace.
Dad switched his employ to a local pole yard,
And often remarked that the work was quite hard.

In looking around he checked at the mill
And found just the job he knew he could fill.
So he got the job, and one worker did pout
When he saw how easily Dad built a spout.

This sketch of the family would surely be folly
If by mistake we'd forget little Rolly.
The fourth in the family and last one to be.
Dad specially named him his "little sweet pea".

The depression set in and the "thirties" were lean.
One almost feels that fate really was mean,
For life seemed to hang on the brink of despair
As many brows knitted with worry and care.

Dad tried out his luck with a truck mounted mill
While Mother got up when the household was still
To fix a warm breakfast and pack a good lunch
As Dad hit the highways to play every hunch.

Many a farmer was happy indeed
That he didn't have to be hauling his seed
To the miller in town- such a long ways away
For this always wasted so much of his day.

Another change in the program was made.
The trade from the farmers now started to fade,
So Dad was obliged to give up the grind
And took to the road some new venture to find.

Grandma was aging and longed for her rest.
She just fell asleep and received her request.
Her things were all packed and put gently away
And quietly she went to heaven to stay.

Again Mom and Dad had a move to prepare
To cold North Dakota so frozen and bare,
As millwrights were needed to rebuild the mill
And Dad stayed on steady the position to fill.

The move to Grand Forks was a change for the best.
Dad went to work with a little more zest.
The kids finished schooling and married-each one.
Then Army life entered to spoil all the fun.

Dee was the first to step into the clan.
Then Vera found Lester and she had her man.
Frank took to Vera, and they walked the isle,
And Rolly with Lois joined up in a while.

But folks here's a story that's not bad at all
If everyone now would just stop and recall
That life for the Young's has been blessed every way
For look at the children that came here to stay.

There's Judy and Nancy and Ronnie and Dick
And Margy and Barby so full of old nick.
Enter Carol and Susan and Janie and Dave,
A nice bunch of children about which to rave.

And last but not least in this rundown on kin
Are two little fellows that each have a "twin".
First Alan then Larry, and Dana then Tom
An increase in Kinder that hit like a bomb."

Then Judy got Michael and Nancy her Russ
They both had a man over which they could "fuss".
When Ronnie asked Mary to join him for life,
Then Dick and his Lorna became man and wife.

So all of us here that are gathered today
Are proud of you folks and we wish to say
We really are glad that you started all this
And gave all the rest here a chance at this bliss.

Dick Young

50th

A walk down memory lane is always fun to do.
We hope the pages following will be fun for you to view.

Fifty years of married life can pass so quickly by.
Seems like only yesterday the knot we then did tie.

In all our joys and sorrows as a couple we did share,
and certainly our faith in God has helped us not despair.

Thank you friends and neighbors and relatives so dear,
for all the joys you've wished us and for your presence here.

Now when this day is over and our guests are on their way,
the memory of this joyous time will ever with us stay.

Dick and DeLoris - October 26, 1941-1991

This poem was written by Dick for the front of the program handed to everyone who attended the celebration event for their 50th Anniversary.

On the reverse side of the program, we included a short synopsis of their fifty years together. We include it here, even though not written by Dick, for others to learn more about their lives together.

Dick was born September 27, 1919 on a farm near Montrose, Minnesota, about 30 miles west of Minneapolis. He moved with his family to Anoka, Minnesota at about age 5, and later, in 1936 they moved to Grand Forks. Dick finished high school in Grand Forks and soon afterwards moved to Moorhead, Minnesota, where he took a position in a machine shop. (Dick's love of working with metal began when he started to build a train and tracks. If you visit Young Mfg. today, you will see those first engine pieces and the tracks made by him at about age 17). Dick met DeLoris while working in Moorhead.

DeLoris (Butenhoff) was born April 9, 1921 on a farm near Baker, Minnesota. She attended country school and graduated from Barnesville High School. After graduation, Dee went to work as a waitress in Moorhead, at the Blue Bird Cafe. A mutual acquaintance introduced Dick and DeLoris to each other and their first date was on Dee's 20th birthday. They were married that fall, on October 26, 1941 at the Trinity Evangelical Lutheran Church in Sabin, Minnesota.

Dick and Dee moved three times during the first few months of marriage. One move was caused because they were living in a house owned by some German people, and they were being 'spied' upon, which made it uncomfortable for Dick and Dee, since they, too, were of German decent. The war was in its beginning stages, and Dick was deferred to work in a defense plant in Minneapolis, so a move was made there in 1942.

Minneapolis Moline was Dick's place of employment. The original jeep was made there, although Dick says it looked more like a 'swamp buggy'. He remained there until the spring of 1944, when he entered the Army at Ft. Knox, Kentucky.

Judy was born in February, 1943 and Dee was a stay-at-home wife and mother during those years. After Dick entered the service, Dee moved to Grand Forks along with Judy to live with her in-laws, a common practice during war time. Dick, Jr. (Butch) was born in Grand Forks in January, 1945. Dick did not receive the telegram announcing the birth of his first son until March, 1945, when he was at the front lines, loading ammunition.

Letters from home reached him announcing the birth before the telegram did. Butch was one year and five days old before Dick ever saw him. The Young house was filled with people and activities and Dee went to live with her parents after the birth of Butch, until Dick returned from service.

After the war, Dick returned to Minneapolis to reclaim his job and when things didn't work out, he moved the whole family back to Grand Forks. The large house owned by Dick's parents was remodeled into a duplex and became the family home until 1963.

During the post-war years, Dick was involved in machine shop work in various capacities. After the war, he and brothers Frank and Roland opened their own repair business. Then, in 1950, both Dick and Rol were called into the Korean Conflict and the shop was closed. The family moved to Ft. Lewis, Washington for a year before Dick went to Korea. After his discharge from the Army, a second time, Dick worked for a short time at Butler Machine and also was a lab technician and instructor in the machine shop at the University of North Dakota. Between the years of 1954 and

1966, Dick was associated with ARCO MFG., Potato Research Lab. at UND and Supervisor of Buildings and Grounds for GF Public Schools.

Then, in 1966, he and brother Rol bought a building on 42nd Street North, off the beaten path, and began working towards what is now Young Mfg., Inc.

In 1953, desire to own 'lake property' caused Dick and Dee to purchase a lot on Maple Lake, near Mentor, Minnesota. The brush was cleared and a cabin was built and enjoyed until 1966.

David, born August, 1958 was a welcome addition to the family. His birth caused the family to start looking for a larger dwelling. In the late 1950's, Dick and Dee bought a house next door to the Young home and gutted and remodeled it completely, including a new basement. They moved into the basement in September, 1963, three weeks after Judy was married. This was to be their temporary quarters for the next two and one half years, while the rest of the remodeling was completed. Dee washed dishes in the laundry sink and used wood orange crates as cupboards for many months, until a more permanent arrangement was built in the basement.

Dick's love for music and the purchase of a theater style organ and a concert grand piano and Dee's desire for a home build all on one floor encouraged a move to 17th Ave. South in 1979. They called that home until December, 1989 when their house was sold and they moved into a rented patio home - which they not so affectionately called the 'cracker box'. After moving from a six bedroom home, into a small rental unit, it was apparent to both Dick and DeLoris that they weren't ready for Condo living just yet.

They both have hobbies and interests that warrant having a larger home. So in July 1991, in their 49th year of marriage, they bought another house on Walnut St. in Grand Forks, ND.

During the years when Dick was busy building up his businesses, serving in the Army and overseas twice, Dee cared for the family needs and took up many hobbies. She is an expert seamstress, and has done tailoring reupholstering, drapery making, learned to knit and crochet, and did painting on wood pieces long before it became the popular art form it is today. She worked at the R.B. Griffith Company in downtown Grand Forks when Dick was in Korea. During those years, she often had a vegetable garden and did lots of canning and freezing. She worked for about 17 years at Young Mfg., running lathes and punch presses and also worked in the office at various times. Her passion over the years is her flower beds. One of her granddaughters said you can always tell which house is Grandma's. It's the one with the most flowers around it.

Over the years, additional members were added to the family when their children married and grandchildren followed. Judy married Mike McNamee and they have four children; Scott, Daniel (married to Patty Bonnet), Paul and Kirsten. Dick, Jr. married Lorna Zenner and they have two sons, Jeff (recently married to Stephanie Keyes) and Brian. David is married to Beth Sundby and their two daughters are Shelly and Jennifer. At present, there are eight family members working at Young Mfg. - Dick, Judy, Dick, Jr., David, Jeff, Scott, Dan and Patty.

Anyone who knows Dick and DeLoris know that their lives are filled with doing the Lord's work - whether it's at church or with the Gideon's or other community involvement. It's a good chance that you, reading this brief history have become involved in their lives through one of these ways.

Thank you, again, for sharing this special day with Dick and DeLoris.

1995

Several years ago, - perhaps 15 or more, my family attended a family get-together at Barnesville, Minnesota. We were in the town park, and somehow the topic of poetry came up. My wife looked at the carved up picnic tables and said, "If these tables could talk" and then she said to me "Why don't you make up a poem about the tables - and see if you can do it in 5 minutes?" And here it is -

A PICNIC TABLE TALKS

I'm just a common picnic table-
But telling tales - I'm really able.
Now at this favorite gathering spot
I hear ALL things - both cold and hot.

It's lovers talks and beer busts too
And sentimental bally-hoo.
It's business deals, and sports - no end,
And stubborn minds that will not bend.

But I'm just glad I'm made of wood
'cause, I hear things - both bad and good.
So I'll just take a neutral view
And be prepared for something new.

R.E.Y.

This little poem was found in Dick's papers.

In the early 1940's, my bride and I
entered an old fashioned street car
in Minneapolis, Minn. A very warm day,
my wife was wearing very short shorts.

A man on the car kept staring at her
legs. I wished he would look elsewhere
or just get off the car. And finally he did,
with the aid of a white cane.

"PRIME TIME" VALENTINES PARTY

FOR BETHEL LUTHERAN
ROYAL FORK BANQUET ROOM
FEBRUARY 18, 1996
REFLECTIONS

When I think of Valentines, I remember as a boy-
Fancy card creations that were meant to bring one joy.

Hearts and flowers grace each card with mushy language too-
Youngsters love it - oldsters also trust the thoughts are true.

The bigger ones, seemed, in a way, to say a little more,
But maybe there's some meaning for the one the card is for.

That pretty girl just down the street - I'd give her my best card-
And if she didn't want it, I would really take it hard.

But---now---on the other hand if SHE gave one to ME-
My rapid pulse would surely show my heart was full of GLEE.

This Romantic day each year, we hope is here to stay-
For many lonely hearts it seems - it is a special day.

I'll be very glad to vote to carry on this 'fad'
Of sending out the message that is meant to make us GLAD.

Ricardo Von Yonke

STORIES

DICK YOUNG RESUME
OWNER AND VICE PRES. OF YMI
May 19, 2004

I am of German descent and traditionally, in Old Germany, the youth were encouraged to work along with their fathers as a practical means to learn various professions. Whether it be farming, woodcrafts, leather work or mechanics, the exposure to various trades takes root in young minds.

Dad saw fit to use me early in life for small chores. At age eight, he allowed me to run a silage chopper, a dangerous machine that didn't know the difference between fingers and corn stalks.

I was 10 years old when Dad bought a wood turning lathe from Montgomery Ward. I was nearby to learn something while Dad made candlesticks, fancy bowls and just some simple experiments. I learned to use measuring tools as I had chosen to make a chess set instead of purchasing one. It was a real challenge to make the chess pieces in a uniform design to look alike.

When I became 16 years old, fully grown and accustomed to hard work, I needed to look for a job. It was still the depression days, but there were projects around town to consider. A new Coca-Cola bottling plant was under construction, and they could use some strong young men for form building and concrete work. Without any experience in job hunting, I spoke to the foreman, asking for work. Without looking up from his work, he said, "We don't need anybody." I said, "Sir, I would like to work for two weeks for nothing just to prove what I can do." He then looked up and said rather crisply, "We pay our men. Be here at 7:00 in the morning." My Dad made sure I took a box of tools so I wouldn't look like a greenhorn.

I worked part time at a sheet metal shop near the high school. I worked after school and on Saturdays. My Dad's family workshop played a vital role in my life. It was in the family shop my Dad offered to help me build a model locomotive. I made the wheels and all the round parts on the lathe. This is what whetted my appetite for a machine shop using professional equipment.

I visited a foundry and machine shop in 1938 and applied for work. I was just weeks from graduating, but available for part time work. The owner favored me with an apprentice rating and I was able to go to work immediately. I was employed full time through 1939 and a few months into 1940. At the age of 20 I was asked to be an assistant to the machinist.

World War II began and a shortage of machine operators created a major problem - training men for war industry. The Moorhead shop was converted into a training school. Using experienced machinists for instructors, I was called to fill the position.

I then was assigned to the well known Minneapolis Moline Tractor Company in Minneapolis. The contracts for the company included steam cylinders for the Navy and anti aircraft guns for the Army. I was assigned to tool-making.

I served in the military until January of 1946. I then took a job at a small welding shop here in Grand Forks.

My brother and I purchased a little machine and welding shop in 1947. Because of the backlog of repair work caused by the war, we became very busy. It was necessary to purchase more machinery and hire workers.

We had many ups and downs during the next few years as my brother, Roland, and myself were called into duty during the Korean War. When we returned we had to start all over. An old pole building that our business started in is now covered with steel and an addition added.

I, now at the age of 84, still come out to Young Manufacturing and work on the presses and do repairs. Young Manufacturing has grown in tool & die making, laser metal stamping and cutting, fabricating, welding and repair, computer assisted design and manufacturing, and employees. Our clients have grown dramatically over the years and look forward to serving more.

THE FASCINATING WORLD OF THE MACHINIST

By: Dick Young, 1965

One reads about almost anything under the sun, so why not hear from the machinist? A master of metals, his trade is to shape and form a multiplicity of items from eggbeaters to bulldozers. The machinist is not confined to metals only since he must possess a knowledge of other materials included in his line of endeavors such as wood, rubber, glass, stone, fabric and plastic, to name a few.

You may stand and admire a sleek train streaking by, or watch with wonder a giant crane hoisting beams to the superstructure of a new skyscraper, or visit a variety store and see counters overflowing with bric-a-brac. You might even include a space ship gliding around in a "no speed limit" zone far above the earth. With all the emphasis on ownership of fine automobiles and gadgets ad-infinitum, if you take a peek behind the scenes, without exception, you will find the machinist.

Undeniably the humdrum of production de-glamorizes the role for many in the clan. Albeit for the more fortunate, namely the general machinists, tool and die makers, model makers, and job shop machinists, the rewards are many. Where else in the entire world would you find a trade or profession that allows one to enter the inner sanctum of literally every other known vocation?

Engineers and draftsmen, the leaders in industry, are saddled with a demanding assignment to summon the total of their resources to keep up with the changing times. Though the world looks to engineering for direction, it is the machinist who has the intimate relationship with the physical end of the program since he must produce that which the engineer designs.

The machinist is somewhat of an egotist. He has to be or he wouldn't feel equal to the problems that are dropped in his midst without warning.

Farmers, millers, bakers, truckers, laundry men, even bankers and numerous others have a diversity of situations that require the machinist to be creative as well as resourceful.

Machinists can be high strung and jealous of each other. No two are alike, fortunately. As may be surmised, their collective heads are better than one and due to the competitive spirit among them, it should be noted that vying for honors strains originality to its maximum. One man designs a machine, and kibitzers detect its "bugs".

Let me invite you on a tour of the trade, par excellence, for a glimpse of the domain of metal workers. Fabulously complicated machines, embodying the ultimate in engineering whirl and grind to produce for the benefit of mankind - machines to produce machines - and machines for the processing of nearly every known commodity for man to consume.

Let us become familiar with shapes, for there are only two - yes two known forms of movement for the machinist to be concerned with. Every machine is designed to do an operation that produces a straight-line motion or rotary motion or a combination of the two.

Then there are the metals. There are hundreds of grades of ferrous (the iron and steel family) and non-ferrous metals to cope with. Some metals are soft, some are hard, some are tough, and others are brittle. The tougher steels that are suitable for heat treating and hardening are created by alloying with other elements such as carbon, vanadium, molybdenum, nickel, tungsten and a number of others. The properties of any given steel are determined by its intended usage. An automobile axle, for example, must be tough while the transmission gears must be hard.

Tool steel, a specifically high-grade shock- and wear-resistant material, also comes in a great variety of tempers and grades. Properly hardened and tempered, tool steel may be sharpened to a keen edge and will cut or shave down the softer and annealed metals. When the object material is too hard to machine, a grinder is employed. When the grinder won't handle the job, it's not the end of the line; there still is an out.

Diamonds, the hardest known substance, are employed in devious ways. A diamond easily cuts an emery wheel, which is the standard means for truing and sizing grinding wheels. (The quantity of diamonds produced for industry by far exceeds the jewelry trade). And how do you cut a diamond? Well, that can be done too, employing other diamonds in various forms. One way is to use diamond dust on a lapidary and another is the use of a special wheel impregnated with diamond particles.

The job shop machinist must be ready to tackle the unusual as well as the standard items of business. One usually thinks of a machine shop as a place where shafts, pulleys and gears are being machined for industry. However, often times, a machinist must be deft as a surgeon, cool as a card shark, and strong as a blacksmith.

In 1937, I started as an apprentice machinist at a local foundry and machine works. I encountered the average type of work expected from the trade. However, the tendency of machinists to drift from shop to shop entered my thinking and I did my share of checking the field before settling in private enterprise on my own. I learned to be ready for almost any request from the company's many patrons.

A frantic father came to me with a small boy whose finger was turning blue. The lad had been thoughtlessly biting on his ring, clamping it deep into the flesh, cutting the blood supply. I had to be careful not to injure a swollen finger while cutting the ring using a sharp nipper.

Then there is the lady who took it upon herself to create a "Hollywood" bed by using a hacksaw to remove the unsightly upper ironwork from an old-fashioned bed frame. Little did she know that by doing so the entire bed would collapse and that she would be down at the machine shop at 4:30 P.M. begging to have the thing put back together again before her hubby came home to find the predicament.

I received a phone call from a fellow one-day who asked me if I could "chop" three feet off five combines. (This is a term applied to the narrowing of a combine to allow it to pass over the narrow bridges in rural North Dakota.) Now this job is not like cutting a board to make it shorter. The entire machine, auger, reel, sickle, feeder pan, and drive parts must be carefully measured, shortened, and machined or welded as needed so that when the machine is put back together again it will still function as before.

If one goofs the assignment he is in for a royal dressing down plus the fact that he still has the job of making right that which went astray. As I have previously said, this is a machinist's domain and the customer has no other place to go EXCEPT to another machine shop. One of the cruelest things a dissatisfied customer can do is to threaten to take his work to a competitor - a horrible blow to the ego.

I received a request from a rubber manufacturer to make three million fly swatter handles out of wire. He would incorporate them in his production run of fly swatters. I didn't get the job but I was intrigued by the report from the successful bidder that a special machine was built for the job. This machine cut, twisted, and counted the handles at a rate beyond the ability of the eye to follow.

One of our local banks had a vault lock problem. A special gear needed to be made and I got the job to make the gear. A locksmith from a distant city came in to engineer the repairs. A brainy sort of fellow, he came with a new lock combination that he had memorized, but he was also trained to "systematically forget" the combination when the job was over. The safe and lock companies follow this method as standard practice lest a written combination be inadvertently wafted into the wrong hands. (Some concerned FBI agents kept their eye on me during this job). Consequently it was time consuming and costly. I was lucky he didn't complain about the bill.

In 1940, I helped another inventor make a bumper jack with a special free-running ball race nut that was designed to raise a car with the least effort. It worked beautifully - except for one thing - the ingenious device that made the jack raise with ease also caused it to run right down again. It wouldn't stay up. What this inventor needed was a quick-off, quick-on wheel assembly to go with it. Ho-hum.

My brothers and I were called upon once to improve on a system for sifting oats out of wheat for grain testing. Wheat is short and fat; oats is long and slender with a whisker at one end of the kernel. Obviously, a sieve with holes large enough to allow the wheat to pass through would also be large enough for the oats to enter. The solution: devise a system where a myriad of small return bend pockets incorporated in a shaker screen would allow the wheat to make the turn and the oats, being longer, couldn't negotiate the turn and had to back out and go another direction.

Back in the late thirties, I worked on an inflatable life belt with a self adjusting buckle. The inventor used a canvas material with a rubber coating for the belt and under his direction, I made the buckle parts out of brass and other non-rusting metals.

In 1941, a burly carnival boss came to the shop with a worn-out drive sprocket from a thrill ride. I had a close race with time to get a sprocket made before the carnival finished its one-day stand.

The headache the machinist must endure is the fellow who frequents the shop with small jobs and after a period of time decides; "There ain't nothing to it." He objects to the bill and states, "Pretty steep for a little dab o' work like that. I could do it myself." But revenge is sweet the day he walks in and asks to rent a machine (for a small hourly rate) and do his own work; save paying for wrecking a machine, he is lucky to get by for double what it would cost him to hire the work done.

I was in business for several years with my two genius younger brothers. The older of the two, also a wizard with electronics, built a unique device for a local bakery for frosting Bismarck pastries. It worked like a bubble fountain with an auger forcing the frosting up through a tube. The swirling motion also aided in uniformity and speed and further saved a young lady a tiresome dip and spread operation with a spatula. All she had to do was hold the Bismarck over the muzzle of the frosting gun.

My younger brother, specializing in instruments and tricky mechanisms, is also a welder. He built one of the first electric golf-mobiles seen in the territory.

Inventors contribute immeasurably to the delights of a machinist for they hold the key to progress. The imagination and perseverance of an inventor is phenomenal and characterizes the calling. Every year the united effort of the society of inventors brings a staggering impact on the populace. New jobs, mounting retail sales, and better living for the consumer may all be credited to the inventors.

The counterpart of inventors, the "crackpot", is also here to stay. Once he has conceived an idea, he believes implicitly he has his fortune "made". Eagerly he heads for a machine shop with models, drawings, documents and all, hoping to find a machinist brilliant enough to interpret him, honest enough to level with him, clever enough to produce his "dream baby", financially able to back production, and too stupid to steal the ideas.

One inventor used the shape of a banana as a basis for his invention. He developed a snout that projected into the firebox of a boiler. This innovation was intended to spray a calculated pattern of water jets into the coal bed to extinguish the inferno in the event of other serious boiler malfunctions. The banana shaped bronze casting was hollow and awkward to hold while drilling each hole tangent to the surface work; save paying for wrecking a machine, he is lucky to get by for double what it would cost him to hire the work done.

Our company built and installed a fire escape on a girls' dorm at the University of North Dakota. I think some of the fellows assisting on the job hoped the project would never end.

During a flood one spring, the National Guard was called out to use their Army ducks for transporting stranded victims to safe ground. Heavy ice flows interfered with the propellers on the ducks. We built and installed grates of steel on the bottom of the ducks that protected the prop yet allowed a free flow of water to pass through.

On one hot August day, two barefoot, vacationing, young ladies drove up to the shop and were very embarrassed to admit most of their clothing was locked up in a trunk they couldn't open. I experienced just a little difficulty in picking the lock.

I learned in shop practice that it is prudent to be slow in admitting being the boss. A most unhappy citizen entered the shop one-day and in a vociferous manner announced he was going to punch the boss in the nose. I am not sure what he was beefing about, however, he growled, "Where the h... is the boss?" I detected he had been in a tavern so I said, "He's not here and won't be back today." The man left. The next day he came back and apologized for his outburst - in the wrong shop.

Because of the enticing nature of the machine trade, it attracts its percentage of screwballs. Hardly a shop escapes having at least one experimenter who hangs dangerously on the brink of wrecking every fine machine in the place. His wild schemes at times hit pay dirt and he credits it all to his intelligence.

Machinists rarely admit being wrong on an error or miscalculation. It is always the fault of the material, or poor light, or the wrong blue print, or the machine jumped a cog somewhere.

Machinists are perfectionists. They bug everybody by noticing such things as pictures hanging crooked, or poor fitting car doors, or bent dinner forks, etc. If you compliment him for his abilities, a machinist will break his neck to prove you were right.

After 28 years in the business, I can truthfully say I would not exchange a machine shop practice for any other trade. For here I am contented in a wonderful association with a host of grand people who continue to bring in a stream of fascinating projects.

A 'SAFE' STORY

By: Dick Young

As part owner and manager of a machine and welding shop, we could expect unusual repair work.

I received a call from First National Bank that the gear used to close the massive door on the main vault was badly worn and some of the teeth were no longer able to be used.

The age of the vault was not known. Apparently ordering a new gear was out of the question. I was asked to look at the problem on a fall day at about 6:00 PM.

What puzzled me was that I was not asked to go through some security check or shake down. The bank vault was on the second floor of the bank.
I entered the bank through a rotary door. Only a few steps were needed to a long flight of steps. At the bottom of the stairway I encountered a security guard. He was not dressed in a police uniform.

The stairway was not well lighted, but a few steps further was another security guard, and I believe there were 4 total on the stairs. There may have been more guards, but I tried not to appear concerned but follow bank officials to the problem.

There in plain view was the problem. Actually the gear was inside the door and was operated by a hand wheel on the outside of the door.

It was necessary for me to assess the job and return for tools. I was the only one called on to attend to the repairs as it did not seem necessary to have extra help.

The gear by definition was a 'worm gear' about 8 inches in diameter. To create such a gear required special tools which was the norm in a shop like ours. I should mention that the gear had a matching unit which is not referred to as a gear but worm which engaged the gear in a rotary fashion.

(Note: This incident occurred in the early 1970's)

TO WHOM IT MAY CONCERN

From: Dick Young, Sr.
12-11-07 *(88 years old)*

I have in my hand a tool I made about the time of the bombing of Pearl Harbor. This shook the whole world and businesses everywhere felt the need to be alert. The date was Dec 7, 1941.

DeLoris and I were married Oct 26, 1941, and I am reminded that there was a major change in shops and factories.

Our little shop in Moorhead was converted into a training school for aspiring machine operators to gain experience for the war effort.

As shop foreman, it was my job to teach practice on the various machines and one young man learning to sharpen tools was machining down a fairly large piece of shafting. The work-piece was not for any particular item, but I had an idea.

The shaft was high quality material, and I proceeded to cut it into slabs for whatever it could be used for, and an idea came to me to make a slide caliper rule.

I could have bought one but the pleasure of making one stuck in my thoughts until I took the slabs and machined them to a uniform thickness.

The job of creating the shape was a relatively simple process, but cutting the V shape of the body and shaping the slide was a challenge. This was, in a general sense, normal machine work. But the marking of the lines to divide the inches into halves, quarters, and the rest of the lines was a major chore requiring utmost care and measuring.

I held the work piece in a shaper vice and made a stop block to measure from using an inside micrometer. I made all the inch lines first, and proceeded to use the same sharp tool for all the other lines.

The lines varied in length as required in ruler making. And it was my job to measure carefully. (A mistake could have ruined the project.)

There is not much more to be said about the tool but it became a regular part of my tools since 1941. At the time of this writing the tool is in existence 66 years and has been used in all the shops I have worked in including Minneapolis Moline and at present Young Mfg. Co.

To the tool and die maker, making special tools adds greatly to our bag of tricks.

A TOOLMAKERS BAG OF TRICKS

On October 26, 1941 I was joined in marriage to my wife, DeLoris. We settled into an apartment in Moorhead, MN and I was employed by a local machine shop geared to serve the general public. On December 7, 1941 the bombing of Pearl Harbor shook the whole world.

The owner of the shop where I worked, Wes Withnell, recognized that there was a lack of qualified machinists available to serve the war effort and thought it wise to convert his shop into a training center for aspiring machine operators.

Though I was still quite young, early training at home and a position at the Grand Forks Foundry helped prepare me to achieve a position as shop foreman. Part of the job required that I teach practical machining techniques to the trainees.

One young man was learning to sharpen tools and tested them by machining down a fairly large piece of shafting. The work piece was not for a particular use, but only to practice on. Knowing the shaft was of a high quality material, I stopped him from machining it completely away. I decided to slice the shaft into slabs to be used for other purposes and for some odd reason had a desire to make a slide caliper (measures inside and outside of parts).

Though I could easily purchase one, the thought of making a caliper stuck in my mind. With no other direct purpose for the slabs I salvaged, I decided to proceed with my plans.

My first task was to machine the material to a uniform thickness, but thin enough so the tool would not be bulky in my pocket. The job of cutting the basic outside shape of the caliper was a relatively simple process and went quickly. Cutting the V shape of the slide in the main body of the caliper, and the slide itself proved to be a bit more of a challenge. The slide needed to move freely but remain in alignment with the body for the full length of the bearing area. Any "slop", even very slight, may allow the jaws to move out of parallel and give false measurements. Fortunately my care in machining paid off and the caliper had a tight, but freely gliding action. I also included a cam action thumb lock to maintain a dimension I may check.

The real challenge came in laying out and marking the measuring lines. Those who have used pocket slide calipers know they are capable of inside and outside measuring. To make sure my caliper was effective for both, I had to take great care in laying out the lines in respect to the jaw configuration.

I scribed the lines in the standard design of a ruler. Each inch was divided into 1/32" segments, and the lines varied in length from halves, quarters, eighths, sixteenths and thirty-seconds of an inch for easy identification. To make the lines I held the work piece in a shaper vice and made a stop block to measure the placement of each line using an inside micrometer. The scribing tool had to be extremely sharp to achieve the thinnest lines possible for accurate measuring. Since the machines I had to use were manual, as there was no Computerized Numerical Control (CNC) in those days, and every movement of the machine was directed by me, I had plenty of chances to make a mistake that could ruin the work I had previously done.

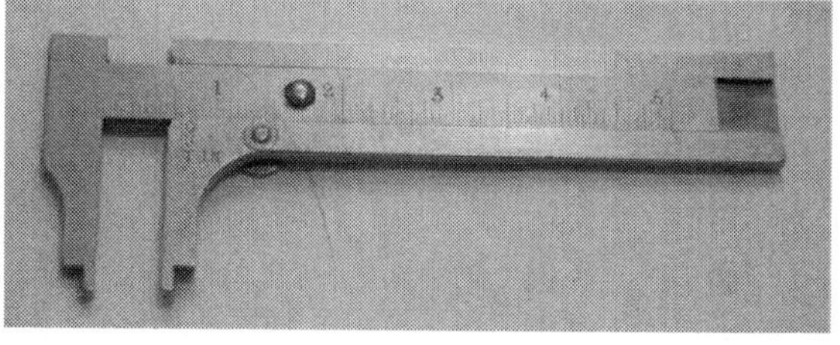

Thankfully, everything came out right and the caliper was very accurate. It has been one of my most regularly used tools since 1941. At the time of this writing, this caliper has been in existence for 66 years, and has been used in all the shops I have worked in over my life. Though it shows some wear from years of use, it still is a functional tool.

To the tool and die maker, the ability to make special tools adds greatly to our bag of tricks.

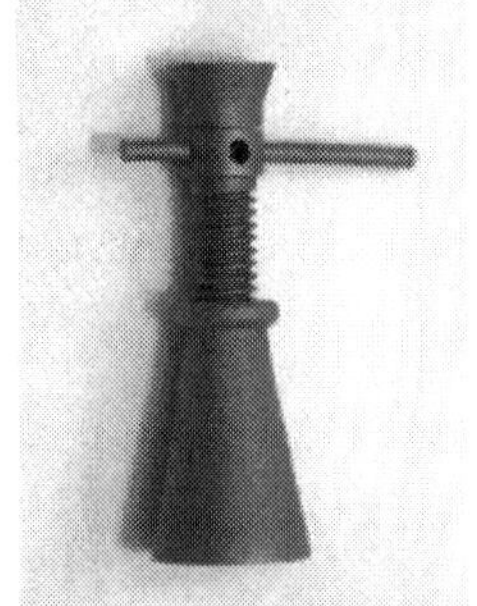

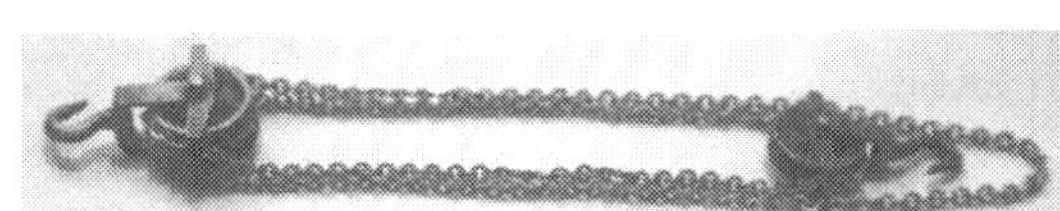

Miniature working version of an old time jack (2-1/2" tall) used for lifting & steadying loads, and a miniature working version of a chain hoist (6-1/2" long as laid out) hand made for fun by Dick when he was 30.

According to brother Roland, "the year was 1949. All three of 'us brothers' decided to make something for Dad for Christmas. Dick made the little chain hoist and jack; Frank made a miniature 'Marquette Welder and I made a miniature Crescent Wrench. I know it was for Christmas because I was able to put the little wrench inside a triple peanut shell. I remember Dad opening a series of boxes and seeing the look on his face when the last thing was just a peanut. I'm pretty sure this was Christmas 1949, the year before we closed our first shop because of the Korean War".

Miniature pieces shown below were turned on a lathe early in Dick's career.

Candle sticks -3/4", chalice -3/4" wide, 1/2" tall

Pawn 7/8", King 2-1/2"

HAIRSTYLING COMBS MADE BY BALD GUYS?

It was the 1960s and big hair was in. Women took great pains to "rat" their hair into large, loose haystacks on top of their heads. Then they doused them with hair spray to maintain the shape. About the same time, Dick and Roland Young opened shop at a new location on 42nd St. North, just out-side Grand Forks. In those days, the company was called Young Tool & Die Works. As always, they were looking for new work. Imagine their surprise when a potential customer showed up at their door and asked if they could make hairstyling combs. A rather ironic request since both Dick and Roland were both dealing with a severe shortage of hair by this time. In fact, because what hair he had left was short-cropped, Dick did not even carry a comb.

After the initial shock at the request passed, the answer came quickly. "Sorry. We can't make combs here." The visiting entrepreneur replied, "A friend of mine said you could." That was the wrong thing to say to a couple of guys who thrived on challenge! Dick replied along the lines of "If someone said we could make them, then we probably can. Let's take a look at what you need." They accepted the job with no real idea of how they would make the product.

The combs were made of aluminum, and the design was unique in that it had a two pronged fork for "lifting" the hair on the handle end. The teeth were of different lengths with eleven "spike" tines evenly spaced on the comb for "teasing" the hair. The remaining tines were shorter and closer together as a normal comb might have.

To create variety the combs were anodized in different colors. Most of them were sold under the name "Style-Her" though some were labeled "Dar-La".

Each comb went through eleven processes from start to finish. As you read through the list of operations, I am sure the question comes to mind: Why were there so many operations? Well, in those days things were different. "Stage" tooling (moving the part from one die to the next) was used almost exclusively due to equipment limitations and because many parts were made from sketches and samples. CAD (Computer Aided Drawing) programs were not available, and draftsmen were hard to find and too expensive for a small shop. Most dies were designed "on the fly" with no blueprints to refer to when creating the die components.

Occasionally, parts were not fully engineered and needed further testing. Though adjustments could be made easily in "stage" tooling, progressive and compound dies will lock the toolmaker into a design with little room for even simple modifications.

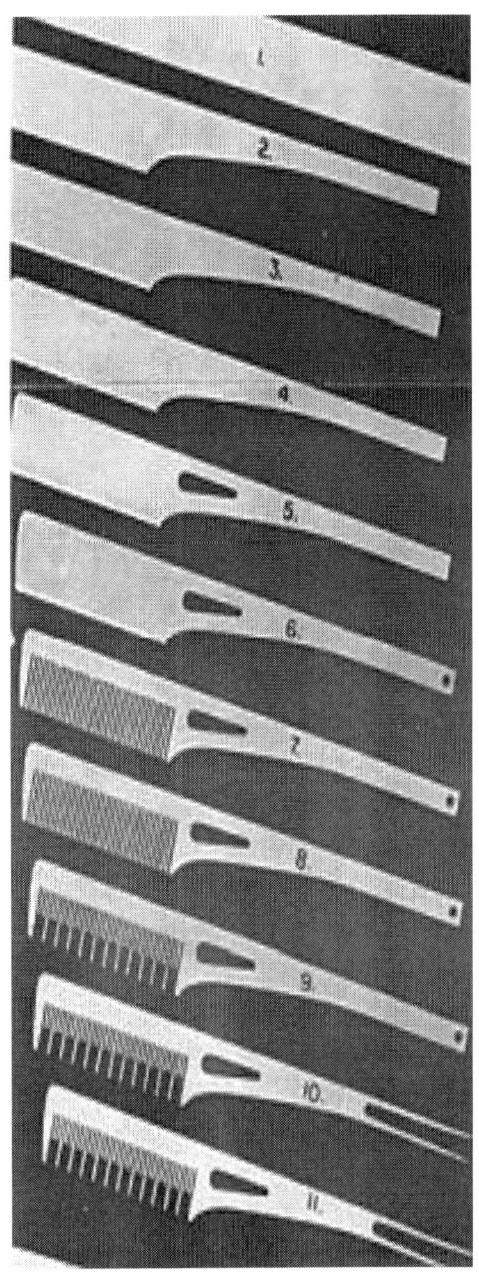

These pictures show the steps taken to create each comb - (1) A sheared blank began the process and then (2) the rough shape was cut in a 60-ton press. (3) A bevel was formed on the edge of the teeth and (4) the name "Style-Her" was stamped into the comb. (5) A slot was punched to add "decor" and (6) a small hole was punched at the handle end to facilitate the finishing process. (7) The teeth were milled with a gang set of slitting blades and (8) then thc ncwly cut teeth were deburred and pre-polished. In step (9) the "hopper" teeth were cut. This process left a single long tooth with two shorter teeth on each side that were cut on an angle (see photos). Next, (10) the lifting fork on the handle was cut and then (11) the combs went through a final buffing and inspection. Actually the combs still were not finished yet. To give the final finishing touch, the combs were sent away and anodized in a rainbow of color.

ALUMINUM COMBS - MAY 2, 2008

Our manufacturing business was often confronted with some unusual requests. Since we were open to new ideas, how does one respond to a customer who asked, can you make aluminum combs? *(This was in approximately 1968).*

My first response was - probably not. But he insisted that he was informed that we could produce a number of items including combs. Since our business was open to metal processing, it was worth taking a look at the possibility. Some of the first work we experienced was heavy tractor wheels. The snowmobile industry required large numbers of track parts, so we had learned to consider each request. But combs?

It took a lot of research to determine the correct material, however our suppliers always were ready to give advice to our benefit. Material for combs was necessarily a durable style that was able to resist bending under normal use.

It is now a number of years since the comb business changed when hair styles were a consideration. We did not pursue a larger market, but completed the styling we agreed to use.

The manufacturing process became quite a challenge. A die for blanking the general shape was first. Following that was the system used for cutting the teeth.

This required a process using metal cutting saws that could be gang mounted on an arbor. This became standard procedure for a milling machine using a vice to hold the comb blank. All the processes were the natural use of the milling machine, and it was easy to train someone for the process.

Some things which could be expected was the rough edges that required sanding or clean-up. A special machine was built to use sanding discs where the combs could be gang mounted for the process.

The finished comb had a forked design in the handle. It was necessary to punch a hole in the handle end of the comb to hold the combs in the polishing process. Later, the part of the comb blank that required the hole was removed with a special die as holding the comb no longer required the feature.

Adding combs to our work load called for many operations. A backward glance reminds me that when a manufacturing company is in business to process metal items for other companies, our reputation hinges on us producing as required. It may be of interest to note that comb production required a total of 13 operations per comb. To complete a comb was to give it a name. The first name was reflecting on its use- and that was - STYLE-HER. Another company interested in our combs used the name DAR-LA.

I have been asked how many combs were produced? I have no record of the total, but it added greatly to a variety of operations in our business that spells success.

MAKING A WARTIME TABLE SAW WAS A SNAP FOR DICK, SR.

In the early 1950s, soon after returning from WWII, my brother Rolly and I felt compelled to join the National Guard to help make ends meet. It seemed like a good idea at the time, but family members warned us that we were just risking another tour of duty. We ignored the warnings. Imagine our surprise when we were both given orders to head west to an Army training camp prior to service in the Korean conflict.

Rolly was first to be shipped out. Just a little later I also prepared to leave. I had attained the rank of Warrant Officer a rather different title and was sent to join forces in Korea. Rolly was assigned to a machine shop in Pusan after arriving in Korea, but I remained unsure of my fate. I was very fortunate to be able to meet him in Pusan when I arrived. We had exactly 1-1/2 hours together before I was sent to a dubious area that our soldiers named the "Punch Bowl."

To my relief, I found I would not be involved in combat. I had enough of that in Germany, already. Instead, I was sent to a large building that was used for repair work on Army equipment. Though I am not sure of the exact location, it seemed to be isolated from combat. From our position we could easily hear the sounds of war and could watch the helicopters carrying wounded back from the front, but we did not experience any direct problems.

The building had many openings spaced around it that allowed plenty of room for a large number of trucks to be backed up to the doorways. The trucks were equipped with machinery lathes, milling machines, drill presses, etc. We were allowed to share the equipment and, all things considered, it provided a pretty fair machine shop, not quite like home, but very workable. Surprisingly, there was quite a bit of material available to handle the various jobs that came up.

It's interesting that we were not given much direction as to our duties while being stationed there. In between jobs we had a lot of free time. One day I noticed a piece of black plate iron that gave me an idea. Though we had plenty of equipment to work on metal, we had few tools available to handle woodworking chores such as cutting plywood and ripping boards.

What we needed was a table saw. The steel plate was about the right size, so I squared it up, cleaned and flattened the surface, and cut guide grooves for the miter gauge. My plan was to a design the saw to handle an 8" blade. With the materials that were available, the saw began to take shape. One important machine tool we were missing was a band saw to trim parts to size so all the parts had to be machined directly from solid stock. There was plenty of time available though. With knowledge of table saws gained from working with my father back home and some patience and persistence, I was able to create all the features found in the popular models of our time.

The saw had a tilt feature and left and right miter grooves. The legs, made from steel fence posts, were cut long enough to position it at a good working height. A "borrowed" electric motor was obtained that promised to give the saw plenty of power.

After the saw was assembled, a slight problem developed. There were no 8" saw blades anywhere to be found. After coming this far, I was not about to be stopped. The closest I could come was a 15" diameter blade. I couldn't rework the saw to fit the blade, but I figured the blade could be made to fit the saw. After checking some dimensions I was pleased to find there was enough room to fit a 9" blade on the machine. The blade was cut to diameter on a lathe, and I used an index plate to create an even number of teeth around the circumference. The exact number of teeth slips my mind today. The teeth were set one by one with a hammer and once the blade had a final sharpening, the saw was ready to go. Because my blade was cut from a larger diameter blade, it was slightly thicker than normal. This actually seemed to be an advantage for the rough things we worked on and the saw ran smoothly.

The saw became a popular tool with several of the men in my group. Though it would have been nice to keep the saw, I was not able to take it home with me when my tour was up. At least I had the pleasure of creating a machine that could be used to make life easier for the fellows still assigned to my unit.

A LEGACY

By: Dick Young - 2002

Young Mfg. Inc. is now in its 55th year. It has occurred to me that the staff and employees of the Young Company may be interested in the factors that worked together to create Young Mfg.

Traditionally, in Old Germany, the youth were encouraged to work along with their fathers as a practical means to learn various professions. Whether it be farming, woodcrafts, leather work or mechanics, the exposure to various trades takes root in young minds.

Teenagers are particularly adapted to the practice simply because they are in their formative years and may not have been influenced in other matters. Working in trade practice not only includes observation, but hands on experience.

Young Family circa 1939

My father, an American born German, believed wholly in this philosophy. My parents, both Germans, were farming about 30 miles west of Minneapolis, Minnesota. I was born at home, the oldest of three sons. My sister was the first of the siblings, but for the sake of this report, the basics involve only the male members.

I would like to give a little sketch of my father, Herbert Young. He was born the son of a German Methodist Pastor. My dad referred to himself as a PK (Preacher's Kid). He was a bit timid about the title as he felt that it required a special life style. But Dad was a morally good man. He didn't force his religion on the family, but his Christian ethics were always evident. Church attendance was the family "norm".

Dad saw fit to use me early in life for small chores. At age eight, he allowed me to run a silage chopper, a dangerous machine that didn't know the difference between fingers and corn stalks. However, his instructions were very clear. (His fear of me being hurt didn't hit him until I was fully grown). Though Dad was a good farmer, his main interest was in woodcrafts. He saw the advantage to leave the farm and move to Anoka, Minnesota where he pursued work in a flourmill. His interest in farming continued, and he bought three cows and rented several acres, which he considered something to "keep his boys busy".

Dad had considerable interest in other professions. One in particular was the turning lathe. In 1929, when I was 10 years old, Dad bought a wood turning lathe from Montgomery Ward. It fit very well in the family shop.

The first use of the lathe was candlesticks, fancy bowls, and just simple experiments. Dad always saw to it that I was nearby to learn something worthwhile.

I joined a chess club in my seventh grade. Rather than buy a chess set, I chose to make one. That turned out to be a real challenge as making chess pieces in a uniform design to look and measure alike was to my benefit. Along with the process, I learned the use of measuring tools.

As a frequent customer in the local machine shops, Dad saw the possibilities in metal turning. In 1933, he purchased metal turning attachments for the wood turning lathe.

Of course, it was only a plaything at first, but here again, the basics were taught to my two younger brothers and me. We learned about speeds and feeds and the sharpening of drills and lathe tools.

My father was a restless man. He had to be involved in some activity right up to bedtime. That included repairing machinery or remodeling the home. He spent hours making drawings of a barn extension or new kitchen cabinets. All this required the involvement of us boys as we each reached an age to take an active part.

In February of 1936, Dad was faced with another job change. The State Mill in Grand Forks, North Dakota required major rebuilding. Grain was distributed through wooden channels in multiple directions. The units were called spouts totally enclosed. The wear was excessive; hence, a continuous replacement was necessary. Several other men from Minneapolis worked on the project.

My father was selected to remain on a permanent basis. After school ended in June, 1936 our family joined him in the move to 1310 University Ave., Grand Forks. This created a major change for each of us. Old farm chores were behind us, but the home workshop was still intact. In May, 1937, we moved to 1523 Lewis Blvd., a rental unit, that had been empty for some time and was in need of much repair. Dad bought the house, where we also did extensive remodeling.

I was 16, fully grown, and accustomed to hard work. Perhaps I had some of my dad's restless spirit. It seemed I needed it in order for me to look for a job.

It was still depression days, but there were projects around town to consider. A new Coca Cola bottling plant was under construction, and they could use some strong young men for form building and concrete work.

Without any experience in job hunting, I spoke to the foreman, asking for work. Without looking up from his work, he said, "We don't need anybody." I said, "Sir, I would like to work for two weeks for nothing just to prove what I can do." He then looked up and said rather crisply, "We pay our men. Be here at 7:00 in the morning."

Here again, my dad got in the act. He made sure that I took a box of tools, and the amusing part, he advised me to take old tools so I wouldn't look like a greenhorn. There were no ready-mix trucks in those days. The gas operated engine mixer was filled by hand shoveling. We had to count out one shovel of cement to five shovels of gravel. A long ramp was built to wheel the mix to the job site. I was able to stay with this assignment until school opened in the fall of 1936.

Construction continued but was not practical for part time. I was able to find work at Nuss Sheet Metal Shop near the high school. This was okay for after school and Saturdays. They specialized in gutter work and furnace installations. This was available to me through the summer of 1937.

The family workshop continued to play a vital role in my life. I have referred several times to the metal turning lathe. It was during the summer and fall of 1937 that my dad offered to help me build a model locomotive. We proceeded without drawings and had no definite plan. We cannot be complimented for that lack of foresight, but we enjoyed our chance to try our skills on what seemed a reasonable approach.

The train parts that occupy the shelf in the front outer office became our expression of design. Dad made the wooden wheel mold that worked well for casting the wheels using high quality nickel babbitt. The wheels and all the round parts became my job to machine on our lathe at home. That whetted my appetite for a machine shop using professional equipment.

After visiting the local foundry and machine shop in the spring of 1938, I applied for work, hardly daring to hope for employment. I was just weeks from graduating, but available for part time work. The owner favored me with an apprentice rating and I was able to go to work immediately. This was like entering magic land. I nearly abandoned the little shop at home. I was able to leave that to my brothers.

The older men at the machine shop treated me very favorably. I was pleased that I was able to put into practice the vital training I had received from a devoted father. Working with older men offered some real surprises. A crusty old railroad machinist said to me out of the blue, "Hey, Kid, you're gonna make out okay around here. At least you ain't a wise guy." I considered that a vital lesson. I also learned much from old Charley, who had many years of experience to share.

I was employed full time through 1939 and a few months into 1940. In February of 1940, one of the men from this shop was asked to replace a retiring machinist who was Foreman in a Moorhead, Minnesota machine shop. After a few weeks, he needed a partner. To my surprise, he asked me to come down to be his assistant. At age 20, this was a new challenge for me. That assignment greatly enlarged my range of experiences.

Still single, I ate my meals in local restaurants. That is where I met the young lady named DeLoris, who would become my wife. We were married October 26, 1941.

The nation was shocked 42 days later when the Japanese attacked Pearl Harbor on December 7, 1941. Young men all over America were in the draft call. Military camps filled rapidly with the country's best. Suddenly, industry became alive with contracts to manufacture war materials.

The shortage of experienced machine operators created another major problem training men for war industry. Within days, the Moorhead shop was converted into a training school. The Minnesota Board of Education took the lead in establishing a curriculum.

Using experienced machinists for instructors, I was called on to fill the position. This was a unique experience. Working with men from the school system, we used tools and machines on hand to create a sort of crash course to men who did not qualify for military duty. These fellows eagerly took hold of a coveted trade, and many were placed in defense plants. My skills became known to employment agencies through the school system. I received notice that I would be deferred for a period of time to enter a defense plant.

My young bride and I found it adventurous to move to Minneapolis, Minnesota where I was assigned to the well known Minneapolis Moline Tractor Company. The contracts for the company included steam cylinders for the Navy and anti-aircraft guns for the Army.

I had no way to know that two men named Richard Young would be employed the same day. I was assigned to tool making. That made me a bit nervous as tool and die work is very specialized. There were no automatic machines in those days and every die maker was on his own. I asked that they reconsider and let me work in the general machine shop. They let me know rather abruptly that they didn't want two men named Richard Young in the same shop. Minneapolis Moline was a massive set of buildings stretching out for blocks. The tool shop was centered in the complex.

The tool room foreman was a Swedish man who learned his trade in Sweden, much like the German young men in Germany. I considered Carl Lansch one of the most important men in my trade experience. His instructions were of the highest order of tooling practice.

My draft notice shortened my employment at this tractor factory, but I am very grateful for the entire special tool and die work that greatly expanded my field of activity.

I had to report for military duty and was sent to Fort Knox, Kentucky. Tank training was the major thrust at this camp centered in the United States. Everything moved swiftly. In a few months and shifting around to other Camps, I was sent to Europe to join combat forces. This report does not include combat experiences, but I was in action until V-E Day, May 8, 1945.

Victory in Europe was welcomed by the ringing of church bells all over Europe. We entered immediately in special training for the Japanese conflict. Those of us who survived combat were happy that the War ended with Japan on September 2, 1945. The balance of my stay in Europe was with occupation forces.

Then, in January of 1946 came the very welcome movement of troops back to the good old USA. The ship ride was routine. However, on a relatively light troop transport, we experienced some of the worst Atlantic storms. As we entered New York Harbor, the sight of the Statue of Liberty gripped me so intensely that I could not speak.

Returning to Grand Forks was next on my agenda. Finding work was easy. The need for skilled workers was ever present. But the luxury of a massive factory was not to be. I took a job in a very small smoky welding shop that had minimal machinery. At least I was home.

Within a few weeks, the two men who operated the little Northern Repair shop chose to break up partnership and the machine and welding shop was offered for sale. My one brother, Roland, had joined me earlier and with the prospect of ownership, a third brother, Frank (now deceased) came aboard. The price of the business was set at $7,000.00. That did not include the building, only the machinery and welding equipment. Dad Young, so much a part of this report, helped with a substantial down payment.

I was 27, brother Frank was 23, and Roland was 18. I was the only one who qualified for military duty, but my brothers had been working for a local electric shop that specialized in wind generators. Their work included welding and machine work.

Our little shop established in 1947 was named by Dad Young as "Young Brothers Machine Works". As could be expected, Dad often reflected on Divine leading in our affairs. Both of our parents deserve recognition for their unfailing devotion and prayers.

Oddly, that smoky little shop did not seem so smoky after we bought it. Because of the backlog of repair work caused by the war, we became very busy. It was necessary to purchase more machinery and hire workers. Since most were unskilled, it was necessary to give training as able. Thankfully, the young men we hired were eager to learn.

An unceremonious interruption in 1950 nearly cost us our business. The Korean War broke out in June of 1950. Since Roland and I were in the National Guard, we had to report for duty.

Brother Frank's injury from an automobile accident prevented him from entering military duty. He declined to operate the business alone, so the shop machinery was put in storage. It seems incredible, but a friend, Earl Sims, who operated a machine shop, offered to store our machinery if we loaned him a machine for the duration. I am sure that he estimated that if our machinery was in storage, it could not be in competition to his business. Brother Frank, highly skilled in machine work and welding, became employed at Minnkota Power Company where he remained until his retirement.

Closing the shop was a devastating blow to Dad Young. Here were his three sons working together with a successful start in general machine work and welding. Added to that was a good start in die work, in both stampings and plastic molding.

Storing heavy machinery was a difficult assignment. We had so little time. Dad joined us after his work day at the mill ended at 3:00 P.M. There was very little conversation. Everyone was tense. I will never forget seeing tear drops from Dad, falling on the machine he prepared for the move.

On the plus side, we still owed $2,000.00 on the shop contract. It seems incredible that our last account receivable covered the debt. I am certain this was Divine intervention.

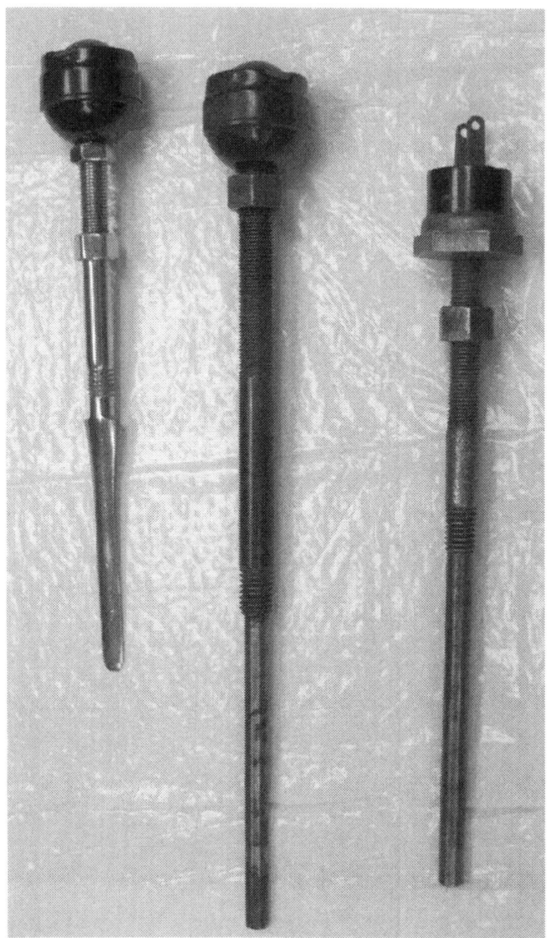

On our return from Korea, my brother and I had to take employment temporarily where we could until we were able to set up shop again.

(Brother Roland added the following: Having acquired extensive skills in machining practice in Minneapolis, MN prior to service during the war, Dick now chose to take a job as machine shop instructor at the University of North Dakota Engineering Department. While employed there he was contacted by Andrew (Andy) Freeman, the manager of Minnkota Power Company. Andy wanted to have a small hole drilled through an automotive head bolt, so Dick drilled the first head bolt for what became the revolutionary

"Head Bolt Heater" invented by 'Andy'. The defective parts were salvaged and made into letter openers. This was the forerunner of the present block heaters commonly used to aid in starting vehicles in old climates.

Andy progressed with development of the Head Bolt Heater design and formed the Five Star Manufacturing to produce the units).

In 1954, we were able to build a 32 foot by 60 foot Quonset on the property now occupied by ACME ELECTRIC CO. We took our machinery out of storage and as before, with limited funds, we put in extra hours to get everything put together with much effort by other family members. It seems we had learned the cooperative spirit early in our lives. The time frame for our new shop was limited to one year. Mr. Andrew Freeman, a well known businessman, who was the Manager of Minnkota Power Company, asked us to join him with several other businessmen to form a new business to manufacture specialty items. The first was a universal motor mount to use with home workshop tools. Also, on his agenda were sanders as seen around our shop today. Included were industrial floor lamps, and he asked all of us to be alert to new ideas for the home and family workshop.

Mr. Freeman was an aggressive person, and did not hesitate to request that we think of him as General Manager of this new enterprise. The name "Young Machine Works" was replaced with the name "ARCO". Most of us believed it was an acronym for "Andy's Research Company". He did, however, say that he wanted to be in the "A" column in the phone book. All this was of little importance to us, as it may be told, it was a major adjustment to have a stranger come in and literally take over our setup. I am sure he meant no harm, but it was very hard to send our customers away who were looking to have work done as before.

These businessmen invested financially. My brother and I were literally stripped of any reserve, so we could not invest as they did. The machinery was ours, and rather than use any of our own money for stock, we were issued stock certificates, which we understood covered rent for our tools and machinery.

This ARCO Company was not interested in general machine work. Hard as it was, we bit the bullet and made every attempt to work in the framework as presented.

Some advantages were forth coming. We no longer had to concern ourselves with taxes and running expenses. So my brother and I could concentrate on developing a wider range of die making experience which has been a benefit to this day.

This stint with ARCO lasted 11 years. My brother and I became disenchanted with a relatively modest production that seemed to have no growth. We decided that we should return to our major type of work.

We left the ARCO Company with good feelings, and in 1966, we purchased a horse training Quonset barn on the property now occupied by our steel buildings.

ARCO needed most of the machinery in use in their facility, but we took a few pieces they could spare and that was the start of building up all over again. The dealings with ARCO were quite involved, but in this time frame, we look back and conclude that all is well after we received some compensation from ARCO when the Company was sold to an organization in Racine, Wisconsin. In 1966 42nd Street was just a dirt road. It was our lot to run a concrete floor in a building that had no running water and only an old oil drum made into a stove for heat. This was the third time we had a grass roots start in setting up shop.

I feel it is worth telling that we were not depressed with this country setting. The property included several acres so we were not cramped for space. But we were back to square one and we had to rebuild our trade.

One of my friends who was the foreman of a telephone line crew had several trucks and other equipment that regularly required repair. I told

Charley that we would try to give him a good deal if he would bring us his trucks during that first winter. We worked on the mechanisms used for auguring poles and other boom equipment.

Since our income was very light, we found it necessary to provide heat with scrap wood. Trucking companies became a great source for our burning wood with cast-off broken pallets. After hours, we used our pickup to gather pallets and cut them up for the next day burning.

Working with the telephone men was like an answer to a prayer. An unexpected bonus came one day when a truck driver stopped in with a truck needing some work and hooked to the truck was a large trailer load of telephone poles.

I asked the driver, Andy Terry, where he was going with the poles. He said, "To the dump". I told him to drop them in our yard. He seemed rather pleased that the chore of going to the dump was over. If that truck hadn't a need for repairs, we may have never seen the drama to follow.

Now with the pole business providing fire wood in addition to the pallets, we felt quite fortunate to have fire wood delivered without any effort on our part.

And, lo and behold, when the city park board learned of the poles being dumped in our yard, they started bringing large loads of trees removed from the park district. Actually the trees mostly dry wood, provided better heating than the telephone poles. But hold the fort, we kept adding to the stockpile of telephone poles. Now we entered into a phase of activity that seemed to be part of destiny. I believe it was my brother who suggested that if we are to add to the Quonset, let's go for pole barn construction. I do not recall the exact time frame, but it was nearing fall, I believe, in 1967. This same Andy Terry, who thrived on extra duty, not only brought more poles but brought the auger truck to dig down the poles after we had marked out the spacing for the first building addition.

The poles were dropped in holes seven feet deep which placed them below the frost line. By this time, we had hired several young men. Some of them were Airmen looking for extra duty. I am pleased to report that the work we were doing was new to them as well as we the owners, and the enthusiastic response was a joy to behold.

These men not only ran machines in the shop, but also eagerly joined in the building program in progress. We did not hire any professional help for the entire project. We needed warm weather to set the poles in place. After the walls and roof were in place, we could work inside on the walls and ceilings. It took quite a few months to accomplish the total building program, all using the pole type construction.

Most people who visit our business would not know that the old pole buildings, now covered over by the modern steel buildings, still stand. The poles cannot be seen.

When we think of pole buildings, we may be inclined to think of unattractive styling. Our main office still stands as the first of these buildings added to the Quonset in 1967.

Judy, Misty and Thora are all in neat offices with new interiors but the original area was actually a machine shop and welding space. Our first main office is now shipping and receiving with work space for Sandra to carry on her work. The redwood paneling was done by Dick, Sr. The small office used by Steff is another one of these pole buildings, and I may add that the tool room, the general machine shop, the VMC (vertical machining center) room, the EDM (electrical discharge machine) room, Jon Heff's space and Scott Peterson's repair shop all have the same styling from a construction standpoint. One other thought I will add to the list is the suite of offices upstairs.

Whereas, the main construction has been thoroughly explained, hats off to Dave Breidenbach and crew for the great job of trim and ceilings. I have not said much about our work load, but going back to the days when pole construction was under way, Roland and I believed we should research other areas for possible custom work. We made a trip to Arctic Enterprises in 1968. We had no knowledge that they were having trouble producing snow mobile cleats in the numbers required. We offered a system to achieve the need and we were favored with a contract to build dies for cleat production.

That opened up the major part of our business as the requirements for cleats for one year was 10 million. That establishes Arctic Enterprises as our largest customer for over 30 years. Cleat work had to be discontinued due to safety regulations; however, other needs have surpassed our first experience.

I have squeezed in thoughts about the building several times, but there is another part to consider that cannot be overlooked. We had to work on the buildings along with production. Placing sheet rock on the sidewalls was rather routine, but the ceilings created a new challenge.

Four foot by twelve foot sheets were heavy and unwieldy. Our first look at the job required scaffolds and extra hands. The inventive nature of Roland brought out the use of a heavy work cart that he rigged up with a system of levers and a cradle to hold the sheets. Using a small chain hoist, we were able to lift the sheets to the ceiling and hold them in place for nailing. The unit could be used by one man. That sheet rock work can still be seen in all of the old shop buildings.

I visited another business in Grand Forks and saw a worker struggling to place a heavy sheet on the ceiling. I offered him the use of our temporary unit.

When Roland learned of the transaction, he considered, if they could use one, who else? That led him to develop a new production model. Young Mfg. did not have space enough to carry on the new project. In 1973, Rolly opened his own factory exclusively for the production of a sheet rock lift he named PANELLIFT. Rolly has added other products requiring telescopic features. He then coined the word TELPRO as the new Company name.

At this juncture, 2002, Roland and I each own separate companies. Space to tell all the intricate workings of our factories would require many more sheets. Family members have been a vital part of our growth and most of our employees know them and work with them.

Dick Jr. spent many years in the Young plant, but he and his wife, Lorna had roots in Fergus Falls, Minnesota area. His desire to run a business led him and Lorna to research that city for a laser shop. He is well established there and is doing well with a major setup of special lasers.

David was eight years old when the Quonset was purchased and he showed interest in the workings of machinery early enough that he came to work on small machines at age 13. Finishing school in Fergus Falls, after graduation in 1976, he came on full time at the Young shop. He found his lovely wife, Beth, at Hillcrest Academy in Fergus Falls, Minnesota.

Judy has had more family members join the force than the others and I am very thankful for all to be working in harmony. If I have forgotten anyone, I am sorry.

The purpose of this report may be obvious. The intent of Dad Young had one central desire, to instill in his sons and other young men in the family the worth of an early introduction to a valuable trade. In keeping with his wishes, my brother and I have tried to carry on the same idea to make the workings of the machine trade available to both young men and women.

There may have been times when we experienced some real challenges. Arctic Cat went broke in 1980, but came back strong in 1982. The military setback when we had to close shop was another scary experience. But Dad Young continued a careful watch for the Manufacturing Company after his retirement at age 72. Even then, he was not a bystander. He built sturdy benches that may be seen in several places in the shop. Dad lived to age 89 just a few weeks short of his 90th birthday. May his memory be blessed.

I wish to thank everyone on our payroll that continues to produce quality work and also the office force that we could not do without. The last sheet covers an entirely different subject matter. I believe it contains thoughts we need to consider.

War affects all of us in different ways. I am almost reluctant to observe that in two cases I was able to benefit in a shop practice through the temporary trade school and then on to the defense plant.

My service time came about as a matter of course, but I do not regret my involvement, The Korean War, as noted came close to shutting us down. I am thankful for the recovery.

Viet Nam, the Gulf War and other conflicts have impacted our government and caused the use of troops on foreign soil. Following the 9/11 attack in New York, President Bush announced, very strongly, that we are at war. At the time we were not sure it may affect young men who may have to answer the call. The attack alerted the entire USA plus other countries.

We all recall that our President asked for prayer, to seek the will of God. Almost immediately, signs appeared everywhere. God bless America. Flag waving became the order of the day.

When a President takes a lead position in Spiritual matters, it ought to remind us of the dedication of our founding fathers. They played a major role in establishing the American way of life.

The Declaration of Independence in 1776, the framers of the Constitution in 1787, and the authors of the Federalist and other papers of the time, have been recognized as the wisest assemblage of men during any single era of human history.

Every one of them emphasized the need for recognizing God. My favorite is Patrick Henry, a truly great orator. Here is his personal quote recorded in numerous volumes in our libraries: "It cannot be emphasized too strongly, or too often, that this great nation was founded not by religionists, but by Christians; not on religions, but by the Gospel of Jesus Christ. For this very reason peoples of other faiths have been afforded asylum, prosperity and freedom of worship here."

There are others; Samuel Adams, Ben Franklin, George Washington and Noah Webster to name a few. They all echoed the same report.

It is my personal conviction, that when our Nation's leaders seek God's will for our country, even a modest business could do well to adopt the same principles.

Dick Young

ZIPEE BELT SANDER

Sometime in the early 1980s Dad (Dick, Sr.) began to have a strong desire to manufacture his own product; an invention that he could design and build in his own shop and sell to the general public. The desire may have come from the fact that some of our largest customers were struggling to stay in business and the future of Young Manufacturing seemed to be constantly at the mercy of our customers. By having our own product our destiny could possibly be controlled a little better. I also believe part of his aspiration was just to create a better 'mouse trap' of some sort.

Dad often told me about a fellow who created an inexpensive electric drill for homeowners. After all his manufacturing costs were covered he added $1.00 to establish a selling price. This businessman supposedly sold one million electric drills, and of course, made one million dollars in the process! Dad always stated that he didn't go into business to get rich. In some ways, I think he was more interested in the idea of making one million of something than to earn a million bucks!

While Dad worked with the ARCO Company, one of the items they produced was a belt sander made for use in home workshops. We had a few of those old machines scattered around the shop that we used for deburring parts and shaping metal. We still have some of those old ARCO sanders in use yet in 2017! Dad spoke often about developing an improved sander, but, at the same time, he thought it would be nice to have something less bulky and heavy. He wanted a sander that could do some real work, but was small enough to carry to a worksite instead of having to carry the work to the sander!

Dad wanted to use a 'stock' sanding belt to build the sander around, instead of designing a sander that used 'specialty' belts that could only be purchased from one source. He wanted the owner of each sander to have the right to purchase replacement belts anywhere he/she could find them and not lock them into a single source and, very likely, a higher price. The belt he found was 3/4" X 20-1/2" long. It was an industrial belt that came in many different grit sizes. Most stores did not stock them, but they could be found without too much trouble through industrial supply companies.

Always on the lookout for what he thought would be the 'right sized' motor, Dad found a small water pump that had a fairly fast running motor and was in the size range he was looking for. After some research, Dad found that the motor was made by a company in Racine, Wisconsin called MAMCO Motors.

The pump motor ran a little slower than what Dad wanted, so he went to Wisconsin and visited the MAMCO plant. After discussing his needs with an engineer at MAMCO, a sample motor was designed that spun about 10,000 rpm with no load. This may sound like a lot of speed, but it was actually necessary to provide the sander with the ability to do some work. Being that the sander was small in the first place, the drive wheels and idlers also needed to be small. By contrast, the ARCO sander used a slower motor, but it incorporated a larger drive wheel, which increased the surface speed of the belt. To get the greatest amount of surface feet per minute, Dad decided that the higher speed motor was the ticket! Even then, the minuscule drag of the idler wheels and slight stiffness of the sanding belts dropped the actual speed of the motor down to about 6,000 rpm and heavy pressure could stop the belt, but it was adequate for most applications.

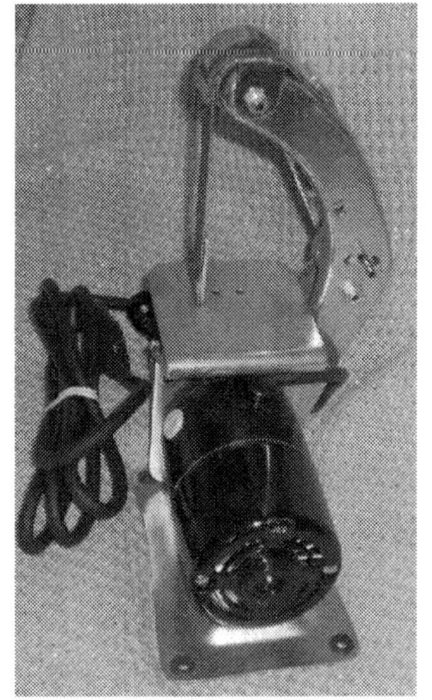

Soon after Dad completed the first handmade sample, he thought it would be interesting to get some feedback from a local company called ACME Electric that sold quality tools for both homeowner and light industrial use. Dad's hope was to find an outlet like ACME to sell the sander through. We took a little time and came up with an estimated price for the sanders. The sander would not be cheap, but it was a quality tool.

Dad made an appointment with the owner of ACME and paid him a visit. At the same time, a man from Taiwan was also at the store. He was a representative of one of the companies that sold imported tools to ACME. The owner of ACME showed Dad's sander to this fellow from Taiwan. He took the sander, set it on the counter, looked it all over, got out a pen, a note pad and a calculator and a few minutes later said he could make one for just slightly over half the price we thought was reasonable! This was a shock for us. Our intention was to gain some local support for the product, and instead we felt totally shot down.

Since there was no other small sander on the market at the time, Dad decided to press forward with the project. We had some young men working for us that wanted to learn the tooling trade and Dad felt that this project was a perfect way to provide needed training to the crew and get his sanders made at the same time. All the sheet metal parts were manufactured and assembled to the motors in our shop. The ZIPEE Belt Sander was a petite size, 10" high and weighed 7-1/4 lbs.

After we had saleable, working models, it was tough to find an outlet for them. Our pricing structure was not appropriate for sales through most stores. This was due to the high cost of the motors and the costs associated with making and assembling relatively small quantities of sanders. Volume helps to bring prices down, but you need sales to increase volume!

Sales were slow, but over time some niche markets came to light. One use was in the jewelry industry. We actually sold some of our sanders through a catalog company that specialized in tools and equipment for jewelers. Another outlet was some woodcarver associations. The carvers found that by using a rheostat they could slow down the sander and get very fine cutting edges on their tools. One other place we sold some sanders in fair quantity was to machine shops that found they could use our sanders to deburr parts right at the CNC (computerized numerical control) equipment. Not long ago, I spoke with a shop owner who commented on how well the sanders worked and was sad that they were no longer available. Over time, we probably sold several hundred sanders but without a good market scheme, sales began to dry up. It's been many years since the last sander was sold, but I know of several that are still in use.

Of note, just a couple months after we met the Taiwanese fellow at ACME, we got a call to come down to their store to look at a small sander they got in for the importer. It had a larger motor and a slightly larger belt, but the same basic idea Dad had was there! I will always believe that Dad's 'idea' was copied that day! Written by: David Young, 2017

MAKING RESPONSE TO CUSTOMERS A TOP PRIORITY SINCE 1947

(Taken from article written for YOUNG TIMES - fall 2007)

From modest beginnings as a small machine and repair shop, Young Manufacturing has seen many changes over the years. But they have not forgotten how that journey began. This excursion started sixty years ago with the inevitable ups and downs many businesses experience. Through the test of time, the business flourishes today.

After returning from World War II in January 1946, Richard E. (Dick) Young came home to Grand Forks, ND to resume a normal life and find steady work. In smaller Grand Forks there weren't any large factory jobs like he had experienced in Minneapolis before entering the war. Instead, Dick found employment at a small local welding and repair shop. Only a short while later, the owners decided to dissolve their partnership and let it be known they wanted to sell the business and equipment.

In 1947 "Young Brothers Machine Works" was established. Dick, along with his brothers Roland and Frank, purchased the equipment for $7000 and set up shop in a rented building.

Just as the business was getting started, it was nearly lost due to an interruption of the Korean War in June of 1950. Roland and Dick had both joined the National Guard and were notified to report for active duty. Frank, a skilled machinist, went to work for Minnkota Power Cooperative where he stayed until he retired. The equipment was moved into storage for the duration of the war.

Upon return from their duty in Korea, Dick and Roland took temporary employment until they were able to build a 32 x 60 foot Quonset in 1954. But after one year this endeavor ended due to a lack of funds.

A local businessman and entrepreneur, Andy Freeman, who was also the General Manager of Minnkota Power Cooperative, asked Dick and Roland to join him and other businessmen to form a new business to manufacture specialty items. The group formed ARCO (which many believed was an acronym for Andy's Research Company), and it was housed in the Young Brothers building.

After eleven years with this organization Dick and Roland decided to leave the ARCO venture and go out on their own again. The brothers were able to take a few pieces of equipment with them when they left.

(ARCO was sold some years later to an organization that moved the remaining machinery and product line to Racine, Wisconsin to provide work in an impoverished area of the city).

In 1966 they purchased a horse training Quonset on a rutted dirt road outside city limits.

Dick Young with David Young 2007 Grand Forks, North Dakota

This is where the business is located today, only now the company is housed in a new steel building, on a paved street (now called 42nd Street North) and is once again within city limits due to city expansion.

After acquiring this new facility, the two brothers started to rebuild their business for the third time. In 1968 Dick and Roland made a trip to Arctic Enterprises in Thief River Falls, MN, hoping to find some tool and die work. They were asked to research a better way of producing the steel track cleats, then used on Arctic Cat snowmobiles. A contract was awarded them to build dies for cleat production, and was probably the break they needed to propel their company into the business that it is today. In 1973 Roland started his own business (TELPRO, INC.) to manufacture and sell a sheetrock lifting device he designed for use in the construction industry, which he called the "PANELLIFT".

David Young, Dick Sr.'s youngest son, is President of the company today. Dave remembers as a young boy spending time at his dad's shop and began working there on odd jobs when he was twelve. Young Mfg., Inc. has expanded over the years from primarily tool and die and metal stamping to a complete metal fabrication facility that includes Laser Cutting, CNC (computerized numerical control) Press Brakes and CNC Machining. The company employs fifty people and continues to have a strong customer base in the area.

Since the early years, the business has seen many changes and many positive results, including other family members who once worked at Young Mfg., Inc. and have left to start their own successful businesses. This year marks the sixtieth year since it all started in 1947.

TRAIN PARTS & HISTORY
Dick Young, Sr.
June 6, 2002

It was still depression days in the 1930s, when my desire to own a model train was very much intact. My father. a very practical German man said he wouldn't buy a train. but would help me build one. His knowledge of shop practice was such that the family workshop became the focal point for the project. His knowledge of steam engines and locomotives was truly the element, which made the project possible.

While I worked on the frame and related drive train sections, Dad carved out a maple wood block with the shape of locomotive wheels. Using high quality nickel babbit, we could melt the metal on the kitchen stove and pour it into the wooden mold.

It worked very well. However, I learned the lesson that the mold should cool naturally and not use cold water to hurry the process. Steam created by hot metal, literally caused the operation to explode. Luckily no one was hurt.

The parts displayed on this shelf (at Young Mfg.) are from our own expression of design and not following orthodox plans. I believe we would have had a difficult time to actually create a working model of the New York Central locomotive we hoped to copy.

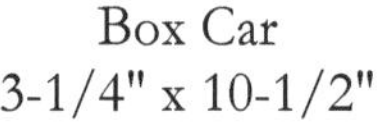

Box Car
3-1/4" x 10-1/2"

All this took place in 1937, when I was still in high school. I had one more year before graduating from high school, but my experience in the family shop led me to a part time job in a local machine shop. I became so involved in the apprentice work, my time was completely used up. Home-made train parts were shelved until a better time.

At this juncture, 65 years later, the locomotive parts plus other train assemblies remain shelved. Hanging on the wall, above the locomotive parts, is the remnant of track parts developed in the home workshop shaped in a "Y".

I sincerely believe that Divine leading was the strong element in creating the background in the home workshop which has been a strong factor in developing the family machine shop and factory, which today is YOUNG MFG.

SPECIAL MOMENTS

(It seems like this article was written by Dick to his brother Rolly, when Dick might have been in his eighties)

Recently I saw an article that got my attention. The suggestion was made that we tap our memories and recall the most outstanding memory of our lives.

We lived in a large frame home in Anoka, MN. I was ten years old and the evening was a soul searching time when several members of the family were afflicted with an inflamed throat problem called quinsy. I had never heard of it before, and for some reason I was spared.

My one year old baby brother could not express his need, but he too was very weak and my parents took turns holding him. I was shocked to hear them say that he may not live until morning.

They tucked baby Rolly in a baby buggy in the front room near their bedroom. The actual time is not clear, but I felt the need to be near. It was a clear morning and I pulled up a chair and sat near his side - just waiting. My prayer life was limited to table and bed time prayers, but I felt that God was near. It would be difficult to express my reaction when, with his last ounce of energy, Rolly sat straight up in bed and that growth in his throat burst. He has recovered very well from that as well as did other family members.

We were going through the lean 1930s, and Dad Young felt the need to find work that would supply our family as needed. He answered an ad for a night watchman in the Twin City (Minneapolis/St. Paul) area. This happened to be an assembly of buildings used by an organization called Western Fruit Express.

We rented a large 2-story home over a mile from where Dad worked. Walking to work in those days was the 'norm'.

Some things happen very unexpectedly, but Rolly experienced a tumble with his sister down a stairway, but fortunately, nobody was hurt.

It seems worth reporting experiences where Dad worked. The actual location was better known at the time as midway between Minneapolis and Saint Paul. If memory serves me correctly a major avenue leading up to the work place was Snelling Ave. However, traffic in those days was not considered dangerous as developed in later years.

The name of Dad's new work place was known as Western Fruit Express. Trains were put together there as needed. To my young mind it was not important how all the offices were used. It all seemed to be the 'norm'. The enclosed rail yard had no activity after dark in any of the buildings. I believe Dad carried some sort of a side arm, but I do not recall any need requiring a gun.

Having a dog was acceptable and Dad had found a beautiful female dog. He named her Lady. I did not object to taking a sack lunch to Dad before dark and it was necessary that I walk about a mile to the rail yard. One night as I came near the yard, I was disturbed to see a police car in the yard. I sensed something wrong and the police were looking at the body of our dog - Lady.

She was guilty of chasing locomotives, and as she tired and gave up the chase, the step up to the cab caught her and skinned her back up to her shoulders. It was necessary to put her to sleep.

Accompanying my dad as he made his rounds seemed as a natural assignment for me. I do not recall hearing my mother question dad's motives.

There were overhead walkways in the rail yards but I do not recall ever needing to use the facility. There were a number of locations where the night watchman was required to key the location and the time of day or night became a factor. I do not remember any activity that seemed unusual.

I recall one day when Dad was required to be on the job in daylight. I happened to be there at the time. What disturbed me was to see Dad sitting near some wall, and he had tears in his eyes. To a kid that had some serious overtones.

I never felt that the job had any real meaning for a skilled craftsman. But kids are subject to the parents' wishes and all we could do was wait for the next move. That job lasted only 3 months. Dad felt that the job had no future, and it perhaps DID occur to him that an 11 year kid ought not be carrying a lunch to him and that to stay all night was not wise.

But those things are past, and by some stroke of luck, Dad was able to return to the Anoka property. I think it is very interesting to note the excitement on the part of little Rolly when we approached the house that dad had not sold, and he exclaimed - 'Daddy goody'.

This message gives a fairly good sketch of Rolly's early life. He didn't realize at that time that his inventive genius would lead him to become a vital member of the manufacturing world. His large factory in South Grand Forks, N.D. is evidence that his energies have been put to good use.

Best wishes, brother Rolly. Sincerely, in Jesus Love Dick

Dick Young

Roland (Rol) Young

2007

ITCHING TO FLY

Startled by their sudden appearance, I was intrigued as a handsome couple entered the open door without making a sound. They moved around, checked everything in sight, and finally settled in what they considered to be the living area. They paid no attention to me.

Within moments they began chattering, almost as if to outdo each other. I could not tell, by their foreign language whether they were arguing or agreeing. I did not see them as intruders, but rather welcomed their unusual behavior. But soon they left, leaving a question in my mind as to what may follow.

Within an hour they returned, and then began one of the most fascinating series of episodes that I have ever had the privilege to witness. Right before my eyes, domestic and family responsibilities unfolded as a beautiful pair of barn swallows chose our modest shop as the site for building their unattractive but functional nest, high in the superstructure above the over-head door.

How that energetic pair knew each other's moves to create the mud, straw, and slime nest is a mystery. Understandably, professional bird watchers have the edge over a novice like me, but in this case, I was a student while our feathered friends taught me.

Our Quonset machine shop had a second floor in its rear which provided us with office space. The front portion of the building was open clear to the ridge. And, in this arrangement, my brother and I could witness from the office window the day-by-day activity of our guests.

The swallows placed the first daub of mud on the upper end of a 2x4 brace which supported the over-head door hardware. Their work appeared to be endless, as progress was accomplished by the beak full. I was fascinated by the team-work of these birds as the black and white nest, held together by grass and sticks, took shape. The final touch was soft material, probably mostly hair, that lined the cavity.

Truly the female was in charge which was, perhaps, to be expected. As soon as the job was complete, she settled down in the nest with a side-to-side motion that suggested she was shaping the liner. Then began a monologue in bird language which I think I interpreted properly. The male sat motionless about six feet away while the female - facing in his direction - chattered more vigorously than before. I later figured out that she was saying to him, "You lazy bum. What are you doing over there? You know what comes next".

In due time, more activity was noticeable. Five smooth eggs were being tenderly incubated by the warm bodies of the expectant pair. I was amazed by the incredibly short space of time it took for five yellow beaks to appear hanging over the edge of the nest. It was the time of year when the weather cooperated; and for what turned out as a convenience to the birds, the large overhead door was open each work day from 6:30 a.m. until 6:30 p.m.

Soon a longer time frame for having the door open became necessary for the barn swallows' food gathering. I then decided that the closest I could come for the birds' convenience was to remove one 5 inch by 12 inch pane of glass from the door for their after-hours activity. I estimated that the wing span of barn swallows was several inches more than the width of the opening.

I couldn't just shrug all this off and treat it as if it was only the birds' problem; but I soon learned that the graceful techniques of these air-borne creatures were far ahead of my concerns. Not a feather was ruffled as their sharp banking and wing tucking allowed perfect entrance for them through this narrow opening. These two adult birds were equal to the challenge.

Growth of the babies was rapid. Before long, I could see gray fuzz above the rim of the nest. Then I saw something taking place that bothered me greatly. It seemed that the nest was literally churning with activity. The young birds were picking at themselves with their beaks in a frenzied fashion that suggested they might be covered with bird lice - a real cause for itching.

Would it be possible, I thought, to provide some means to rid them of such pests? But, I knew that any interference on my part would cause greater problems for the birds, so I merely continued to watch with interest as their strange picking continued. But the picking appeared to be regulated. After awhile the picking ceased, the nest became quiet and I supposed that the baby birds were sleeping.

During feeding time every beak was open wide. Bugs and moths were the main course. And again, how all five babies were fed equally was another mystery to me. I failed to record the length of time of development of the little birds, but I was continually surprised at their rapid growth.

One early afternoon, I walked into the shop below the nesting area and looked up and saw what I believed was a visit from full grown birds. Not so. There, sitting on the rim of the nest, were five fully developed orange-breasted birds, all facing one way. This was the first I had seen the entire brood still clinging to the comfort of the nest. But all were serene. No picking. Had the lice disappeared?

One of the adult birds, presumably the mother, began again with the language of birds. Sitting nearby, giving instructions, she swooped down in a looping fashion and returned to the spot. This she did several times. Suddenly in one grand sweep, all five young birds followed the female out the door, and were as graceful in flight as experienced swallows.

What a thrilling sight as these colorful young birds mounted up into the wind. Trees blocked part of the view, and I was certain they had scattered. Later, I saw birds sitting on a high line wire several hundred feet away and wondered, could they be the same ones?

Closing time for the shop approached and I felt a twinge of the feeling that goes with saying, "goodbye". The nest was empty and there was not a bird in sight. What now? My sense of duty suggested I stay awhile with the big door open. I thought, "How would the fledglings get in otherwise"?

About an hour later, a call from home reminded me that supper was growing cold and I should close the door and close down operations. As I left the shop, a warm evening breeze seemed to dispel any real concern I had for our feathered friends.

The next morning I witnessed one of the most rewarding sights that could greet anyone. There, sitting on a wire in the height of the Quonset interior, as close as the knuckles on my hand, were five orange breasts; all facing toward the main door. The great Instructor we refer to as "instinct", and perhaps more correctly "Providence" had brought the family together again in the Quonset through the door's narrow opening. That was the last I saw of this entertaining troupe.

That feverish picking - it still puzzled me. It all took place while the young birds were developing. No doubt, as each new feather pierced their tender skin, the itching sensation was alleviated by their picking. Whether the experts would agree with me or not, I can't say. I am inclined to believe it was nature's way of accomplishing two things - preening feathers with a great form of exercise truly preparing the bodies of these creatures who were "itching to fly".

Dick Young

"Waifs" In Want

By Richard E. Young

It is over twenty years ago that I became aware of worldwide poverty. I had heard of poverty, which, for the most part, seems to describe a condition belonging to someone else. I was able to take a philosophical point of view of the misfortunes of the population in general, yet never wishing to rid myself of the duty of lending a hand where able. However, it seems one generally becomes engrossed in personal pursuits, and the needs of others are left to fate.

As a boy, I recall judging poverty as a relative thing. Whoever was financially better off than my father was rich, and whoever had less than our family was poor. Though my father felt the full brunt of the depression, I don't remember ever going without food. Clothing to a boy is only a necessity, which in our case was adequate. The poverty of my parents, if any, went by me entirely. I perhaps never would have known if there was actual suffering. We always had a garden, a few head of cattle and a bunch of chickens.

At age sixteen, I took a job as a carpenter apprentice; and from that day, I have been blessed with steady employment. Poverty is not felt by one like myself who only experiences an occasional financial uncertainty.

Far flung as my encounters with those in need have been, the start of it was in France during World War II. We had unloaded from trucks and marched through the strife-torn city of LeHavre. Small faces peered through the crowd of civilian onlookers in sheer wonder at the sight of American soldiers, who, in their thinking, were filthy rich. Their inexhaustible source of chewing gum, chocolate, and cigarettes never ceased to amaze especially the younger set. Hollow-eyed youngsters, many of them orphans, were among those who watched hundreds of well-fed soldiers march in full combat garb to the bivouac area in the outlying parts of the city.

Snow covered the ground; streets were slushy, and the chilly wind whined through our helmets. Trying hard to give a moment of feeling towards those in need, the verity of the situation climaxed as a small boy dived after an apple care tossed by a soldier.

I knew I would never see the little fellow again, yet he left an indelible imprint on my mind - that hunger gripped Europe. Another element entered into the picture, the lack of warm clothing.

During my first night in camp my wool-knit cap was stolen. Perhaps I should say it was merely transferred to a head that needed it worse than I.

It was not the work of a GI, but some youngster. Small boys hung around all military establishments looking for candy or cigarettes. Nearly all of them smoked regardless of age. A smoldering cigarette had only to lie for a new seconds when it was promptly snatched up for a few more puffs.

I needed a wool-knit cap. There were none in the supply truck, and neither could I find anyone who had an extra cap. A slight French boy, about nine or ten years old, was standing near the PX truck. He wore no coat; his shoulders were hunched from the cold. He was puffing on a cigarette he had just picked up. The cigarette was really too short to be held, but the boy managed.

He asked me for "chocolate" and a cigarette for "Papa". I was more interested in the wool-knit Army cap he wore. "How much for the cap?", I asked. His only answer was "Cigarette um Papa".

I bargained for the cap. It was not the one I had lost, for my own was plainly marked. The boy must have worn it day and night for weeks. The rim inside the headband was thickly coated with grease from his hair, and inside the earlaps he had stored wads of chewing gum for the future.

After I had made the deal, I nearly changed my mind, except, I did need a cap before going to the front. I carefully carved the gum out of the earlaps and washed the cap in cold water using face soap. The perfumed aroma remained in the cap almost all winter serving one purpose - to remind me of a little lad in want. He, no doubt, could have used the cap, but he had an unusually thick head of hair. His real need was a coat.

The incidents of little children wearing tattered clothing, and waiting near the chow lines wherever field kitchens were set up, was a common sight all over Europe. In Karlsruhe, Germany, a little girl with stringy brown hair stood expectantly, watching men emptying their mess-kits of leftovers. She held a battered gallon can and kept a large spoon poised, ready to reach out with a quick swipe at some edible morsel remaining on a mess-kit.

When chow was over, GIs of all ranks lined up for cleaning mess-gear. All utensils were washed in boiling, soapy water after passing the garbage cans. Into the garbage went unused coffee, hunks of bread, small pieces of meat, or a spoonful of cold mashed potatoes topped with a smashed cigarette. Several inches of coffee in the bottom of the can, hid the heavier material that went to the bottom. Cigarettes and pieces of bread floated in the coffee. As each man banged his kit on the edge of the garbage can, immediately three youngsters quickly bent over the can scooping out anything they could grab. One lad came up with hands clasping a few peas and chunks of carrots. After several dives into the can, he had enough for 'essen', and dashed home with his prize.

Occasionally, an obliging GI bent down and helped sort out a few remnants from his mess-tray. I believe some soldiers went back for 'seconds' in order to present a more appetizing offering to those little 'waifs' in want.

Our commanding officer issued a edict, that no cigarettes would be extinguished in mess-trays; and that some consideration be given to hungry youngsters who may have otherwise gone unfed.

Our units rarely stayed anywhere long enough to get to know any of these little personalities, yet the behavior of the children of the continent was the same everywhere. I witnessed youngsters and grown-ups alike, scrounging around the Army mess dumps; and some went home with nothing more than a few potato peelings.

The scene continued to shift to Nuremberg, Munich, Wolfgang, Salzburg, Linz and others. Every Army mess was frequented by the hungry. Some of the more enterprising youths had learned to perform some service, thereby qualifying for a more consistent dividend.

It was amazing what one could do with a package of chewing gum. As First Sergeant of my unit, I was required to see that the area was 'policed' around headquarters. Unidentified tots, constantly waiting for a handout, stayed in close rage of our operation. I recruited five boys and girls, about age six. I demonstrated how a piece of paper, or some other refuse, should be gathered and placed in waste containers. The eager youngsters quickly caught on, and did a most satisfying job for the payment of one stick of gum each. It was heartwarming to see the delight registered in their faces. Five dirty faced little kids hurried down the street when the work was done to "tell someone" they had some "choon-gum".

My military duty took me from Europe back to the States, and eventually to the Far East for Korean Service. Poverty was even more pronounced, it seemed, in the ravaged South Korea. The language barrier and the indoctrination of the youth by Communist leaders present most difficult situation.

American food was not known to Korean children. Communists had told them the Americans 'poisoned' the chocolate. Children, dwarfed by malnutrition, often shrank away from servicemen who offered them some "favor", their eyes filled with fear.

I shall never forget the night our train carrying troops to the front was waiting on a side track for the box lunch break. The lunches came in a white cardboard container with a couple of ham-in-a-bun sandwiches, a pickle, an orange, a hardboiled egg, and a candy bar. Undoubtedly, the operation was well known to many of Korea's orphans near Pusan. When the truck arrived, children came out of cardboard boxes and shipping crates. From under the loading docks, and wherever a small body could find shelter, a stream of three to ten year olds hit for the train.

Their bare legs were blue from February temperatures. The only known footwear most were able to possess was a small low-cut rubber shoe. Dirty little hands with long uncut nails, cracked from the cold, and rough as turkey claws, were held out as the children begged in strange utterings.

I doubt if there was a man on that train who hadn't offered something, and many turned over their entire lunch. The haunting, dark-eyed small fry backed away and stood, clutching an orange or an egg, perhaps not knowing what to do with it. Soon the train chugged away, and the fate of that group remains a mystery.

In the course of time, I returned home. Year after year the radio, and the newspapers carried the message that we should CARE. Shortly before Christmas 1963, I received a letter from the Holy Land Christian Approach Mission in Kansas City, Missouri. An appeal was made to help donate to the orphanage in Bethlehem.

I was very busy, but I recall considering my bank balance and managed to slip a 'twenty' into an envelope, mailed it, and forgot it. I don't remember giving it anymore thought than dropping a coin in the Santa workers' kettles.

Sometime after Christmas, I received a letter from the Mission Director's wife. She named a little girl that was associated with my 'gift' and sent a picture of her. I had not known until then that I would be a foster parent. The little girl is Nawal Tumm, born in Kwait, Jordan in 1959. Her father died shortly after she was born. Her mother, unable to care for the entire family, released her to the orphanage.

After receiving the letter and picture, I made the decision to continue a $10.00 monthly check for Nawal's support. Her caretaker wrote me one day that Nawal was able to have a beautiful Christmas because of the donation. Words are not able to describe the feeling that gripped me as I read further in the letter, that though she could not speak my language, she wanted me to know that SHE prayed for ME every day.

WHO'S HANDICAPPED?

In March, 1972, Dick wrote an article for consideration to be published in the Reader's Digest. The OPPORTUNITY TRAINING CENTER is still operating in Grand Forks under a different name some forty four years later. Since it was a part of Dick's 'life' after his wartime experiences, we are including it in this book.

Little did I dream that a casual comment to a stranger would trigger an unusual and rewarding experience. Much less did I imagine that a leadership role would be placed in the hand of a novice.

My regular occupation was supervising the maintenance program in the public school system. I frequently went with other school personnel to one of the popular restaurants for a mid-afternoon coffee break. New faces were seen every day in the coffee shop which gave opportunity to meet some new comer to our city.

I met Joe Wilson, a mild mannered young man, who was employed by the area association for the handicapped. I felt a little awkward trying to make conversation in a completely foreign field, but Joe and I talked for a few minutes about elements relating to the handicapped. Paralytics, amputees and mentally retarded all came under the general heading of handicapped.

I recall saying to Joe, "It's unfortunate that there isn't some industry in our area where the handicapped could be employed." Joe agreed, but since time was limited we did not pursue the point and we went our separate ways.

I doubt if I ever spoke to Joe again but some things we talked about lingered in the back of my mind. He pointed out that ordinarily, handicapped people don't talk about their handicap for sympathy. They prefer to be thought of as 'normal'. If they can do the work or perform some feat expected of someone who has all of his faculties, then no handicap exists.

Shortly before Christmas, a man named Vic applied for work in the schools maintenance department. He had lost his right hand and part of his arm, but he was outfitted with an artificial arm. Since we needed a man, I put him to work. No favoritism was shown him. His handicap was obvious but we didn't talk about it.

We were building a loading dock in the supply room. Vic took hold like a veteran. He could pick up lumber with his mechanical arm, and also seemed to have more than average ability with his left arm. When it came time for him to help with the nailing, he disconnected part of the mechanical arm and attached a hammer.

Judging from the way he used the tool, he had become fairly well adjusted to it. At lunch time, Vic left the hammer attached. Since he was new on the job, the rest of the crew acted a bit stiff - not knowing what to say. I took a chance. I said, "Well, there's one man who won't have to look for his hammer." Vic grinned and sort of let me know that he appreciated the little ice breaker. It didn't take long for him to become one of the regulars.

Perhaps my conversation with Joe Wilson had something to do with my hiring a handicapped person, but that seemed to be about the extent of my contact with the handicapped.

One day, sometime later, I received notice that I was to attend an afternoon meeting. Nothing was said as to the purpose of the meeting. Not being the suspicious type, I didn't pay much attention as to the why of it, nor did I particularly think it strange that the meeting was to be help in the public schools Special Education Building.

I believe I was last to make an appearance at the meeting. By the time I passed several people to find a seat, I realized the room was filled with many of the persons known to be associated with the handicapped or mentally retarded programs.

Mr. Irv Bitz, the director of Special Education was there; one principal and three or four Special Education teachers were there as well as several parents who had retarded children. I was the only one in the meeting without a given reason for having any contact with the mentally retarded program.

Moments after I was seated, Mr. Bitz called the meeting to order, and before I could collect my wits, I was nominated, and elected as chairman of a newly formed organization with a central purpose of establishing a center for mentally retarded youngsters. I was shocked. I said, "You people don't know what you are doing. I don't know a thing about this business. There must be some mistake."

"Oh, we know what we are doing all right," Irv said very calmly. "We want new blood in our organization - someone who isn't so near the forest he can't see the trees. And, besides that, we heard about your interest in the matter from Mr. Wilson."

There I was, suddenly boxed in - thanks to Joe. Truthfully, I immediately considered some excuse to withdraw from the assignment, but that wasn't the answer. The meeting was official, so I knew I had my work cut out for me.

Even after the short meeting adjourned, almost everyone lingered still talking about the area needs, so I moved about in the group trying to gather information. One of the parents ventured to let me know that for some time they had tried to establish a re-hab center, but each meeting seemed to gravitate into buzz sessions reflecting on the problem, but no action.

Then it dawned on me that the problem could be resolved. I couldn't help but notice that everyone was sincere. They talked constantly of the elements involved in the problems of the handicapped. There wasn't a lot of time wasted on trivia or small talk. I made up my mind that the same people who saw fit to make me the chairman, were the ones best qualified to do the work in organizing their center.

When I called the next meeting to order, a day or two later, I made it known that I needed plenty of help. But I didn't publicize the fact that I had already been confronted with unsolicited advice from a couple of members of the association who gave me the low-down on who's who and best qualified to serve on the different committees. So, it was easy for me to quickly name committees to specific assignments. There was a building committee, a committee for selecting a director, and a finance committee.

Considering how the committee performed, I knew my secret advisors were correct. The committee system proved to be the way to get the job done with dispatch. I believe the personnel committee had secretly selected a director before the formalities, but several people were interviewed for the directorate. The man who qualified for the number one position was Mr. Clarence Knudson, a retired postal employee. With his excellent leadership abilities, the details of establishing the center promptly got under way and the OPPORTUNITY TRAINING CENTER became a reality. A board of directors was selected to assure protocol to the center's operations.

Funds to operate the center were made available through grants and donations. The Myhra Foundation, a local enterprise, provided capital to purchase on old church. The stucco building needed some remodeling to take away the 'churchy' look and give it more of a school-like appearance. The main auditorium became the general shop area. The balcony was closed to provide counselors' rooms, and the front of the church, below the balcony, provided space for three offices. A full basement was easily divided into kitchen, recreational, and special crafts areas.

We purchased woodworking equipment for the shop and outfitted the domestic training area in the basement with refrigerator, range and cabinets. Items were accepted from interested citizens who contributed to the center training needs. This included games, furniture, tools, blackboards, musical instruments, etc.

The (Red River) Valley association for mentally retarded children helped to enroll about fifteen boys and from six to ten girls for the opening of the center. With a director, two counselors, a secretary and a shop supervisor, the training center became a beehive of activity.

Local firms provided work for the trainees. The Coca-Cola Bottling Co. brought in broken bottle cases to be repaired. The shop supervisor worked closely with the boys in making surveyors' stakes, lawn fence, yard ornaments and simple furniture. In time, the center took on the more involved task of manufacturing unpainted chests of drawers. Girls learned cooking, sewing and painting. Special crafts such as leather-work and weaving were available to anyone wishing to expand his skills.

One of the main elements of the center was to create an industrial atmosphere. Making a profit was not allowed, but the sale of goods made by the trainees helped provide part of the funds required to operate the center. The trainees were paid a small sum in order to acquaint them with handling money and also learn something of the ways of our country's economic system.

After the center was operating in full swing, my one official duty was to sign checks. The trainees called me "the man with the hat". They knew when it was pay day and they were on the lookout for the man with the hat.

When time permitted, I looked at some of the projects being worked on. One pudgy young lady took special interest in painting religious pictures. I noticed how carefully she worked as she put finishing touches to 'THE LAST SUPPER'. I asked her if she would paint a picture for me and that was all it took. The next time I visited the center, Mr. Knudson told me the girl had a picture for me.

I stayed in the office while he went to get her. She came to the office, her face aglow, and there she handed me a beautifully painted picture of Jesus. She did not speak a word, but took a good look at my face and then slipped out of the office, closing the door as she left.

I said to Clarence, "Wait a minute. I have to give that girl something for her effort." Clarence stopped me. "Don't try it," he advised. "She was not looking for pay. She just wanted to see the expression on your face."

In time the trainees increased in their range of activity. More and more was learned by the staff in dealing with the mentally retarded. I was disturbed to know that many people in the community were somewhat interested in the center but were actually afraid to visit. Nothing could have been more wrongly judged. There was no violence or any misconduct which would put the trainees in a bad light. They had come from several areas, so they were not previously known to each other. Learning to get along with one another was part of their training. They knew the center was friendly territory, and they conducted their affairs commensurate with treatment they received.

The director announced to me one day that "graduation day" was near. Several of the trainees were ready to leave the center. Some had even become gainfully employed. Customarily, special events and regular meetings were scheduled to be held in the evening for the convenience of those who had other daytime duties. Since I was chairman of the board, Clarence asked me if I would give a little talk which I suppose could be considered the commencement address. He had prepared an agenda which included participation by trainees.

Everyone connected with OPPORTUNITY TRAINING CENTER was present for the center's first graduation. Board members, staff members and trainees nearly filled the lunchroom where all such functions were held. As Mr. Knudson rose to start the program, the room quickly fell into order. Each boy and girl who had something to say or demonstrate seemed to know exactly what to do. One young man played the accordion. As he strode to the front of the group, he faced the same people I would have to speak to. Very casually he adjusted his instrument, and then with a big smile he looked over the assembly and asked, "What would you like to hear?" (as if he had a great repertoire). Of course, the other young people knew what songs he could play, but he listened and noted each request until he heard the one that appealed to him. Needless for me to say, he performed astonishingly well. He seemed to know that, too, which prompted him to ask if he should play another number, but the applause had already established that.

Frankly, I envied him for his confidence and stage presence. As my turn to speak approached, I became increasingly uncomfortable with a feeling that I would be quite inadequate before that assembly. The one thing I relied on, however, was the same courtesy and attentiveness the trainees gave to each other. That is how the first season of operations at OTC ended - a complete success.

It had been a great privilege to see a dream come true. Here was a group of youngsters - girls and boys from teenage to early twenties with a variety of skills they had acquired - who could laugh heartily with (not at) each other over minor mistakes or some provocation. They clapped enthusiastically for speeches and performances. A reverent attitude prevailed when grace was said at lunchtime. Complete respect for the director was the order of the day and that was caught, rather than taught.

I served as chairman of the board for the first four years of the Center's operation. Mr. Knudson retired after two years of duty, but the training center, a well-established part of our community for over nine years, goes on under the very capable direction of Ret. Air Force Col. Roy Kimbrell; his assistant, Ret. Col. Elmer Lian; and shop supervisor, John Lynch. The Valley Association for the Mentally Handicapped continues to give complete support to the center's operations.

I will always feel very close to the trainees of OTC. They were friendly and courteous and showed a remarkable degree of self-confidence. I shall never forget the candor and behavior of that group of youngsters which prompts me to ask myself once in awhile, "Who's handicapped?"

NEWSPAPER STORIES

YOUNG MANUFACTURING BUSINESS IS BOOMING

Matthew Okerlund

Saturday, October 14, 1989
GRAND FORKS HERALD
Used with permission

Dick Young Sr. is a tool and die maker. Which is also to say he is an artist.

Young runs Young Manufacturing, Inc. on North 42nd Street in Grand Forks. He has been out there for almost a quarter of a century making metal stampings and dies for manufacturing firms in the region.

The 70-year-old Young is not given to brash theatrics. During most of its history, his company has been kind of quiet, too. But lately, Young Manufacturing has started to make a little more noise, so to speak.

The company is close to completing a $300,000 expansion after starting the project a year ago. The extra space was needed because orders for its metal stampings and dies have been coming in one after another the past couple of years.

Not many people know anything about the tool and die business. In fact, it would not surprise me if there are more people who know the rules of squash or what the state flower of New Mexico is. But in simple terms, tool and die makers produce metal parts companies use to manufacture their products.

Young Manufacturing stamps out almost 500 different parts that Arctco Inc. needs to make its Arctic Cat snowmobiles in Thief River Falls. Most of these parts are small - things such as brake brackets and clutch guards - and cannot be seen unless you turn the snowmobile over or peer inside its hood.

Young Manufacturing makes hundreds of other parts for companies throughout the Upper Midwest. And it is adding to its list of customers almost every day.

Dick Young landed his first job in the tool and die business at the Grand Forks Foundry while he was still in high school.

Young recalls attending classes in the morning and working at the foundry in the afternoon. Because of the job, it took him two years to complete his senior year in high school. He says the job didn't pay much, either. "But my idea was to get in there and learn the trade and let the salary take care of itself."

After working for a couple of other companies, Young opened his first tool and die shop in 1947. Nineteen years later, he moved the business to its present site. But there is more to the story than that.

The building Young moved into in 1966 happened to be a barn that had been used to train show horses. Young says at that time there were no other buildings between his shop and US Highway 2 several blocks away. He says 42nd Street was a dirt road. "My father thought we wouldn't get any business out here because we were so far off the beaten path."

Young didn't get much business at first, either. But he says in 1969, the company talked Arctic Enterprises - the predecessor of Arctco - into letting it make some parts for its snowmobiles. While there have been some ups and downs since then, that job was the break it needed.

Sales at Young Manufacturing this year should approach $1.5 million. The company now has 31 employees, which is more than twice as many as only five years ago.

Young is not exactly certain why his company has been expanding so quickly of late. He says it has never advertised. He says any new business is through word of mouth, and it appears that word simply has been spreading faster these days.

"The integrity of our business is what brings more work in here," Young believes. "It has really been that way as long as we've been here."

Young is devoutly religious. Much like his grandfather - a German Methodist pastor - Young has been actively spreading the gospel as a member of the Gideon Society for two decades as well as being an elder in his church.

Young does not hesitate to attribute the longevity his company has enjoyed to his belief in God. "Much of what we do here is still considered a venture of faith. I frankly believe that our faith in God has an awful lot to do with the success of our business. I really do."

Three generations of the Young family work at the company, including his three children. A year ago, Young was seriously considering moving the company eight miles south of Grand Forks to Thompson, N.D. He was contemplating this for a couple of reasons. Some of his family members live there. And the city had just notified him that it would annex his company into the city limits and onto the city tax rolls in 1991.

But after talking to Mayor Michael Polovitz and some economic development folks, Young said he decided to stay put even though only a small part of his business - 5 percent - comes from Grand Forks companies. "We chose to reconsider the move," he says.

Young is well past the age most people retire. But it is for love and not for money that he continues to work.

Young admits tool and die making might not seem like a glamorous job to most people. But he says his profession is as much an art as an exact science because when he designs something, "It is my creation. That is the fun of this work. The pleasure."

Sounds like the words of an artist.

ONE HOT IDEA

Head bolt heater revolutionized cold-weather starting for cars.

(NOTE: This article is included because Andy Freeman was a great influence to Dick and the beginning of his career in the manufacturing business).

By Jonathan Knutson

January 16, 1999
THE FORUM
Used with permission

The next time you mutter darkly about a cold winter morning, add a word of thanks for Andrew Freeman.

Freeman invented the Freeman Head Bolt Heater - the granddaddy of modern plug-in heaters used to warm car and truck engines for cold weather starts.

He also was a champion of rural electric cooperatives and a nationally honored leader of the electrical industry.

"Mr. Freeman was a remarkable man who had a major impact on this area," said David Doer, general manager of Minnkota Power Cooperative in Grand Forks.

Freeman, who died in 1996, was a co-founder of Minnkota and served as its general manager for 42 years.

A native of Upham, N.D., Freeman graduated from the University of North Dakota in 1932 with an electrical engineering degree. Because of the Depression he bounced from one temporary job to another before becoming manager of North Dakota Five Star-Cooperative in 1939.

In 1940, he was instrumental in founding Minnkota Power Cooperative in Grand Forks. Investor-owned utilities strongly opposed the cooperative.

Today, Minnkota serves nearly 100,000 cooperative and municipal customers in northeastern North Dakota and northwestern Minnesota.

In his spare time, Freeman was a inventor. He began working on the head bolt heater in the 1930s. At that time, motorists in this area had to warm auto engines with light bulbs, hot water and even blankets.

Freeman fashioned his heater using copper tubing that he found in some rubble and a heating element from an old flat iron.

In a 1966 interview, he said he lived by the philosophy that "Winners never quit and quitters never win."

"I threw that head bolt heater in the ash can several times, but I dug it out and continued to experiment until it worked," he said.

In 1947 he got a patent on the device, which consisted of a brass cylinder about the size of a finger. It replaced one of the head bolts in the engine, and the cylinder with the heating element extended into the engine water jacket. A cord attached to the top of bolt plugged into an electrical outlet.

(The Head Bolt shown is in the 1949 Ford pickup truck owned by Sean Allan).

Five-Star Manufacturing Co., the business he helped start, sold the head bolt heaters for $10 each. He later sold his interest in the firm.

As cars changed, he also invented a frost-plug heater that attached to the side of the motor and an external tank heater. The head bolt heater was the only invention he patented. The patent expired in 1964.

Freeman also invented a remote control car starter, so motorists could start their car without leaving the house. The device didn't catch on with motorists.

While best known as inventor of the head bolt heater, Freeman also played a leading role in the area's electrical industry.

For one thing, Doer, said, Freeman "championed using North Dakota lignite" to generate electricity.

Press accounts from the 1960s and 1970s show Freeman to be a tireless booster of exploiting lignite coal from western North Dakota. That meant building plants near the coal mines, rather than building plants close to where the electricity is used.

And Freeman proposed the dual heating system, in which customers switch from electricity to another source of fuel during time when demand for electricity is at its peak.

Doer, who worked with Freeman for 15 years at Minnkota, called Freeman a hands-on manager who respected employees and their ideas.

"Mr. Freeman always listened."

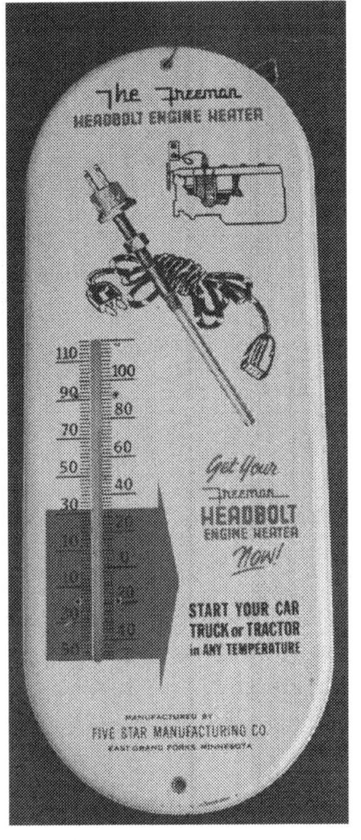

Antique thermometer showing Freeman Head Bolt Heater is found hanging in the Lyons Auto Supply Store in Grand Forks, North Dakota.

After speaking with third generation family member Jim Lyons, who now owns Lyons Auto Supply with his sister, Jane (Lyons) Bohn, and younger brother John Lyons, I learned that the Freeman Head Bolt Heater was such a success because of the flat head engines in automobiles. It was the only technology around until the middle of the 1950's to keep the engine warm. Prior to that invention, some folks would even take hot coals and place them in a pan under the oil pan for easier car starting in the cold winter months. Jim said many hundreds of the Head Bolt Heater were sold though the family business, before sales slowed down with the invention of the overhead valve engine. *Notes given to Judy in 2017*

DICK YOUNG PUTS MEMORIES OF WWII DOWN ON PAPER

Marilyn Hagerty

Sunday, December 9, 2001
GRAND FORKS HERALD
Used with permission

For 60 years since Pearl Harbor, Dick Young shoved memories of World War II into a corner of his mind. Now 82, he has started writing about those days. Especially about 1944 and 1945 when he was in Europe in a hot spot in southern France at the same time as the Battle of the Bulge. And as he writes, he says things are becoming vivid.

There is so much he never wanted to talk about and so much he never even told anyone in his family about his tank battalion attached to the third infantry division. "There were a lot of casualties," he says. "I took no pleasure in killing. But war is war. Either you get them, or they get you."

Young says, "Those of us down inside and driving tanks couldn't always see the results of shooting. But we knew. Lots of times we'd load infantry guys on the tanks and move out to secure territory and take prisoners." He shuns those memories, but he likes to remember the way the church bells were ringing all over Europe on V-E Day on May 8 of 1945. With the battle over in Europe, Young's battalion went into training to go to Japan. Then, came V-J Day on Sept. 2, 1945, and it was a matter of working and waiting to go home in January of 1946. He didn't enjoy closing in on Germany because he is of German extraction. He was pleased to be stationed in Austria at the end of the fighting.

He finished his tour in Europe as a First Sergeant. After World War II, he was called up for a two-year stretch and spent nine months in Korea in the early 1950s. In these years, Dick Young is semi-retired, but he spends part of every day at Young Manufacturing Co., 2331 42nd St. N., a business he started with his brothers. He is among the dwindling ranks of World War II veterans. As he is starting to write about his experiences now, he says he doesn't want to embellish them. Young is a rather quiet, methodical man. If a job needs doing, he figures a way to manufacture the parts for almost anything. If he sees a need, he invents an answer. He writes poetry. He has been an assistant organist at Bethel Lutheran Church. He is a member of the Gideon Society that places Bibles in hotels and motels and in prisons and schools.

He is a board member of Child Evangelism Fellowship. "I believe God gives us our talents," he says. "I trust in the Lord to direct my life. As I get older, I am more aware we need to rely on the Lord for everything."

His words come clearly, thoughtfully. He sits in the second floor loft where offices of Young Manufacturing are located. In the next office, is his son David who is now president of the company, which employs 50 on day and night shifts. His daughter Judy McNamee and two grandsons - Daniel and Scott McNamee - work at the plant. Another son, Dick Young Jr., has a plant in Fergus Falls.

Young Manufacturing dates back to a boy who wanted a train for Christmas in 1937. Dick Young says his father told him he wouldn't buy him a train, but he would help him build one. The first die he ever made was for that train. And it created a desire within him to work with machinery. As a Central High School student, he went to work for Grand Forks Welding. In 1940, he went to Moorhead, Minn., to work for Withnell Machine Works. When Pearl Harbor was hit, he was asked to go to work for Minneapolis Moline where war goods were being built. But there was a time limit, and he was called up for military service.

Born on a farm near Montrose, Minn., Young came to Grand Forks with his family in 1936. He graduated from Central High School. He and his wife DeLoris, who now look back on 60 years together, had been married 42 days on December 7, 1941. When World War II was over, he started working again at Minneapolis Moline. But there was a strike, and he came back to Grand Forks. With his two younger brothers, he bought Northern Machine Repair Shop. His brother, Frank, is now deceased, and his brother, Roland, operates Telpro Co. in Grand Forks. Along with developing his own machine shop here, Young was an instructor at UND for several years.

OATMEAL, RAISINS AND A PRAYER

This article was written for her column, *In The Spirit*, by Naomi Dunavan, a columnist for the GRAND FORKS HERALD on September 20, 2008.
Used with permission

I have read with great interest this week the story of the founding of Young Brothers Machine Works in Grand Forks.

It was 1947 when Dick Young, the eldest, and Frank and Roland Young first opened a small repair shop that through the years saw many changes. Today we know it as Young Manufacturing, Inc.

Dick wrote the history in 1987, when his company was nominated for special recognition by the Small Business Council. At the close of the document Dick states, "If I were to offer a motto for this type of operation, I would say we should be ready to 'give a kid a chance.' "

Dick has given throngs of kids a chance not only in the work force but also when it comes to hearing the Gospel message.

Young Manufacturing, Inc. is 61 years old, and for more than half that time, Dick has faithfully helped carry on the local ministry of a worldwide interdenominational organization called Child Evangelism Fellowship (CEF). He does that monetarily and through prayer.

CEF's purpose is to make the Gospel known to children who might not hear it because their parents are not church goers. CEF offers 5-Day Clubs, which meet in neighborhood settings during the summer and Good News Clubs held in school after school hours. CEF workers sing with the children, tell them Bible stories and offer them treats.

Doug Berntson, Manvel, N.D., is a director of the northeastern North Dakota/northwest Minnesota region of CEF. His wife, Ruth is his volunteer assistant.

They witnessed Dick's love of children the first time they met him in 1977. "We had a 2-year-old daughter, and he wanted to play with her," Doug said.

"You could just sense the kindness in him" Ruth added. "He's one of the kindest people I've ever known. He's very generous and he puts others before himself."

The Rev. Jeff Stephan, Dick's pastor at Bethel Lutheran Brethren Church, Grand Forks, vouches for Dick's generosity. "If he's not here on a Sunday, he'll come to the church to hand-deliver his offering," Pastor Stephan said.

Like all ministries, CEF sometimes struggles. "Dick always prays for my wife and me as we serve the Lord," Doug said. "One time, the money wasn't there to pay us. Dick called the treasurer. He told her to give us a paycheck and he would see to it that the money was there. You don't see too many people do things like that. He'd been our prayer chairman I don't know how many years. He and I talk often about prayer and we pray together. He's always there to encourage us and to help any way he can."

For years, CEF has held a monthly prayer breakfast, first in restaurants and since 2000, hosted by Grant and Genie Jensen in the atrium where they live.

Lots of prayers will be offered at the breakfast set for 9 a.m. Sept. 27, but it's also Dick's 89th birthday and he'll be recognized for all he's done for CEF.

Grant Jensen recalls that Dick always ordered oatmeal and raisins when they met in a restaurant. He and Genie have served many fancy dishes, but never oatmeal and raisins, so for Dick's birthday, it will be oatmeal and raisins.

Dick was born in Montrose, Minnesota. His family moved to Grand Forks when he was a teen after his Dad was hired by North Dakota State Mill. Dick married DeLoris Butenhoff, who was from Moorhead. DeLoris died in 2004.

Dick's children are Judy McNamee and David Young, both of Grand Forks, and Dick Young, Jr., Fergus Falls, Minn. He has eight grandchildren, and 17 great-grandchildren.

"In a lot of ways my dad reminds me of the way his mother lived," Judy said. "It was by example. My dad's mother was a wonderful Christian lady. She led her life quietly, and she had a servant-type attitude. He emulated that in his life and his business."

When I visited with Dick in his home, I could tell he was proud to have been a soldier. He spoke of what people did in the 1940s to stay out of the military.

"Some people had all their teeth pulled, "Dick said. "I stood straight and tall and let them look me over. I decided if I had to go, I might as well look alive."

He spent two years in France and Germany during World War II. "I had bullets whistle around my ears," Dick said. "Whenever we were confronted with real war, we had prayer thoughts, and we had prayer books in our duffel bags. Some of those things really mature you."

When he returned to America and "when I saw the Statue of Liberty, I was gripped in the throat," he said. "I couldn't talk."

On Dick's davenport is a comfy throw that reads: "Blessed is the man whose confidence is in Him." A fitting verse for Dick!

Brother Roland lives in Grand Forks. Brother Frank and sister Vera are deceased.

No longer in management at Young Manufacturing, Dick does retain his office. "I go there to write letters and poetry," he said. "My mother was a poet."

To be called a born-again Christian is "one of the hallmarks of our faith," Dick said. "It's our testimony."

He'll always thank God for the ability and the opportunity to serve CEF.

"It's a worthy involvement, I thoroughly enjoyed."

OBITUARY

In my darkness Jesus found me
Cleansed mine eyes that I may see.

Broke sins chains that long had bound me
Gave me life and liberty.

John W. Peterson

Jesus answered, "I am the way and the truth and the life. No one comes to the Father except through me.
John 14:6

All those the Father gives me will come to me, and whoever comes to me I will never drive away.
John 6:37

In Memory of

Richard "Dick" E. Young

September 27, 1919 November 23, 2013

Services
Saturday, Nov. 30, 2013 at 11:00 AM
Faith Evangelical Free Church
Grand Forks, ND

Officiating
Rev. Scott Connolly

Special Music
Tyler Cullen –pianist
Dick's Grandchildren
Joan Karner, organist

Casketbearers
Scott McNamee Dan McNamee Paul McNamee
Tim Cullen Thomas Grandouiller
Paul Dionne Tyler Cullen

Honorary Casketbearers
Gideon Members

Military Honors
North Dakota Army National Guard
VFW Post # 3817, East Grand Forks, MN
American Legion Post # 157, East Grand Forks, MN

Interment
2:30 PM, Nov. 30, 2013
Memorial Park Cemetery
Grand Forks, ND

Richard Emory "Dick" Young went to his heavenly eternal home to be with his precious Lord and Savior, Jesus Christ on November 23, 2013. Dick was 94 when he passed away quietly after living several years at 4000 Valley Square in Grand Forks, ND. Dick was born September 27, 1919 to Herbert and Alta (Volkenant) Young on a farm near Montrose, Minnesota. The family moved to Anoka, MN when he was about age 5 and later moved to Grand Forks in 1936. In 1938 Dick graduated from Central High School.

Soon after, he moved to Moorhead, MN where he worked in a machine shop. In April 1941 he was introduced to DeLoris (Butenhoff) at the Bluebird Cafe where she worked as a waitress. They were married Oct. 26, 1941 in Sabin Minnesota. In 1942 Dick was deferred to work in a defense plant in Minneapolis. Daughter, Judith (Judy) was born in 1943, and the Minneapolis Moline factory became Dick's place of employment until the spring of 1944. He then entered the U.S. Army and left for Ft. Knox, Kentucky. In 1945, while loading ammunition at the front lines, Dick received word he had a new son, Richard Charles. The news took 2 months to reach him and Dick Jr. was already one year and 5 days old when Dick Sr. first saw him. After the war, Dick returned to the Minneapolis Moline factory, but a prolonged strike caused him to move the family back to Grand Forks. They lived with Dick's parents in a large house that was remodeled into a duplex. Son David was born in 1958. In 1963 Dick and Dee bought a house next door to his parents. They completely remodeled the house and added a basement, where the family lived for two and one half years as the rest of the remodeling was completed. (The house is now owned by daughter Judy and her husband Michael.) In the "post-war" years Dick was again involved in machine shop work. His brothers Benjamin Franklin "Frank" and Roland "Rolly joined him and they opened a repair business. Then, in 1950, Dick and Roland were called into service for the Korean conflict and decided to close the shop. Dick and family moved to Ft. Lewis, Washington from 1950-1951 before he shipped out to Korea. After his discharge from the Army the second time, Dick worked a short span with Butler Machine and as a lab technician and instructor in the machine shop at the University of ND. From 1954 to 1966 Dick worked with Andy Freeman of ARCO MFG. during which he helped develop the "Head Bolt" heater, which was first car engine heater to go into commercial production and use. He was also associated with the Potato Research lab at UND and was the Superintendant of Buildings and Grounds for GF Public Schools during this time frame. In 1966, Dick bought an old Quonset building on a rutted dirt road that is now known as 42nd St. North. When Dick and Roland opened the shop they called it Young Tool & Die Works. Dick seldom turned away any job. He always felt that if the work could be done somewhere else, he could figure a way to do it, too. An early customer asked him to make aluminum hair styling combs. The combs were produced very successfully and some of those combs are still in use today! Around 1980 the business was renamed Young Mfg., Inc. (YMI) and is run by son Dave. The company initially produced metal stampings for many local industries but now also performs laser cutting, machining, welding and some assembly. When Dee's health began to fail she was moved into assisted living at Parkwood Place.

Dick sold their home on Walnut St. soon after and lived near her in the same complex, but on the independent living side. DeLoris passed away on January 12, 2004. Dick and DeLoris were long time members at Bethel Lutheran (Brethren) Church in Grand Forks. Music was a huge part of Dick's life. He loved playing the piano, the church organ and singing. He personally owned a theater style organ and baby grand piano and also owned and played an accordion! Many times Dick, his two brothers and their father Herbert would gather around the piano and sing while mother Alta played Gospel hymns. Dick also enjoyed singing duets with his daughter Judy and singing in the church choir. Dick was known for his poetry and composed a new and unique Christmas poem each year. He also enjoyed sharing his war stories both verbally and in writing and was always happy to provide printed copies of his memories to anyone who had an interest. Dick's love for the Lord Jesus Christ kept him involved in various ministries over his lifetime. He was active in the Gideon's Bible-placing ministry and regularly spoke in area churches to promote the Gideon organization. For many years he would hand-out pocket New Testament Bibles to children and college students as they went to their classes. He was also on the board of Child Evangelism Fellowship. CEF's purpose is to make the Gospel known to children who otherwise might not hear it. This is accomplished through 5-Day Clubs in the summertime and Good News Clubs which are held in some schools after the class day is done. CEF workers sing with the children, tell Bible stories and offer treats and encouragement. The Grand Forks Mission, now known as Northlands Rescue Mission, was also dear to Dick's heart. He worked with Rev. Trankina in the early days as they endeavored to help people who were struggling with life issues by providing a safe haven where food, shelter and spiritual encouragement could be found. Dick also helped to establish the Opportunity Training Center in Grand Forks, ND and was Chairman of the Board for four years.

Dick is preceded in death by his wife DeLoris, his parents, brother Frank, sister Vera and her husband Lester Soberg, sister-in-law Lois McIntyre Weston (Roland) Young and daughter-in-law Lorna (Zenner) Young.

Survivors include: daughter, Judy (Michael) McNamee, Grand Forks; sons Richard, (Lorna, deceased), Fergus Falls, MN; David (Beth), Thompson, N.D.;

Grandchildren: Jeff (Cyndi) Young, Brian (Noemi) Young, Scott (Katrina) McNamee, Daniel (Patricia) McNamee, Paul (Amy Jo) McNamee, Kirsten (Paul) Dionne, Shelly (Tim) Cullen, Jennifer (Thomas) Grandouiller;

Great-grandchildren: Declan, Isaac, Kieran, Calder, Arielle, Amber, Savannah, Caleb, Rachael, Megan, Tanner, Trinity, Alexis, Monique, Tyler, Emma, Abigail, Elizabeth, Matias; brother Roland, sister-in-law Vera (Frank) Young; and many nephews and nieces.

MEMORIES OF GRANDPA

One of Dick's granddaughters, Jennifer (Young) Grandouiller gave him a gift. Dick describes it here.

March 10, 1996

It is my pleasure to share something quite unique that I was blessed with, on Valentine's day - 1996. Jenny Young, age 11, our youngest granddaughter has a special talent for unusual ideas, and this was her "Valentine" to me.

I received a plastic container with a screw-on lid, and the container was filled (packed in) with dozens of hearts cut out of colored craft paper. Each heart had some message on it. Many were Bible verses, or references that Jenny selected from her own study of the Bible. I was amazed at the selections. They were all very good, but I feel she was led to a type of verse that is certainly a meaningful "thought" for <u>any</u> adult, and she chose me.

Here is a listing of the verses and thoughts I gleaned from a total of 105 hearts.

1. Ecclesiastes. 2:26 For GOD giveth to a man that is good in His sight wisdom, and knowledge, and joy: but to the sinner He given travail, to gather and to heap up, that he may give to him that is good before God.
2. Isaiah 9: 6,7 For unto us a child is born, unto us a son is given, and the government shall be upon His shoulders. And His name shall be called Wonderful, Counselor, Mighty God, Everlasting Father, Prince of Peace. Of the increase of His government and peace there shall be no end, upon

the throne of David, and upon his kingdom to order it, and to establish it with judgment and with justice from henceforth even forever. The zeal of the Lord of hosts will perform this.

3. Prov. 3: 5,6 Trust in the LORD with all thine heart and lean not unto thine own understanding. In all thy ways acknowledge Him, and He shall direct thy paths.

4. Romans 5:8 But GOD commendeth His love toward us, in that, while we were yet sinners, Christ died for us.

5. John 15:5 I am the vine, ye are the branches; He that abideth in me, and I in Him, the same bringeth forth much fruit; for without Me ye can do nothing.

6. Ps. 141:3 Set a watch, O Lord, before my mouth; keep watch over the door of my lips.

7. Genesis 9:1 And GOD blessed Noah and his sons, and said unto them, Be fruitful, and multiply, and replenish the earth.

8. Proverbs 6: 16-19 These six things doth the Lord hate: yea, seven are an abomination unto Him. A proud look, a lying tongue, and hands that shed innocent blood, an heart that devises wicked imaginations, feet that be swift in running to mischief, a false witness that speaketh lies, and he that soweth discord among breathren.

9. John 17:6 I have manifested Thy name unto the men which Thou gavest me out of the world. Thine they were, and Thou gavest them me, and they have kept thy word.

10. John 3:16 For GOD so loved the world, that He gave His only begotten Son, that whosoever believeth in Him should not perish, but have everlasting life.

11. Genesis 1:1 In the beginning GOD created the heaven and the earth.

12. Psalm 119:133 Order my steps in Thy word, and let not any iniquity have dominion over me.

13. Ecclesiastes 12: 13,14 Let us hear the conclusion of the whole matter. Fear GOD, and keep His commandments; for this is the whole duty of man.

14. Acts 3: 6-10 Then Peter said, Silver and gold have I none; but such as I have I give to thee. In the name of Jesus Christ of Nazareth rise up and walk. And he took him by the right hand, and lifted him up, and immediately his feet and ankle bones received strength. And he leaping up stood and walked, and entered with them into the temple, walking, and

leaping and praising God. And all the people saw his walking and praising God. And they knew that it was he which sat for alms at the Beautiful gate of the temple, and they were filled with wonder and amazement at that which had happened unto him.

15. Revelation 22:21 The grace of our Lord Jesus Christ be with you all. Amen.

16. John 11:32-36 Then when Mary was come where Jesus was, and saw Him, she fell down at His feet, saying unto Him, Lord if thou hadst been here, my brother had not died. When Jesus therefore saw her weeping, and the Jews also weeping which came with her, He groaned in the spirit, and was troubled. And said, Where have ye laid him? They said unto Him, Lord come and see. Jesus wept. Then said the Jews, behold how He loved him.

17. Genesis 4 This chapter reflects on the well-known story of Eve bearing sons and the account of Cain slaying Abel. (I won't print the whole chapter).

18. Revelation 22:20 He which testifieth these things saith, Surely I come quickly. Amen. Even so, come Lord Jesus.

19. Galatians 3:22-23 But the scripture hath concluded the whole world is under sin, that the promise by faith of Jesus Christ might be given to them that believe. But before faith came, we were kept prisoners under the law, shut up unto the faith which should afterwards be revealed.

20. Isaiah 55:6 See ye the Lord while He may be found, call ye upon Him while He is near. (Jenny calls this her favorite verse).

21. Matthew 5:44 But I say unto you, Love your enemies, bless them that curse you, do good to them that hate you, and pray for them which despitefully use you, and persecute you.

22. Romans 1:16 For I am not ashamed of the gospel of Christ, for it is the power of God unto salvation to every one that believeth, to the Jew first and also to the Greek.

23. John 14:15 If ye love me, keep my commandments.

24. 3 John 1:11 Beloved, follow not that which is evil, but that which is good. He that doeth good is of God, but he that doeth evil hath not seen God..

25. Proverbs 17:17 A friend loveth at all times, and a brother is born for adversity.

26. Ecclesiastes 7:9 Be not hasty in thy spirit to be angry, for anger resteth in the bosom of fools.

27. Hosea 10:12 Sow to yourselves in righteousness, reap in mercy, break up your fallow ground, for it is time to seek the Lord, until He come and rain righteousness upon you.
28. Proverbs 18:24 A man of many companions may come to ruin, but there is a friend who sticks closer than a brother.
29. Song of Solomon 8:6,7 Set me as a seal upon thine heart, as a seal upon thine arm; for love is strong as death, jealousy is cruel as the grave. The coals thereof are coals of fire, which hath most vehement flame. Many waters cannot quench love, neither can the floods drown it. If a man would give all the substance of his house for love, it would utterly be scorned.
30. Proverbs 1:7 The fear of the Lord is the beginning of knowledge, but fools despise wisdom and instruction.
31. John 12:26 If any man serve me, let him follow me; and where I am, there shall also my servant be. If any man serve me, him will my Father honor.
32. John 16:14 He will bring glory to me by taking from what is mine and making it known to you.
33. 2 John 1:6 And this is love, that we walk in obedience to His commandments. This is the commandment, that as you have heard from the beginning, ye should walk in it.
34. Proverbs 27:6 Faithful are the wounds of a friend, but the kisses of an enemy are deceitful.
35. Psalm 33:6 By the word of the Lord were the heavens made, their starry host by the breath of his mouth.
36. Psalm 5:3 My voice shalt Thou hear in the morning, O Lord; in the morning will I direct my prayer unto Thee and will look up.

Jenny's 36 Bible verses were picked at random and were not organized in her decorated container, but were mixed with 69 other hearts with many thoughts and, some were questions she asked. She perhaps knew the answers but her desire to learn will, no doubt, be answered. Also, a few of the hearts were just hearts with some of her own decorative styling.

But, along with the selected Bible verses were thoughts I believe are worth recording from an 11 year old girl, and here they are in her own wording.

Do not use God's name in vain - Remember Sunday 4 rest - Have a nice day - Remember to love others as you want to be loved and treated - Never lie - Do things for other people all day - Smile a lot -Tell someone you love them today - Try to stop a habit 4 a day - Give a gift today - Tell someone your favorite verse - Give up something for the day 4 someone - Smile today - Don't give up on something tough - Be kind - Make a donation to your favorite charity, soon - Honor God - Pray - Read the Bible - LOVE - Give a big hug to someone - Honor father and mother - Smile at everyone you meet -Be good - Have grace - Give somebody a hug - be nice - Have peace - I love you - Have no other gods before the living one - Do good things - Worship our God - Read about Jesus birth - Read about Jesus rising from the dead - Share your testimony today - Be gentle - Have joy - Be honest - Have patience - Have faith - Loyalty - Smile - You shall not covet - You shall not commit adultery - Don't make any idol - Do not steal Treat others the way you want to be treated -Read the ten commandments - Choose good friends - lead a man to Christ -Love your neighbor as yourself Have self control - Share something with someone - Give a gift

I love you Gramps.

She had 8 hearts with questions - What is an angel? - What is sanctification? What is hades? - What is Pentecost? - What is resurrection? - Who's the Devil? - What is genealogy? - Do you know what a hypocrite is? (I'm sure I will be sharing these with Jenny).

On the lid of the special container Jenny prepared - she wrote - DRAW A HEART EACH DAY - DO WHAT THE HEART SAYS

Well, I tried that, but it is like trying to eat one potato chip. I took out several a day - and finally I separated the Bible verses from the other hearts and decided it was worth sharing.

(Dick wrote out each Bible verse and the other ideas Jenny shared on each heart contained in her Valentine gift to Grandpa and he distributed those typed copies to other family members).

We recently found a notebook filled with questions for Grandpa - something his granddaughter Kirsten (McNamee) Dionne gave him for his 75th birthday - in 1994, when she was 13 years old. There was a question each day of September, which were answered by Grandpa Dick.

Turned 75 - Sept 27 - 1995

Grandpa,

Hope you had a very happy birthday! And that you have many more!

Happy Birthday!

Love,
Kirsten
McNamee

Grandpa, Hope you had a very happy birthday and that you have many more. HAPPY BIRTHDAY! Love, Kirsten McNamee

Sept. 1 - Grandpa, tell us your most embarrassing moment.

It happened on a windy day. My hat blew off near Valley Jr. School. I had to chase after it and hoped nobody saw it. I tried three times to grab it, only to see it blow away again. Finally, when I did get my hand on it, I heard a loud cheer and clapping. There, outside the school were the entire lunch program workers - about 16 of them. They saw the whole thing and made the most of it.

Sept. 2 - Grandpa, what was your high school goal?

My high school goal was to finish with at least a "C" average. I did not get into sports, but my 'extra' was music. I was in boys quartets, octets, and solo work. The highlight of each year was operetta! I took shop, but they made me the assistant instructor. I got "A" for this.

Sept. 3 - Grandpa, tell us about some of your friends as a child.

Kenneth Gonyea - loved to tick bread in syrup and suck it out. ALL of his teeth turned black. Brother Jimmy Gonyea - even as a kid growing up - he talked suc baby talk it was hard to understand him.

Ray Christianson - a really smart boy. He loved to 'fake' watching a ball game and give a play-by-play.

Archie Holden - loved guns and motorcycles and girls. But, the girls liked Archie's brother Graydon better. He was handsome.

Cleda Watson - a girl. I thought I loved her. We were both about 6 or 7 and played 'house' under a folding clothes rack.

Sept. 4 - Grandpa, have you ever been very angry at someone? If so, how did you resolve it?

Yes, some smart-aleck at school, older than I was. He called me names. I wanted to smash him. (I called him names under my breath). My mom would NOT have approved. It was never really resolved, but we both grew up. I think he moved away.

Sept. 5 - Grandpa, when did you become a Christian? Explain.

I grew up in a Christian home. I heard about Jesus all my life. But, there comes a time when we make a commitment - or should. I was headed for Korea, and spent time at a chapel with Chaplain Nally. The things we talked about made me know I needed a deeper walk with the Lord. I liked Isaiah 55 verse 6 - Seek ye the Lord while He may be found. Call ye upon Him while He is near. Just knowing a Bible verse is not enough. We must put it into practice. We never get too old to admit we need Jesus.

Sept. 6 - Grandpa, draw a sketch of your house that you lived in as a child.

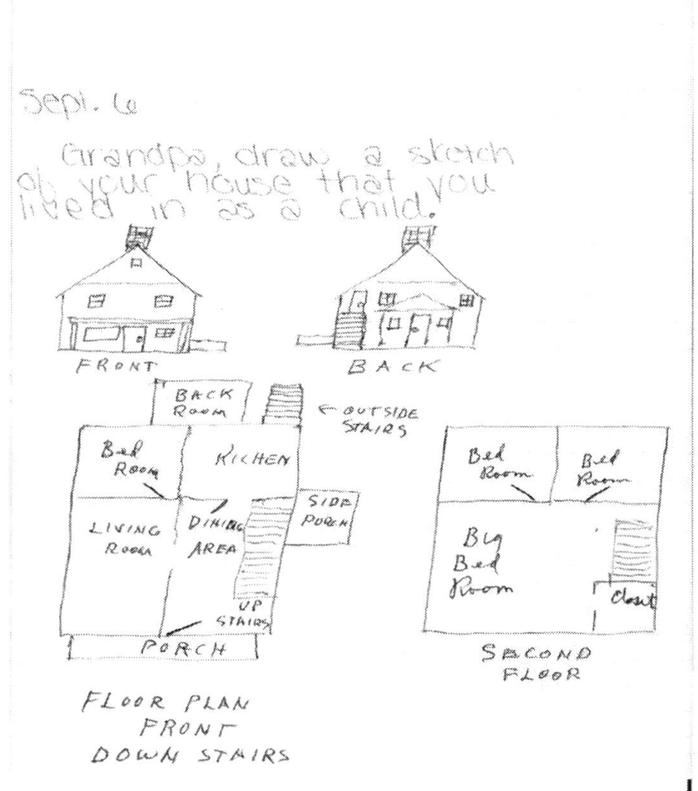

Sept. 7 - Grandpa, when did you meet Grandma? Explain your feelings.

She was a waitress in the Blue Bird Cafe where I ate my meals. She was petite, very blonde and liked to dance and bowl. I maybe tried NOT to show it, but I was pleased to ask her for a date. It was her 20th birthday- April 8th - our first date. We didn't go to shows, but Dee and I and some friends like to picnic, bowl and go dancing. Dating was simple in those days. We didn't spend much money, but would just drive around in the car, listening to the radio. Dee lived on a farm near where Floyd Butenhoff lives now. We drove out there a lot. Dee's home was on the farm, but she roomed in Moorhead to be close to her work.

Sept. 8 - Grandpa when did you know that Grandma was the one you wanted to spend the rest of your life with?

After we dated a few months, I found out she was German. Since I am German, I thought we could raise a German family. And, we did!

Sept. 9 - Grandpa, what was the lowest grade of your entire school years?

I don't remember. I had so many chores to do at home, I hardly ever studied home work. I never failed any grade, but I think my freshman year may have been the worst. As I mentioned earlier, I was very much a "C" student.

Sept. 10 - Grandpa, why did you want to start your own business?

I wanted to be able to do my own planning and also do the kind of work I loved. Machine work still intrigues me and has become my way of life.

Sept. 11 - Grandpa, explain the worst day of your entire life.

That one is hard to come up with. I don't remember for sure. I remember the day we encountered German tanks during the war. I thought I was going to be killed. Those tanks were really big, but I fired large explosive shells at them and beat them off. One other experience happened *at night.* We dropped our tank in a water reservoir. Two of our men nearly drowned. But, the Lord was with us.

Sept. 12 - Grandpa, what was the happiest day of your life?

Here again, it's hard to say. I have had many really great days, but I think when we entered New York harbor with the very small ship I came home on - I saw the Statue of Liberty, and I was so choked up, I couldn't talk. Thousands of soldiers *never* came home and I was among those who were spared an evil end. Probably another day would be one where I knew for sure my sins were forgiven.

Sept. 13 - Grandpa, what was the most valuable thing you owned when you were a child?

A small American Flyer train set. It was the wind-up kind, but I loved it. The value was not in the price so much as it was in the pleasure of ownership. I had to share it with my brother, Frank.

Sept.14 - Grandpa, what were your feelings while in your first war?

Very jittery - many times. I knew I was where I could get hurt. But, like other things, I got used to it and took it in stride. Mainly, I believed we would win because we felt our cause was just. I have begun writing about my war experiences and hope to finish in a few months. That will give you the really broad picture of my WWII experiences.

Sept. 15 - Grandpa, what were your feelings when you walked into the first house that you and Grandma owned?

That house happens to be the one you now live in - 1513 Lewis Blvd. Other homes were rental units. But, we bought a really beat-up piece of property to rebuild it, and put a basement under it. And that is what you see today. We had to raise the house 24 inches so we could put in the foundation and have room for the basement windows. Entering the home after we bought it was no thrill. It smelled bad, and I can explain THAT some day.

Sept. 16 - Grandpa, what were you like in school? (class clown, smart one, etc.)

I was a very quiet kid. Some thought I was not with it because I had to work so much of my time at home, I thought of myself as being rather dull.

No way could I have been class clown.

Sept. 17 - Grandpa, what was the best Christmas that you spent with your family? Explain.

Perhaps the first after returning from the War. I spent four Christmases away during my two military tours of duty. It was good to be home and everyone on deck for the family gathering.

Sept. 18 - Grandpa, did you ever get so nervous you felt like you were going to throw up? Explain.

No, I didn't feel like throwing up, but when we were hit with artillery shells after we lost our tank in the reservoir, I was standing outside with no protection and the shell bursts made me REALLY move fast to cover.

Sept. 19 - Grandpa, what was the most foolish thing you ever did?

Dragging a big log chain up into a big willow tree. I hooked it over a branch and came down. I didn't want to climb up to get it down, so I grabbed the loose end and whipped it until it let go up top. But the big hook came down and hit me in the eyebrow above my left eye. The blood ran like a stream, and I had to go to the hospital for stitches. The scar is under the left eyebrow. You can still see where the stitches were made. Oh, I forgot to tell you, I was about 9 years old.

Sept. 20 - Grandpa, what was the most terrifying moment of your life?

The storm at sea in the North Atlantic Ocean. We came close to capsizing. The storm was so bad, they couldn't cook coffee for four days. The waves pounded over the ship so hard, it broke glass 3/4 inch thick. Several men had to go to the ship hospital. The ship rolled on its side so far, I thought we were going on over. This was in January of 1946.

Sept. 21 - Grandpa, what was the first thing you ever made that you were really proud of?

When I was about 13, I made a small chess set on a lathe in our basement when we lived in Anoka, Minnesota. Since many of the pieces were the same shape, my job was to try and make them look alike, and measure the same. That was in 1933. That set is over 62 years old, and I still have it. Even though the set was made of wood, it taught me a lot about running a lathe, and that ultimately became my major life work and the shop on 42nd Street. I have to thank my dad for the early training on a lathe.

Sept. 22 - Grandpa, did you ever have the feeling that your life was ruined? Explain.

Emphatically NO! I believe all of us <u>think</u>, at times, that we really goofed. My parents were Christians and I know their prayers made a big difference. There may be people who ruined their lives with booze or drugs and maybe died early. But, I feel that God has helped me to avoid really bad things, or even picked me up if I fell. A Bible verse says, "<u>All</u> have sinned and come short of the Glory of God" - Romans 3:23. Praise God for sins **forgiven**.

Sept. 23 - Grandpa, what was the funniest thing that ever happened to you?

When I was 17, my family arranged a birthday party that I didn't know about. I was at work, and my dad came and detained me past the supper hour. I was wearing sooty coveralls. I worked for a furnace company, and really got messy at times. They wanted me to come home in yucky clothes - on purpose - and there was a house full of school friends just waiting. Well, I tried but was too embarrassed to stay in such clothes. So I went upstairs to clean up and slipped into some school clothes. The pants I wore were really tight, but that was better than soot. We played a game where we had to bend over, and wouldn't you know, when my back was turned to the party bunch, the seam in back let go with a ripping sound, and now you know the rest of the story.

Sept. 24 - Grandpa, what was the biggest and most excellent decision you ever made?

I really find it hard to answer that because there have been so many things that could fit that. But I believe there are times when something happens that we may <u>think</u> was a personal decision when it well could have been the hand of the Lord giving direction. I worked in Minneapolis at a huge factory - Minneapolis Moline - and had everything I could need in a shop. But, I couldn't bring my family to Minneapolis after the war because there was no housing. So, I went back to Grand Forks and took a job in a smoky-dingy little shop. Only about 3 or 4 people worked there. But the one owner drank a lot and his partner asked if I would care to buy the little machine shop with practically no machines. Guess what? That was the birth of Young Mfg., Inc. in 1947. My two brothers joined me at the time.

Sept. 25 - Grandpa, what was it like gathering eggs?

Fun. If the hen was done, we just picked up the eggs and put them in a basket. My grandmother always took them when they were brought in. Sometimes my brother Frank would help. He would hold the eggs in his hands up against his mid-riff. Once he put a golf ball between his little fingers, and just when Grandma reached for the eggs, he let the ball go and it bounded on the hard wood floor. Grandma said "Oh! Oh!" and went after it - not realizing it was only a ball. Talk about funny!

Sept. 26 - Grandpa, name the funniest thing that ever happened while milking cows?

Forgive me if I use my brother, Frank, on this one, too. During fly time, the cows tail really went after the flies. As you sit milking, that old tail really comes around and slaps whoever is milking. Just imagine a tail kind of soggy from the gutter. Frank caught a few good licks. He thought he would fix old Nelly. He went and got a brick and tied it to the tail to hold it down. The next thing that hit him was a soggy tail with a brick added. True story.

Sept. 27 - Grandpa, what was the best birthday you ever had?

My second birthday. My dad had carved out a horse, and I rode that old piece of wood by the hour. Dick Young Jr. is now the owner of the rocking horse made of basswood.

You can see it at his house. This year the horse is 73 years old. The tail and mane are made of hair from my Aunt Frances. It is still a rich brown color. But, I have had many good birthdays. It is hard to just pick one.

Sept. 28 - Grandpa, have you ever been lost so much that you felt you wouldn't ever find your destination?

Not in good old America. But one time in WWII, in Germany, we lost a tank and had to abandon it. I got separated from my buddies in the night, and I wandered around - and so tired - I crawled up on top of a pile of ammunition to rest awhile. An artillery shell burst over head, and I got up to try and find someone I knew. It was pitch dark, and I finally found a tent. I went in and crawled under some blankets on the ground to rest awhile. There were other men in there- some wounded. In the morning, I could see I was in the wrong outfit and had to leave to find my own platoon. But - lost - I was!!

Sept. 29 - Grandpa, what is your biggest fear?

This may have some spiritual overtones to it. Fears change, as we get older. As a kid at home, my Grandma talked so often of the end of the world, that I was really scared. I envisioned all sorts of things - fire - darkness - destruction and even pain. I hoped I would be old before it happened. Christians have fear about loved ones not being right with the Lord. I would never write down any names of whom I believe need to get saved, but I have friends that I pray for and hope for the day they make a commitment. To name a certain fear as the biggest one is a bit elusive. Some people fear to give a speech. Some may be afraid in a storm. I have been caught in several winter storms and the fear of not being able to come out of it is scary. Trusting in the Lord for deliverance cures fears. At present, there is nothing in my thoughts that is overwhelming.

Sept. 30 - Grandpa, explain your wedding day.

In a way, I wish I wouldn't have to, but here goes. I was like in a fog, but I think that is natural for grooms. I was supposed to pick up the flowers, and I forgot them. It was a country church wedding. Here I was, at the church, and no flowers. The wedding was due to start, and I had to drive back to town - about 15 miles, and get the florist to open up his shop. Some guy grabbed me, and said I should leave town and forget the wedding!! But I finally got there and in a few minutes the ceremony began. Like I said earlier, I was in shock. I felt stupid and embarrassed and glad when it was over. Everybody gathered at Dee's farm home and the rest of the day was spent visiting and eating. I was told not to let my new bride out of sight. As we sat in the living room, somebody came and said, "Dee, you are wanted in the kitchen." She got up and left - and, guess what? Her uncle grabbed her and took off. Stealing the bride is an old trick. Dee got very cold and when she was finally brought back, she was sick and had to be warmed up with hot water bottles.

LETTER FROM CHUCK BENNETT

February 23, 1993

Dear Judy,

This special letter which is 50 years old
Contains a message that now can be told.
Truly a Prayer that was meant just for you
But when it was written no one really knew 'who'.

Old friend, Charles Bennett, a good solid chap
Was mentally holding 'that one' on his lap.
It may be a girl or it may be a boy,
The newcomer of course would truly bring joy.

So read over the letter and read it again,
And realize of course, that when "Chuck" took his pen
He wanted to tell about Jesus, you see
And be sure you'd discover - Salvation is free.

Affectionately Yours, in Love, Mom and Dad

February 28, 1993

Dear Chuck and Minnerva,

Last evening reached a milestone in the life of one first identified as either "that boy" or "that girl". That girl, now 50 years old, received the letter created by C.O.B. Jr. and mailed to a Minneapolis address.

Dee has guarded the letter for many years and recently said that if Judy is ever to receive it, we had better get into the act. So a few days after her birthday, which is the 23rd, everyone who has been under the weather felt good enough to have a dinner meeting and present the birthday girl with the very special creation by you, Chuck, and for your interest in the birth of an unknown, we enclose a copy of the letter. Do you remember?

If there is anything that Dee and I have been blessed with, it is the first one born in both families who has been only a blessing. If all children were as much of a delight as our Judy, this would be a different world. She would be embarrassed by some of these thoughts, but there is another element in this whole story.

Anyone who would take time to write a terrific testimony and prayer filled message to one not even born, the net results would have to be as we see and experience. God's hand in that life.

Dee and I have been sponsors for several new born children and the admonition in each case is to pray for the little one. How soon we forget. But a letter, carefully considered by one truly interested the spiritual welfare of a little child is certain to bear fruit.

Dee and I have thought about it a lot in recent days. All of Judy's family are born again, church going members, and what better in these distressing times?

We have other solid Christian family members on both sides of the family and one bears witness to the other.

I am sorry that much of my middle life, I didn't have the courage to witness as one ought to.

But you, dear friends, have been very important in our lives and we look forward to another get together when possible.

Dee may want to add another line or two, so I will leave some space.

May the Lord richly bless you.

Sincerely, in Jesus Dick & Dee

Note: The following letter was actually written the SAME day that Judy was born. "Uncle Chuck" had no way of knowing that when he penned the letter, which is why he addressed "that Boy or Girl". Interestingly Chuck mentioned receiving a letter from Dick, dated January 24(1943). That is the exact date, two years later, that Richard Charles Young was born, 1/24/1945, when Dick was serving in WWII. "Charles" was given as the second name to honor a good friend - Charles Bennett.

2-23-43

My dear Friend, "that Boy or Girl",

Your father wrote me a long letter - it was dated January 24th - but because the Minneapolis postman by mistake, sent it to Baltimore, I did not get it until yesterday.

But your father wrote some very good news, good news which at your age now cannot very well understand, but which will mean more and more to you as your years on earth go by, day after day as you grow older.

A lot of things will have happened to you until the time arrives when you are able to read and understand this letter by yourself. You will first learn to eat, then you will learn to walk, then your Mother will take you out on the streets of Minneapolis, and she will introduce you to the world.

You will be taken to church and Sunday School; you will be taken to the store as Mother goes to buy the milk and oranges that make your body strong.

Then some day you will go to school, and there you will meet other boys and girls your age, who are eager like you, to learn to read and write. You will draw, and color pictures, first, but later you will do greater things.

In Sunday School you will first see pictures draw pictures, hear stories, and then read stories about God and His Son Jesus, and about the prophets and early Christians.

When you are old enough to read and understand all these things, you, like all the rest of us, will be left to choose for yourself in this big world in which God has placed.

But then you will learn that you are you and that God has a purpose behind your being brought here, and that through His Son our Heavenly Father seeks to show you that way.

When you come to the time when you face this reality, you will be able to look back upon the time, brief though it be, that you have already spent here - and you will then be able to thank our Heavenly Father for placing you in such a good home, where you learned to know, early, that God provides all things that are good, and that men must be thankful to Him for the concern He has for them.

You will then know why your Mother and Father insisted in their urging you to pray daily for help from God, for His care, for his watch over you as you work and play. You will then know why Mother and Father and you always bowed your heads in thankfulness before eating the food that was set, each meal, before you.

But best of all you will learn then that God cares even more for you than mere food and a good home here on earth can provide. You will come to know that He cares most about your soul; and that He sent His only begotten Son Jesus into the world to die for you that when you pass on your soul might go home to Heaven with Jesus.

And what a privilege you will learn it, is to be able to take Jesus with you, by prayer, into everything you do each day, until earth's work is all done and Jesus calls you home.

Jesus will be coming again, maybe during your lifetime, maybe later, to call all those who love Him and have accepted Him as their own. And you, with your Mother and Father, can look forward to that.

Right now you don't understand all this, why men are fighting, why some of us are away from home, and when it is all over you might read about how men fought back in 1943 - why some of them had to die.

But you will see that it is all because something called SIN causes all the trouble - and that Jesus came here to free you from sin and the cares of this world.

I am sending you something now, it's just a little picture of Jesus. I don't know whether Jesus looks like that or not, but the man who painted it thinks that that is the way He looked when He was praying for you and me in Gethsemane.

Other men have painted other pictures of Jesus, written songs about Him. Maybe you will do that, too, or maybe Jesus will have something else for you to do. You will see.

But, please accept this picture as a gift from me - your Father's and Mother's friend, and your friend. And I hope you will like it.

If I can get away, I am going to go home for a few days, and I am coming to see you. And to see your father and mother.

If I can't get free from my work I can nevertheless be satisfied that you are born into a good place in life, and that your parents will together endeavor to provide a home for you that is built on the solid Rock.

Homes are supposed to be built on rocks - that's why Jesus spoke of building on Him, the Rock.

But remember that seeds don't grow so well on rocks, so plant your seeds on good ground. That is why Jesus said that the seed of the Word of God must fall on good soil (hearts) and not on rocks.

So may your "acre of ground" in this life so contain a Rock on which to build your soul's home, and soft ground in which to sow the seed of God's Word.

Yours respectfully, Charles Bennett

This picture was taken in 2004 when Chuck came to visit Dick in Grand Forks.
Judy McNamee, Charles (Chuck) Bennett and Dick Young

ABOUT THE AUTHOR

Richard (Dick) Young was born to German parents and his father insisted, at an early age, that he learn many skills working with his hands. In his teenage years, he fell in love with the properties of metal and what he could make with it. His fierce love of trains, caused him to begin making model train pieces and tracks, with the help of his father. Other skills were carried into his adult life, including "work ethic", which is also evident in the telling of his WWII memories, writing poetry and stories, and in the business world.

After his U.S. Army service, he opened a machine shop with his two brothers. It was temporarily closed while Dick and one brother served in Korea. He returned to begin a career as a tool and die maker and operated his own company, metal stampings contract manufacturing. He remained active in his business until he retired, well into his eighties.

His Christian faith was very important to him. He was a member of Gideons International, the group that places Bibles in many places and gave away many Bibles to students. He was also a long serving board member of Child Evangelism Fellowship. Dick loved music, sang solos and duets with daughter Judy, played the piano and organ at his church.

Made in the USA
San Bernardino, CA
30 November 2017